Of God, Rattlesnakes & Okra
a preacher's boy tells
his growing-up story

J. Bennett Easterling

For information, contact:

MSI Press
1760-F Airline Highway, 203
Hollister, CA 95023
Orders@MSIPress.com
Telephone/Fax: 831-886-2486

Library of Congress Control Number 2013951729

ISBN 978-1-933455-75-4

Cover design by Carl Leaver

Front cover photo, left to right:
sister Geraldine, sister Iris, the author

A long, slow sip from a delightful vessel of remembrance about growing up in the old south as a struggling preacher's son with God right smack dab in the middle of all of it – it just doesn't get any better than this happy yarn!
- Tom C. Tsui, Former Director, World Bank Group, Washington, DC

I am truly blown away by this memoir – very sophisticated story telling of simple lives.
- Ke Ke Lowe, Montgomery College Staff, Maryland

A tale of bullfrogs and Baptists, butterbeans and blessings. A story of prospects, preachers and possums, but certainly not prosperity. This telling is worth the reading. A true voice, singing a song of Mississippi.
- Barbara G Beck, Barrister and Solicitor of the High Court of New Zealand

This is a gem of a book. You have found a way to portray a sense of time, place, and character that most experienced novelist seldom achieve. I expect that is because your stories are true and from the heart.
- Harry Peebles, Former Deputy Assistant Secretary, U. S. Department of Energy

This takes me back in time to when life was simple and sweet.
- Mike Walters, Professor, Mississippi State University; former Superintendent of Schools in Tupelo & Petal

Read this book, please! It will lift your spirits and make you laugh and cry, often at the same time.
- Frank Pedreira, M.D., Pediatrician, Washington DC

Fascinating, entertaining and original tales of life in the old south where God, family and nature have a great influence on a young boy's view of the world.
- Larry Frank, Ophthalmologist, Maryland

Makes the Duck Dynasty folks look like Harvard graduates.
- Jimmie and Hulda Bennett, Missionaries, Czech Republic

"Delightful Mississippi tales from a time I remember well"
- Mary Beth Beck, musician

This book is terrific! Amazing detail! Unique style of writing! Vivid language, rich in humor and southern 'isms"! Amazing life lessons revealed through the art of story telling! The last section was stunning, and I will never think of rattlesnakes the same again.
- Vivian Farley, Moms in Prayer International, Maryland Area Leader

Ben has told the true tale of a southern preacher's boy and his world that is mischievous, hilarious, touching, frightening, and memorable all at once. A wonderful story told with innocence and a hint of a smile that brings us right into Ben's boyhood—a place he cherished and one that we readers don't want to leave.
- John Fitzgerald, J.D., Chief, Chevy Chase Village Police Department

I will not get another thing done because these stories are so fascinating, and I just want to keep reading.
- Alice Brown, Leader, Hope Alive Cancer Support Ministry, Church of the Redeemer

The book, through its many short stories, relays the deep love this monetarily poor but love and faith rich family shared, which was strengthened by the strong influence of God and prayer... a wonderfully interesting and entertaining book.
- Alan Cutler, Professional Photo Refinisher, Maryland

Well-told true stories from the Mississippi Delta...
- Mary "Mac" Beck, Professor, Head of Poultry Science Department, Mississippi State University

Sweeter than a real Dixie Iced Tea, this tale of faith-filled innocence will provide more Southern Comfort than Jack Daniels ever could.
- Antonio Nedimala, Consultant to U. S. Department of Energy

A fascinating story of simpler times, of life's many challenges and hardships, and a bedrock faith that is anything but simple.
- Amy Freese, missionary to Guinea, West Africa

To beloved wife Dot
& for daughters
Linda, Jan, and Talisa,
& grandchildren
Heather, Alex, Parker, Harmony, Angela, Tyler, and Kaitlyn

Contents

J. Bennett Easterling

ACKNOWLEDGMENTS

To all the characters in this story, both living and long-dead, thank you for enriching our lives. Though your names may have been changed to protect your privacy, you are not forgotten. Your quiet dignity and courage live on. Your lives still entertain and inspire us.

Julie Castillo has been teacher, mentor, and cheerleader, helping an unpublished writer survive rejections and keep plugging away until something good happened. Linda Collier provided wise counsel and countless hours of professional editing and proofing. James Culpepper offered excellent organizing ideas. Appreciation to Gregg and Amy Freese, missionaries to Guinea, West Africa, for their encouragement and support. Mark Ernstmann, Matthew Fitzgerald, and David Rhodes patiently coaxed and tutored us into the electronic age. Alan Cutler, photo rescuer par excellence, restored the ancient family photos. Dean B.F. Ogletree and Professor Frank Buckley deserve tribute for seeing something salvageable in a Perry County mud-caked kid. Christi Richards shared Uncle Abie's dramatic handwritten account of being bitten by a rattlesnake. Pastor Steve Homcy has been spiritual mentor, brother, and friend. To all who graciously reviewed specific stories for good taste, sensitivity and accuracy, and who provided suggestions for invaluable improvements. Betty Leaver and MSI Press, thank you for turning a bundle of memories into a book. Fond remembrances to the Courtney family; your decades of loyal sacrifice greatly helped a struggling preacher. To the family of the late Otis Russell, thank you for sharing this good man with us—he was indeed the preacher's soul mate. Dr. Christopher Campbell, director of communications, USM, and Chris Vennetti, missionary to Asia and India, for timely advice and encouragement.

Last but not least, to my beautiful wife Dot for keeping the love fires burning and keeping us connected to family and friends while I hunched over a cold typewriter. Our God kissed a sunbeam on the dew when He created you.

INTRODUCTION

Diamondback rattlesnakes are a curse of the South. They thrive in delta lowlands, rolling hills, cotton fields, and backcountry roads. On our Mississippi farm, they slithered back and forth terrorizing kids, leaving their crooked tracks in the dust.

Okra makes the title page simply because it's the most dreadful of all farm chores. You'll find out why as the story unfolds.

Our farm lay 100 miles north of New Orleans, 100 miles south of Jackson, the state capitol, and a hard day's mule ride west of Mobile, near to nothing but forgotten graves of the aboriginal Choctaw Indians.

These stories are of real people triumphing over hard times. Names have been changed as appropriate to protect their privacy; some of the dialog has been reconstructed from memory.

It's about a time and place lost to history, at least to recorded history, because poor folks don't often get their names in the paper unless they rob a bank or steal a cow. Yet, it doesn't seem right to let their stories slide into oblivion because they overcame incredible odds. Their stories shine a light on who we are and what kind of stuff we're made of—and they tell us if they did it so can we.

There was never a doubt with a preacher father that God must occupy a place of honor. Then its these colorful characters, beloved animals, and childhood shenanigans that make growing up so special.

Nothing enriches us like the fascinating people and four-legged soul mates we find along the way in this life.

A farm boy's days are filled with raw fibers of life. As each new day unfolds, he breathes in sights, sounds—and, yes, the smells--of God's creation.

There with a father and mother who loved us and invested their lives trying to civilize us, we grew up dirt poor but royally rich.

No kid ever grew up happier. While some memories are sad or bittersweet, they couldn't steal the joy of being alive when life was fun, people were kind, dogs were loyal, fish were biting, girls were icky, and the outside world just didn't much matter.

This story takes you to places you've never been, to people you'll enjoy getting to know. You'll revisit your own childhood, entertained as you sit ringside. Maybe you'll decide to create your own story.

So, come along, dear reader, past your big cities, your busy towns, your tiny villages, back to the soil from whence we came, back to America's open countryside where our hearts were hatched.

PART I

EARLY MEMORIES

*About a baby-snatching eagle, beloved bulldog,
killer rattlesnakes, dumb turkeys,
angry sisters, and hard times.*

J. Bennett Easterling

Attacked by an Eagle

What chance would a kid with a penknife have against a starving eagle? The Hattiesburg American, our daily newspaper, reported that a huge eagle had seized a baby and flew off with it. The baby's mother had placed her infant in a cradle to be near as she hand-washed its clothes in an outside tub. The hungry bird was apparently watching the baby. When Mom turned her back, she swooped down without warning.

The baby's attacker was thought to be a mother eagle feeding her young. She likely had a nest nearby. As the paper went to press, the baby was still missing.

The story made a deep impression on mothers of our rural area. It was a call to arms, the hot topic at Sunday schools and ladies socials. "Our babies must be protected!"

The episode etched itself deep into my gizzard. Search parties launched into nearby woods and swamps. The baby was never found. Time passed; the nightmare faded.

One day Daddy sent me to bring home our milk cow. She was in a far back pasture. I was jogging along, thinking boy stuff, when something caused me to look up.

A monster eagle was standing erect in the path up ahead. Her gaze was fixed on something off to my right. She was a towering fright to behold—and I was all alone.

The old gal was blocking my path—or what would've been my path. Now, I was not sure which way to turn.

Deadly still, she was silently watching whatever had attracted her attention. Her great wings were half-raised like she was poised to attack. I froze in my tracks and melted to the ground.

The giant predator looked as tall as a man. Maybe she hadn't seen me yet. I was hyperventilating.

"Thank the Lord, she's looking the other way."

News flashes at the movies had been showing our WWII troops flattening themselves on the ground when they come under enemy fire.

"How long can I cower here before she turns and sees me?"

Every sin of my young life paraded before me. Why did I give Momma such a hard time? Why didn't I go forward when Daddy made those altar calls?

"You gotta scat outta here!" I told myself.

Hugging the ground, gulping field dust, I began crawfishing—backing away, inch-worming and slithering snakelike, straining to see if she'd detected me. The great feathered carnivore was still watching for prey, looking in the opposite direction.

"Lord, you've spared me so far—don't quit now!"

Heart thundering in my temples, one elbow bleeding from shimmying across the dirt, slowly I was gaining ground....buying time ... putting breathing room between me and that hungry mother.

Then, God be praised, I remembered my knife. Daddy had given me a little pearl-handled pocketknife for my birthday. I rolled over on my back, fumbling in my overall pockets. Trembling hands grasped the knife. Opening the blade, I gripped the handle with a spurt of adrenalin. As the distance between me and that flying dinosaur grew, so did my bravado.

"Well, Mrs. Eagle, you think you're going to kill me and feed me to your hatchlings like you kidnapped that baby, but—and here my fingers lock in a death grip on the tiny pocket knife—you're going to have the fight of your life!"

My imagination soared. When she attacked, if I could slit her throat, the battle would quickly turn in my favor. Instead of being dead meat, I'd be a hero. The *Hattiesburg American* would run a story about the baby snatcher meeting her fate.

"BOY KILLS THE BABY KILLER" scream tomorrow's headlines. "SLASHES HER THROAT WITH A KNIFE."

A photo would show me holding the dead monster, her jugular vein clearly severed, her windpipe still pumping blood. In my fevered brain, the thrilling headlines continued: A MUTILATED KID FIGHTS FOR HIS LIFE AND WINS....MOTHERS, YOUR BABIES ARE SAFE. DOWNTOWN PARADE PLANNED.... HERO TO RIDE IN MAYOR'S OPEN CONVERTIBLE. PRESENTED KEYS TO CITY...MADE HONORARY MEMBER OF RESCUE TEAM.

Of course, I'd accept all honors with genuine humility, regardless of how greatly deserved. "I only did what had to be done to make sure no more mothers go to bed at night grieving over an empty cradle."

Suddenly, I awoke with a start. How long had I been daydreaming? I was still lying in the dirt with every muscle trembling when it dawned on me the songbirds had stopped their chatter. The world was strangely silent.

Maybe the creature had circled around to attack from behind. Turning my head ever so slowly, my eyes locked-in on the adversary. All my courage melted.

"Better a living dog than a dead lion," said a wise man. Got it!

Still, she hadn't spotted me.

"Am I far enough away to get up and run? Or will that attract her attention?"

Maybe the great bird's asleep, but for how long? Terror was clutching at my windpipe, strangling me. To escape, I must risk being seen. Gripping the knife like my life depended on it, my confidence came creeping back.

"You big overgrown buzzard, you think you will tear me to pieces and feed me to your little eaglets, but don't count on it! This is not a helpless baby you're messing with!"

All the time I was talking trash I knew deep down it was a bunch of baloney. "Who am I kidding?" I told myself, "You better scat while the scattin's good!"

Rising up on all fours, I resumed crawfishing inch-by-inch, putting more space between us. My elbows were screaming. By now, I was half a football field upwind from the she-devil.

"Time, that's all I need, a little more time."

Encouraged by my grip on the open knife—and the growing distance between me and the death-fowl—I lifted myself up, half-crouching half-standing.

I scanned the horizon one last time and fixed on the enemy. She hadn't moved or turned her head.

She may be trying to fool me into thinking she's not stalking me. That idea fired me up with another shot of adrenaline. By now, Daddy's cornfield is a mere bunny hop away; the tall corn stalks beckoning. If I could dart into that head-high thicket, she'd have trouble tracking me or attacking from the air, but what if she smelled me? Animals can smell a person who's afraid of them. Not a comforting thought. I must have been leaving quite a scent.

At last and still alive, I melted into the tall corn. God is so good! The rows were running in the direction of home. I sprang to my feet, gripping that precious pearl-handle lifesaver, and raced like a terrified jackrabbit toward safety.

Bursting through the back screen door, I nearly tore its hinges off, collapsing on our back porch. Gasping for air, I rolled back and forth. Daddy and Momma rushed out to see what all the commotion's about. They see me rolling on the floor, open pocketknife still in my clenched fist.

When I'd caught my breath, I told them my hair-raising tale. Daddy listened with no trace of a smile. When I finished, he explained, "I put a scarecrow in the peanut patch yesterday."

This new information hit me like a ton of bricks. How could I be so stupid? Will I ever live down the humiliation? What will my friends think when this story gets out? Momma saw the wheels turning in my head.

"You don't have to worry; we're not going to tell anyone about this. It could've happened to anyone." Truly, mothers are God's gift to the careless and clueless.

The preacher said he'd dug a hole, set a post into it, and nailed two-by-four boards crossways on the upper part for "arms." Then, he put an old raincoat on the arms and hung a baseball cap on the top of the post to look like a man.

"Or an eagle with her wings stretched out, looking the other way," said I.

"I'm so sorry I forgot to tell you," Daddy apologized as he reached out to hug me. He really was sorry. Momma felt terrible too, but, not nearly as terrible as me.

What Happened to Lucky?

For the life of me, I can't remember what happened to the milk cow, but none of us will ever forget what happened to Lucky. It's September in the cotton fields. Bones Courtney, our cotton-picking straw boss, is dragging a seven-foot long sack behind him, grabbing handfuls of the fluffy snowballs.

Mississippi's subtropical sun is shooting thermometers skyward. Shimmering heat waves dance on the horizon. Snow cone mirages are beckoning.

Perspiration is melting the leather bands of our straw hats. Sweat runs down our foreheads into our eyes. Gnats and dog flies are trying to eat us alive.

Bones is huffing and puffing. His gnarled old hands dart swiftly between two rows of tall cotton stalks. Stripping off stubborn bolls of cotton, he stuffs them into his sack as he's done for five decades. He's singing his own version of an ancient Negro folk song:

> *You got to jump down, turn around,*
> *Pick uh bale uh cotton*
> *Got to jump down, turn around*
> *To pick uh bale uh day.*
> *Me an' my Margie gonna pick uh bale uh cotton*
> *Me an' my Margie gonna pick uh bale uh day.* [1]

Because I was skinny as a rail, Bones nicknamed me Big Ben. He was a great kidder, lifting everyone's spirit:

Me an' Big Ben gonna pick uh bale uh cotton
Me an' Big Ben gonna pick uh bale uh day [2]

Bones was patriarch of a wonderful black family sharecropping a farm next to ours. He and his wife, Margie, lived just down the road. Margie and their kids were also helping us that day.

Anybody showing up for dinner was welcomed at their table—and if they needed a place to sleep Margie threw a pallet on the floor.

A salt-of–the-earth soul, Bones limped from childhood polio. Yet, he moved like a gazelle, picking more cotton than any of us. As soon as the Courtneys finished picking their cotton every fall, they moved over into our fields to help us.

Daddy weighed and emptied our cotton sacks as we filled them. Keeping a running tab for each picker in his spiral notebook, the preacher paid in cash when we knocked off for the day. As Daddy weighed, we watched his scales to see how many pounds we'd picked.

"Big Ben, do you think Preacher Man's gonna have some ice cream for us at the weigh-in station?" Bones teased.

Daddy was Preacher Man to our black neighbors. They would do anything for him. They looked to Daddy for pastoral duties when no black minister was available.

Bones knew no ice cream would be waiting. What horror awaited us back at the cotton shed, no one even imagined.

A windowless log cabin served as weigh-in station and storehouse for the cotton. When our sacks became too heavy to drag, we'd load them on our backs and tote them to the shed be weighed and emptied.

By midmorning Bone's seven-foot-long sack was stuffed full. Finally Daddy called, "Weigh-in time!"

This was the break we'd been dreaming of. Momma would be bringing us a bucket of chilled water. We headed for the cotton shed, a cup of cold water, and the nearest shade tree.

"Come on, Lucky!" Bones called to his ferocious looking bulldog. Lucky was so named after surviving a life-and-death fight with an angry otter.

The otter chewed him up and almost drowned him before Bones jumped into the creek to rescue Lucky. We all loved this miracle dog, a gentle white giant following Bones' every step.

Bones had brought Daddy a dozen cotton picking hands that day—his wife, Margie, plus their kids, in-laws, and whoever happened to be sleeping under their roof.

Now, Lucky was thrilled to be getting out of the sun. He ran ahead of us, crawling under the cotton shed floor. The shed rested on concrete blocks, leaving just enough room for Lucky to hunker down and slide under it.

Daddy waited at the scales for us to line up with our full sacks and then began weighing them. Bones is ribbing us, "Now we'll see who's been working and who's goofing off!"

Nobody expected to beat Bones. He once picked 400 pounds a day in the cotton-rich Mississippi Delta. Or so he claimed—and none of us doubted it. We called Margie "Deputy Dog" because she picked almost as fast as her husband. All the Courtneys picked fast. My pigmy-sized sack was a joke.

Just as Daddy started weighing, a bone-chilling cry erupted from under the shed. Everyone froze. A pitiful howling came next.

Lucky dragged himself out from under the shed, collapsing at Bones' feet. His smooth white skin was quickly turning reddish-purple. Breathing hard, his great chest heaving, unseeing eyes rolling in his head, Lucky fought for his life. It was no use. Within minutes he was dead.

What had happened to Lucky? What was lurking under that shed?

"Rattlesnake!" someone whispered. We all looked at each other, knowing it was true.

An ugly wound on Lucky's nose told the story. He'd confronted the monster but with no room for Lucky to avoid his strike, the Diamondback had sunk his fangs deep into the bulldog's nose.

The poison shot straight to his brain and heart. Lucky's luck had run out. He hadn't stood a chance. Everyone gathered around his still-warm body. We couldn't believe our mascot was dead.

The old warrior had been a born fighter. Coons, possums, and fox were no match for him. Even the otter died after their brawl. Lucky was all heart; he took on all comers and gave no ground. Now this!

What happened next is seared into our memories. Big brave Bones, hero of our cotton fields, reached down and picked his beloved dog up in his arms. Looking up to heaven, he began bellowing like a Brahma bull.

Never had we seen a grown man cry so. Soon, we were all weeping. How long did he carry on like that? It seemed forever. Daddy, meanwhile, found a long slender pole to flush the rattler from his lair. Poking and jabbing, he punched the foul critter out and killed him. The Diamondback measured nearly six feet long. It took both of Daddy's hands to reach around his thick belly.

"Will you say a prayer for us?" Bones asked Daddy.

"Let's do that!" Daddy quickly agreed, sensing the distress gripping everyone. I don't recall his prayer, but it helped us cope with our sorrow.

Bones finally stopped crying. We helped him carry Lucky home. He dug a grave out back, behind their privy. Together, we buried Lucky.

Bones revived enough to say a few words about what a good friend we'd lost and how we'll always remember Lucky—- which indeed we do.

Postscript: Daddy couldn't talk anyone into going back into that field. We feared more killers were lurking. The Courtneys were too spooked after what happened to Lucky, and the preacher didn't have a heart to make his own kids do it. So, the dry cotton bolls hung on the stalks until they rotted and were disked under next spring.

A Boy Talks to God

The painful loss of Lucky was a preview of things to come. God knew I had a lot more growing up to do.

Daddy made sure we heard good things about God. Maybe it was a guilty conscience, but God seemed to be lurking around every corner—with more rules than cotton has boll weevils.

We couldn't dance, smoke, or play cards. No movies on Sunday—or comic books, hunting, or fishing. Skating rinks were off limits. So were pool halls and slot machines, not that we'd ever seen one. So Sunday seemed a kid's day to suffer quietly. "Remember, God is watching you!"

We enjoyed this old preachers' story:

> Two boys are wondering what God is like.
> "I think He's very old, has white hair, and frowns a lot," says one.
> "Yep," agrees his buddy, "and He's watching to see if anybody's having any fun so He can put a stop to it."

Growing up in the Bible Belt made us think maybe those little guys got it right. Thankfully, like teenagers who think their parents are hopelessly dumb until they grow up and have teenagers of their own, God's reputation improved.

If God wasn't out to get us, though, surely Satan was. Momma spring-loaded us with fear: "If you're bad, the boogerman[3] will get you."

Bless her soul, she had to try something. Her dire warnings of being impaled on Satan's pitchfork worked wonders. In nightmares, I was chased by Old Slewfoot. He visited me in his red suit, wagging his long tail and brandishing evil horns. Crawling under my bed, he poked his pitchfork up through the mattress, trying to impale me on its barbs.

Momma assured us the old boy keeps accounts. Like Santa, he knows when you've been good or bad. A normal red-blooded boy didn't stand a chance. He knew my name and address; of that, I had no doubt. On those frequent days I slipped up, he was watching, counting, and gloating.

How I managed to stay one step beyond the thrust of his pitchfork, I'll never know. My wife declares I still sleep in the middle of our bed. Why take a chance?

Caught between God and the devil, a boy's life seemed precarious—like being squeezed between a backhoe and a bulldozer.

Eventually, God emerged as a better choice. Keeping God's rules was better than facing that big fork, or maybe Momma's colorful warnings were more inspirational than Daddy's sermons.

So, to improve my chances of survival, I learned to pray. Confessing blackest fibs and dastardly deeds must've paid off. God didn't strike me down with lightning. He never answered my confessions aloud, sparing instant cardiac arrest, but clearing the air seemed to help. Call it fire insurance for boys.

Eventually, I grew less terrified of God, but dare I ask Him about life's great mysteries? Actually there were two: *rattlesnakes and okra.*

My question was this: "Why did you invent rattlesnakes and okra? We all make mistakes, but you're perfect. You see the misery they cause. So, why don't you snuff them out like you did Sodom and Gomorrah?"

Diamondback Rattlesnakes were a constant threat. We kept a wary eye out for them in fields and woods, playgrounds—everywhere we roamed.

Rattlesnake bites are dreadfully painful, sometimes fatal. Word traveled swiftly of sightings and bitings. Newspapers frightened us with photos of Diamondbacks killed, some as thick as a man's leg.

To see a victim suffering from a rattlesnake attack is sobering. Daddy's brother was bitten by a Diamondback while surveying timber in remote backwoods. He stepped over a fallen log; the startled snake buried it's fangs in his leg.

"He struck with no warning," Uncle Abie recalled.

"Knowing time was critical, I asked my companion to suck as much venom out of the wound as possible. He gladly obliged. I made a tourniquet with my handkerchief, tightening it above the wound, to slow the poison from racing to my heart. Then, I hobbled a mile back to a lake, crawled into a canoe, paddled across, and was driven to the nearest hospital.

When I visited him in the hospital a week later, his leg was purple, swollen twice its normal size. He was still on anti-snake venom and antibiotics. Doctors were keeping his leg wrapped in ice and elevated 90 degrees, but he was alive, telling everyone, "God answers prayer."

So, I talked to the Lord about sending the Death Angel to wipe out rattlesnakes. It didn't seem fair. In my childish mind, God owed us an explanation. It turns out some people eat rattlesnakes. Maybe that balances the scales for you, but it didn't help me.

And if dodging rattlesnakes made life miserable, harvesting okra was worse. Of all the farm chores to hate, cutting okra topped the list. But why not let okra tell her story?

> My name is Ora Mae. I'm a pod of okra, a hibiscus out of Africa. They say I'm a kissin' cousin to King Cotton. Don't know about that, but I remember this:
>
> Descended from the royal courts of the Aztecs I am. They treasured me more than their pots of gold.
>
> When Cortez conquered my people he took their gold and okra back to Spain—repaying the Indians with cholera and whooping cough.
>
> So, I found myself in Spain for a spell, but the conquistadors never embraced me; shipped me back to Mexico.
>
> By this time my Latina friends decided I was too tame for their taste; apparently they don't cotton to stuff not as smoking hot as their jalapeno or fan dancers.
>
> My next stop was Texas where I felt more at home with the spiny cactus. Texas, though, proved to be just another way station on my pilgrimage.
>
> Wild Bill Hickok gave a few pods to Jesse James who ate them as he pillaged and robbed trains. Jesse shared his okra with the womenfolk he robbed (beautiful Southern Belles from romantic towns like New Orleans, Natchez, and Vicksburg). Those grateful damsels slipped me home to their beaus.
>
> The rest is history. Every true son of the South became addicted, esteeming me above rubies and rhubarb. We found ourselves swimming in their gumbo, fried with their chickens, boiled with their

collard greens. Like the weary Israelites stumbling out of Egypt, I'd found my promised land, my inheritance from Jehovah.

To be spoken of in the same breath as Confederate General Robert E. Lee is a rare honor. Could I ever violate that sacred trust? Not in a coon's age!

Sadly, I was never allowed north of the Mason-Dixon Line. Yankees turned up their pointy noses, called me slimy and yucky. (Remember, they also hated my brother Grits. As the Good Book says, "They hated him for no reason.")

But now all's forgiven. I've found my destiny in Dixie. Content am I, down on the Swanee River, bringing joy to those who truly love and appreciate me."

Meanwhile back on the farm, okra grows best where it's miserably hot and humid. The Magnolia State wins a blue ribbon for this. By July, even our dog-flies were sweating.

Daddy insisted we cut okra while dew was still on the plants. When the sun sucks the dew off okra leaves, they begin wilting. He was convinced it damages okra stalks to cut the young pods off after they wilted.

"What about us? Aren't we drooping, too?" I was tempted to ask. Since the preacher wasn't one to suffer foolishness, I bit my lip and groaned silently.

So, we hit the fields at dawn, strapping a sack over our shoulders to shove the okra pods into. Did I mention that a prickly bone-seeking fuzz covers okra?

Armed with knives, long-sleeved shirts and gloves, Daddy's suffering serfs waded into those humid, bug-infested fields. Every kind of insect Moses turned loose on the Egyptians was waiting.

Bloodsuckers zoomed in to feast on our exposed body parts. With sweat running off in rivulets, we cut okra, fought off biting and stinging bugs, and prayed for a windstorm to blow the little boogers into the Gulf of Mexico.

Maybe the Lord would send hordes of seagulls like those he once dispatched to Utah to gobble up the locusts, saving Brigham Young's Mormons.

As the buzzing tormentors sucked our blood, we swatted our faces, ears, and necks with gloved hands now covered in itchy fuzz. This fuzz added burning fire to our bug bites. Swollen lumps soon turned us into giant whelps. Back on the chain gang, Daddy's leading the charge.

"Gotta work fast! Sun's up; okra leaves will be wilting soon."

I'm thinking, "And maybe they'll die if we're lucky."

My warped little mind by this time was rebelling against God. I pictured Him up in heaven enjoying air-conditioned splendor. Reclining in a giant rocking chair, sipping iced tea as angels flew back and forth fanning Him with their wings. A kid couldn't help getting a little miffed.

Today when people speak of the good old days, I smile agreeably and keep my mouth shut, but those okra fields are laughing out loud and screaming, "Who do you think you're kidding?"

Yet, in my agitated state, I prayed. Maybe God would send a killing fungus to rid the world of okra. Or maybe Lord Byron was right:

> *Even my chains and I grew friends*
> *so much a long communion tends*
> *to make us what we are.*
> *Even I regained my freedom with a sigh.*[4]

And sure enough out of those hell-holes, lo a silver lining appeared. One day while fighting dog-flies, besieged by hungry gnats, swatting mosquitoes, stung by okra fuzz, came a still small voice:

"Pack up your ditty bag and go to college!"

It's not always easy to know when God's speaking and when it's your imagination. Surely, this had to be God. It was time to begin plotting escape: dreaming of a day when suitcase in hand, a boy is traveling down a dusty lane, looking back and waving goodbye. Until that blessed day, though, more hard times must be navigated.

Surviving Hard Times

Daddy, an unsalaried circuit-riding preacher, raised six kids by hustling and scrambling. He and Momma began as sharecroppers, living in a tenant house on the landowner's property.

Momma kept pushing until Daddy borrowed money to buy 80 acres of timberland and then carved our homestead out of virgin forests with a crosscut saw, an axe, and a grubbing hoe.

A few years after wooing and winning Momma, Daddy scraped up enough cash to buy a Model A Ford, but preaching, raising hogs, and trapping mink didn't bring in enough to buy gas and keep it running. He finally parked it in the barn where our cows ate the seat covers and Momma's hens moved in to roost and lay their eggs. For the next 25 years, the preacher walked or hitch-hiked with kindly neighbors.

Winters found the preacher trapping fur-bearing animals, nailing their skins to our smokehouse wall, and then selling the cured hides to traveling fur-buyers.

My earliest memory is not of family but a brown teddy bear dubbed Ted Roundhead and his pink sidekick Monk the Skunk. Our next door neighbors lived a mile away. With no playmates nearby, Ted, Monk and I quickly bonded.

We spent so many happy times together that Ted's ears fell off and Monk lost his button eyes. Years passed.

When my pals grew filthy from being dragged through dirt, Momma insisted on throwing them in her wash tub, soaking them with Octagon soap and scrubbing them. This proved too much for their ancient bodies. They fell apart, having given their lives to make a lonely kid happy.

Yet, a boy is never alone. Throw him outside; he lands in the dirt, perfectly content among fireflies, worms, bats, and tree toads.

Toys were unaffordable. A kindly neighbor, sensing how much every boy needs a red wagon, spoke to Santa. Christmas morning it was sitting under our tree. Years later, older siblings pooled their piggy banks to buy me a flaming-red B.F. Goodrich bicycle.

The only present Daddy ever gave me was a toy woodpecker on a pole. Woody was spring-loaded. If you pushed him up the pole and turned him loose, he pecked his way down. That old red-headed bird entertained three generations of kids; it still sits in a place of honor on my roll top desk.

Of course, Daddy gave each of us so much more than presents—faith in God, unqualified love, and a sense of belonging. Strictly speaking, the Great Depression was petering out when I came along. Yet, memories of it still struck fear in survivors. Afraid to discard anything, Momma saved everything—bottles, cans, twine string, faulty coat hangers, and bags.

To keep shoes and clothes on six school kids Momma bartered the eggs we didn't eat and Daddy peddled his animal furs. Momma bleached fertilizer bags, sewing them together for our sheets and pillow cases. To their shame, my sisters wore blouses and skirts Momma made from Purina chicken and hog feed sacks.

Daddy used a cast iron shoe lathe to patch and resole our shoes, handing down the same pair several times. Being the youngest, my hand-me-down shoes were scuffed and well-worn, but breaking them in was never a problem.

Not knowing where his next dollar was coming from, Daddy held on to the precious few in his pockets. Getting a nickel out of Daddy when he was almost broke was harder than prying ticks off our hound dog, Ole Pup.

"Doing without builds character," claimed the preacher. We got awfully tired of building character.

Except for the *Hattiesburg American* newspaper and *Progressive Farmer* magazine, our only window to the outside world was a battery-powered radio. From it, Daddy and Momma learned how our troops were faring in WWII—son Bruce was fighting with General Patton's allied forces to liberate Normandy and France.

The all-important weather forecasts told Dad when to plant and harvest his crops. The Chicago Commodities Exchange told him when to sell his cotton, corn, beef, and pork.

We never went to bed hungry, but we vowed if we never saw another Crowder pea or speckled butterbean it would be too soon. Momma's pantry was a makeshift room off the smokehouse. Her shelves overflowed with half-gallon and quart jars of peas, butterbeans, corn, tomatoes; a groaning board of veggies and fruits. An entire wall was filled with preserved figs—a staple of Momma's country breakfasts.

Daddy's peach orchard attracted city folks. Daddy took buyers out to the orchard to pick their fruit, insisted on filling their bushel baskets to the top, then he kept picking and piling them on until not another peach could be added. This was his way of following the *Bible's* teachings of giving good measure, pressed down, shaken together, and running over.

Since everyone knew Daddy needed every cent he could get out of his peaches, this simple act of generosity did not go unnoticed. Peaches the preacher couldn't sell Momma cooked down with five pound sacks of sugar for her high-energy workers.

Three varieties of pears supplied fresh fruit in summer; the overflow Momma canned for wintertime cobblers and desserts. To keep us from burning out on pears, she mixed coconut or pineapple with her pear preserves.

Daddy's apples were his one flop. Small, wormy, and half rotten, our hogs gobbled them up with no complaints.

At our smokehouse door, mouth-watering aromas of sage, garlic, and spices, mixed with smoked, dried, and salted pork, wafted into the air.

Daddy grew palmetto stalks in a back pasture, using them to hang fresh pork from smokehouse rafters. Hickory chips he used to keep a smoldering fire on the dirt floor. Hanging his meat high above the fire pit, he slowly smoked and dried it; thus, it was hickory-cured.

Jimmy Carter, the peanut-growing former President from Georgia, would've loved us. Our barn was crammed full of peanuts. Irish potatoes, beans and grain.

"Sweet potatoes are like manna from heaven," the preacher claimed. To keep his potatoes from freezing during the winter he improvised.

He shoveled dirt into a mound, leveled off the top, and lined it with pine straw, piling his potatoes on top of the straw. Then, he covered them with another layer of straw, topping it off with more dirt. His "potato bank" was ready except for building a frame over it and covering it with a tin roof. When Momma needed potatoes for a meal, she sent one of us kids out with a galvanized bucket to dig them out and wash them.

When she cooked turnip greens, she saved the pot liquor to pour over crumbled cornbread. By adding pork cracklings to her cornpone, we're talking gourmet vittles!

Daddy found novel ways to keep us out of the poorhouse. In late summer, the rivers ran low, allowing him to wade up and down the shallow waters fishing with his hands. The technique is called grappling. Here's the way it works. Big catfish look for a place to spawn. One of their favorite places is to find an underwater hollow log, lay their eggs, and move inside to guard it from intruders.

The preacher took a brown burlap bag, wrapped it around his hand, and waded into the rivers probing into these hollow logs. When he shoved his gloved hand into the mouth of a submerged hollow log, a catfish with eggs to protect attacked the intruder. Daddy would grab it and haul it out for dinner.

What awaited the preacher's hand in those dark underwater cavities —a prize catfish or a water moccasin—a snapping turtle or a disturbed alligator? That thought sent goose bumps racing up my timid spine, causing cowardly hairs on the back of my head to quiver. Maybe the preacher felt he had to take risks to feed a house full of kids, but grappling appeals not to faint-of-heart. No sir, threading worms on fishhooks is for us cowards.

In dry seasons, nearby Bear Branch stopped flowing and dried up into dark pools. Small sunfish, Goggle-eyed perch, Red bellies, and catfish became trapped. The fast-evaporating mud holes were also full of tadpoles and harmless little black bugs (Mellow bugs) floating atop the water. If you catch one and press it, they give off a fragrant vanilla-like aroma.

Also skimming across the mud holes were queer-looking mosquito-like creatures that walked on water like Christ once did. Daddy called them water-walkers. To us kids, they were Jesus bugs.

Grabbing a bucket and hoe, Daddy went looking for those muddy water holes. When he found one he'd take his hoe and begin stirring up sediment from the muddy bottom.

As suffocating fish rose to the top, gulping for oxygen, he slapped them out on the bank with the back of his hoe. My job was to grab' em before they flounced back into the water.

We were not the only predators fishing those dried-up stream beds. Cottonmouth moccasins gathered for a feast. It was wise to step carefully.

Momma took the tiny fingerlings, battered them with flour or cornmeal, deep frying them in lard. When they were golden brown, we ate the whole fish, crunchy bones and all.

Little time was left for relaxing. Once in a blue moon, some kindly soul took us to town to see a movie. Famed WWII radio announcer Gabriel Heater with his deep baritone voice set our hearts pumping even before the movie began:

> Hello, Americans! There's good news tonight from
> across the oceans! Our fighting men are advanc-
> ing against the enemies of freedom. Allied forces
> are overwhelming Hitler's Nazis and the powers of
> Japan.

Dramatic propaganda scenes of our GIs mauling the enemy followed.

The preacher frowned on Hollywood but tolerated westerns because the good guy always won. We paid a dime to see Roy Rogers and his horse Trigger rescue Dale Evans and other beautiful ladies from flint-eyed lightning-fast gunslingers. Or, the Lone Ranger hopping on Silver and thundering off with Tonto, six-guns blazing, after a pack of scalping savages or godless outlaws. Violence in those days featured the Three Stooges mauling each other with feather pillows—or Wile E. Coyote chasing terrified rabbits.

Vacations were something we could only dream of. Once I escaped the farm for a 4-H Club sponsored weekend to Pensacola, having never seen an ocean, built a sand castle, chased sand crabs, or marveled at dolphins, gulls and pelicans.

The mini-break was too soon over, and we headed back to the farm. Another chore was always just around the corner. Yet, there was one redeeming quality: farm kids do not go hungry.

Bedbugs once invaded our home; Momma declared war. Stripping sheets and pillowcases off, she ordered us to drag all the mattresses out into the hot sun, turning them over two or three times until sunset. Taking a stiff rod she fiercely beat those sun-soaked mattresses to dislodge any surviving eggs or larvae.

Momma birthed seven babies at home. Her most tragic time came when son Hobert died of spinal meningitis when he was 11 years old. Momma fell into deep depression. Her heart healed agonizingly slow. Really, does a mom ever fully recover from losing a child?

This happened before I was born, yet years later Momma was still bringing fresh flowers to his grave. She'd cut a bouquet of her saucer-sized tea roses in summer or camellias in winter, arranging them in a half-gallon Mason fruit jar, and then walk to the cemetery.

She allowed me to share her lonely pilgrimages. The routine never varied. The graveyard lay just beyond tiny white clapboard Prospect Church where Momma worshipped.

The church was vacant during the week but never locked. Momma would open the door and set her flowers on one of the pews, slipping inside to pray. She did not invite me in; she needed a moment to be alone.

Afterward, Momma was ready to mosey on out to the cemetery, stand over Hobert's grave, shed a few tears, and relive memories of him as a playful kid.

A local farmer had kindly donated land to bury family and neighbors. A metal fence topped by a strand of barbed wire kept roving cattle and animals out. Since few could afford tombstones, most graves were left unmarked. Sunken graves lay sprinkled amid fescue grass, cockleburs, and bitterweeds.

A few wooden markers had been driven into the dirt by loved ones. Names were bleached out by sun, rain, and weather. Granite markers announced the remains of those wealthy enough to afford them.

Hobert's grave was marked by a tin nameplate left there by the funeral home. Sadly, only the rich were honored by marble markers while most poor folks lay forgotten in the weeds.

But this didn't tell the whole story. Graves of the affluent were adorned with faded plastic flowers. Momma had come to grace Hobert's resting place with a fresh bouquet of her gorgeous tea roses. When those petals faded, Momma would be making yet another pilgrimage to replace them with fresh ones.

Gathering up the old dried-out flowers, Momma lovingly arranged her fresh bouquet on the grave. Then, she turned stoop-shouldered toward home, a home without Hobert. Sad indeed, but the ritual helped her to cope and go on.

Fifty years would pass before Momma lay down beside her lost boy—seventy before Daddy joined them. Now they rest in a lonely country graveyard, forgotten by the world but together at last.

Siblings say I was an accident of nature, an unplanned afterthought. When Momma became pregnant with me, my sisters were furious at Daddy. Momma had been sick, fighting high blood pressure, heart trouble, and rheumatism.

"She's suffered enough" was their attitude. They had a point, but Momma felt God was giving her another son to mend her broken heart. I don't know, but that's what she believed.

Trips to see a doctor were rare. After Hobert's death, Momma obsessed about keeping us healthy with home remedies: Syrup of Black Draught, Chill Tonic, Carters Little Liver Pills, and One-A-Day Vitamins.

Once when Momma couldn't find Syrup of Black Draught, she found it in a dry powder and mixed it with homemade molasses. A tablespoon full was supposed to cure everything from consumption to constipation. We were tempted to keep our ailments to ourselves rather than suffer Momma's cure-alls.

Horse liniment was one of her sure-cures, the kind used to treat swollen legs of racehorses. She doctored her own painful joints with it as well as our bumps and bruises. Oddly enough, this old home remedy is making a comeback. You find it today in drugstores under the name "Arth Arrest." You can run down to a pharmacy and pick up a roll-on applicator for your racehorse or yourself.

A critical illness once left Momma paralyzed from the waist down. Daddy found a charity hospital to treat her in Laurel, a Mississippi town of decent hard-working folks who gladly reach out to help their neighbors.

Sadly, Laurel suffered the misfortune decades later of gaining notoriety as the home of hatemonger Sam Bowers, Imperial Wizard of the White Knights of the Ku Klux Klan, whose terrorists firebombed homes, synagogues, and more than 40 black churches, killing children and civil rights activists.

Granny moved in to cook for Daddy and his kids, wash them, send them off to school, and clean house. Stepping in to take care of his children, she freed Daddy to keep preaching, work his crops, run trap lines, and visit his sick wife. Daddy never forgot her kindness.

After being hospitalized six months, Momma finally came home. She had laid in bed so long her back and hips were ravaged by sores, penetrating all the way to her bones. Daddy and Granny rolled her over in bed several times a day, rubbing her down with alcohol. Finally, the infection subsided.

One day Momma screamed out for Daddy. When he ran to her bedside, she was crying. "Watch this," she whispered, moving her big toe just a fraction of an inch. God had answered their prayers. Momma would walk again. Her little ones would have a mother.

"With God, all things are possible," the preacher was fond of saying. However, grinding poverty was so relentless that it was tempting to give up on God—or hold on so tightly one's knuckles turned white.

"We're just scraping by." Momma said. Still, we were a happy bunch, surrounded by family and beloved pets. We laughed and played with kids no better off than us.

In fact, a million dollars wouldn't have added to our joy. We didn't know we were poverty-stricken. If sociologists had discovered us, they might've stolen our bliss. Yet even in happy times, unwelcome clouds arise. Teenage sisters blamed many of their clouds on me.

Momma, Do Something!

That would be my sisters complaining about me. They started dating when I was barely a school-age urchin. When their suitors called, Momma sent me out on the front porch to entertain them while the girls finished primping. Taking this duty seriously, I poured my heart into it. Sadly, my efforts were not always appreciated.

One of Edith's beaus was plagued with teenage acne, which left ugly pockmarks. Trying to make conversation, I asked if someone had shot him in the neck with buckshot.

Sister Iris fell for a fellow whose notable feature was big tobacco-stained front teeth. As we sat on our porch swing making small talk, my beloved hound dog Ole Pup joined our waiting party. I noticed his teeth looked a lot like Pup's.

"Do you know that your teeth look like Ole Pup's?" I asked him. He must've thought it funny because he laughed nervously. Iris failed to enjoy the joke.

Geraldine's first boyfriend was a lanky teenager who wore western jeans, cowboy boots, and a Stetson hat. Grandpa nicknamed him "the Gunman."

On the front porch swing one evening, I asked Geraldine's new admirer if it were true he carried a pistol in his jeans pocket.

"Momma, please do something about him!" the girls pleaded. Instead, when Iris and Geraldine were old enough to go to church socials, Momma insisted they take me along. Was she sending me to spy on them, or did Momma simply need a break? She never said.

One starlit evening, I sat on the roots of a giant Live Oak tree, watching as my sisters' youth group played "Spin the Bottle." This was during WWII when meat was rationed.

A particularly bashful boy took the Coke bottle and twirled it around in the sand. To everyone's delight, it landed, pointing to a girl who weighed about 300 pounds. As he reluctantly took her hand and sauntered off down the road, I loudly pip squeaked, "Well, meat's not rationed with Robert Ford!"

When we got home, my sisters told Momma, "We'd rather stay home than to take him along!" Don't you think they overreacted?

Sister Edith went away to Mississippi Normal College (for teachers) when I was just a sprout. There she met Archie, who owned a car. We're not sure if Edith was smitten with Archie or his car. Their friendship blossomed; Edith brought him out to meet her family. He apparently passed the parent test, becoming a frequent family guest.

One day Edith asked if she could invite Archie out for Sunday dinner. This was exciting news for a kid living out in the boonies. Momma would be cooking big time. Her groaning board would overflow with fresh corn, tomatoes, peas and butterbeans, cornbread, and banana pudding. The highlight of Momma's home cooking would be her southern fried chicken with buttermilk biscuits and gravy.

So, preparations began. Only one thing was missing. Daddy hadn't yet killed a chicken by wringing its neck and chopping off its head with his axe.

Eager to be a part of the festivities, I grabbed a heavy broom from the kitchen closet and went looking for a chicken. Slipping up behind a sweet hen, I knew she was the right one. Lifting the broom high overhead, I struck her a horrific blow breaking her back and causing a great deal of panicky squawking.

Daddy rushed out and, seeing her distress, finished off the poor thing. The preacher was not happy, and Momma for once didn't rush to my defense. Archie and I bonded after that, though. Knowing my heart was in the right place, he took me into his bosom. I still think he would've made a fine brother-in-law.

How Dumb is a Turkey?

Despite a troubled past with chickens, my future in turkeys looked brighter. Daddy's farming, trapping and preaching kept us one step from the poorhouse, and to help make ends meet, Momma raised turkeys.

She sold her turkeys at Thanksgiving and Christmas. Town folks enjoyed driving out into the country to buy a fresh turkey for their holiday dinner. Momma sent me out with customers to pick out their bird. Banging on a feed bucket, I threw out shelled corn to the unsuspecting flock.

While they were gobbling it up, the buyer looked them over and fingered his holiday meal. Slipping in back of the chosen bird, I would suddenly lunge, grabbing a leg. Customers enjoyed the show.

After we tied the bird's legs together, the buyer paid Momma five or ten bucks and then headed back to town, with his main course fluttering in the rumble seat. Most of Momma's customers were city folk with money—doctors, lawyers, judges, merchants. Anyone with two dimes to rub together was a big shot.

Momma used her turkey money to buy things Daddy never dreamed of like decorations to beautify our house or a "store bought" dress for the girls. Since Momma's turkeys turned into instant cash, we seldom found turkey on our Thanksgiving table. Momma said not to worry; a good, fat hen is more tender and tasty. Who was going to argue with Momma?

I'll never forget how dumb those turkeys were. Young turkeys have a stupid habit of turning their beaks skyward when it rains. Unless someone comes to their rescue and literally drives them into a shelter, their snoot fills with water, suffocating them.

Once a thunderstorm struck so suddenly we had no time to gather in Momma's turkey chicks. By the time we found them, they'd collapsed on the ground, drowned. Daddy had us quickly gather them up into a basket and bring them into the house. He took each little unconscious bird, opened its beak, and blew into its mouth.

Miraculously, the little creature blinked its eyes and began breathing. Daddy kept blowing air into their mouths until he saved every last one of them. Resurrection Day it seemed to us when those drowned turkeys breathed again.

Naturally, the preacher found a spiritual parable in all this. People and turkeys share a lot in common. Too often we wander off on our own, oblivious to danger. We're not much smarter than those silly turkeys, sticking our noses in the air until we drown. We refuse to acknowledge God or let Him help us. Then, after we've ruined our lives beyond recovery, we expect God to bail us out.

Now Daddy's on a roll: Why does the good Lord put up with us? He knows we're as clueless as those dumb turkeys. So, he hangs in there with us, refusing to let us go. When it looks as if we're all done for, he brings us in out of the rain and breathes life—eternal life—into our drowned spirits. Who but a preacher could find a sermon in a basketful of drowned turkeys?

It's a mystery why farm-raised turkeys and their wild cousins are so different. The tame turkey is so heavy he can barely lift off the ground to fly. He doesn't have sense enough to get out of the rain. He's big, fat, and slow.

A wild turkey is just the opposite. He's incredibly wary, born with an uncanny sixth-sense to avoid hunters. He rotates his neck 90 degrees in both directions so it's nearly impossible for a predator to slip up undetected. He runs like a bullet. When pursued, he flushes into the air like a quail, flying as fast as 50 miles an hour. Like white-tailed deer, wild turkeys survive despite shrinking habitat and human encroachment.

Today, wildlife experts say more than seven million wild turkeys are strutting and gobbling up and down the hills and hollows of North America—with frustrated hunters in hot pursuit. Now, you tell me, who's the turkey?

J. Bennett Easterling

PART II

REMEMBERING THE PREACHER

A preacher's faith is fire-tested as he tries pastoring, farming, trapping, bounty hunting for rabid foxes, and building ships and army camps to feed his family.

J. Bennett Easterling

Pastor, Farmer, Trapper

After my siblings grew up and escaped the farm, Daddy needed help more than ever. Momma and I were the only ones left.

This did not appear in the sky as a blessing. Work was hard, rewards scarce. Yet, looking back, it's amazing how one's feelings change. Now I know what a privilege it was to spend time with my father.

At just five foot-four inches, he was a little guy with a huge heart, throwing around hundred pound sacks of fertilizer like they were five pound bags of sugar. Preacher, farmer, trapper, woodsman, hunter, and fisherman, he'd go to Kalamazoo or Timbuktu to feed his family or serve his God.

Working in fields until noon Saturday, he rushed in to bathe and shave for church. I remember him in his seersucker suit, starched white shirt, tie and Sunday straw hat, holding his big leather-bound Bible in one hand and his suitcase in the other.

Since he owned no car, a neighbor picked him up and took him down to New Augusta where he stood on Highway 98 to catch a Greyhound bus to Mobile or another church. Momma and I were left to feed livestock and keep things going until the preacher did his God thing and landed back on the farm.

After weekend services, he'd catch a Greyhound back to his drop-off point. If some politician or kind soul found him walking the eight miles home, they would give him a ride. Otherwise, he hoofed it.

Shedding his preaching clothes for overalls and rubber boots, he headed for the barn to check on his animals. Sunrise Monday found him and his ill-tempered mule back in the fields, battling weeds and grass.

Living on the edge of poverty, sometimes over the edge, brought anxious moments. Yet, he never showed it. People loved to hear the preacher laugh. His great, big, booming laugh carried through the crowds.

His prized possession was a gold-plated 17-jewel Burlington Special pocket watch given to him by a deacon. "It's the same watch used by train conductors," he told the preacher. A heavy gold chain allowed the preacher to keep it in the bib of his overalls. That watch was his only luxury.

One day while clearing and burning brush, his watch chain was caught in an armload of limbs he was tossing in a brushfire. Before he discovered what happened, it had melted into a lump. Another church member who ran a watch repair shop came to his rescue.

"Don't worry preacher," he told him, "I'll keep my eyes out for one just like it." True to his promise, he found a gold-plated Hamilton and presented it to Daddy.

"It was like lightning struck twice," the preacher marveled. It was not the first or last time we saw good simple country folk, despite being poverty-stricken themselves, follow the golden rule to help their pastor.

Daddy knew the blessing of giving as well as receiving. Once he saved his teacher's life. A rowdy bully attacked the teacher with a switchblade. He wounded the man and was trying to kill him when Daddy grabbed a heavy two-by-four board and stepped between them. He held the crazed attacker off until help arrived to overpower him. We kids begged him to tell that story over and over. Admiration and awe of our giant-slaying Daddy grew with each retelling.

He made us proud. This cotton-picking, sharecropping man of God could dig postholes and string barbed-wire all day and then rattle the gates of hell with fire and brimstone, preaching at night.

Daddy had a place for everything: his coffee cup, his hat and boots, and his heavy King James *Bible*. At midnight, he often got up and, sleepwalking in a dark room, walked straight over to find a sweet gum toothpick he'd whittled out and used after supper.

I had a terrible habit of borrowing his tools, then dropping them in the spot where I'd finished with them, driving him into conniption fits.

"Why can't you put things back in the same place you got them?" Obviously, not all gifts of the Holy Spirit are given to preachers: Daddy was still reaching for patience. Momma worried I was sending him to an early grave.

Hard times, yes, but humor he found in dire circumstances. When Hurricane Camille walloped the Gulf Coast with 150 MPH winds after Momma died, the preacher was living alone. The wind roared all night, blowing down hundred-year-old pines and live oaks. Next morning, some of his church people came to see about him.

"Brother Ira, what were you thinking last night with the wind howling and your house shaking?"

Said he, "I was thinking maybe the good Lord's hearing from some of his little children he hasn't heard from lately."

We lived in the tiny community of Prospect. Seldom did a name seem so ill-conceived. In post-Depression rural Mississippi, one's prospects in that little dustbowl appeared dismal.

"I'm nobody going nowhere" was a prevailing attitude. Yet, Daddy never bought into a woe-is-me mindset. He believed that if one lived right and honored God, things would turn out okay.

Years later, my brother Ray lost his job and surrendered his car to Daddy, who took over the payments. The preacher went to New Augusta, the county seat, to take his driver's license test.

"Reverend, who drove you here?" the highway trooper asked, seeing no one with him.

"Nobody, I drove myself," Daddy answered innocently.

"Brother Easterling, don't tell me that! It's like spitting in my face."

Then, he laughed and said, "Let's pretend we never had this conversation."

Good folks, struggling themselves to survive lean years, were glad to give the poor preacher a break.

One Sunday before he was called into ministry, Daddy was down to his last two dollars. He gave them both to the preacher. When he came home and told Momma, she was shocked. "How could you leave your family penniless?" she demanded.

Daddy explained he'd felt led by the Spirit. His attitude was: If I do as the Lord leads, He'll take care of us. Momma's point was valid, but Daddy had followed his conscience. Did disaster follow? It did not.

So, what are the prospects for one who sacrifices to follow his convictions? Maybe Prospect wasn't such an ill-conceived name after all.

Elder Ira Easterling, author's father, "the preacher"

Clay Hill Church

It took little imagination to come up with a name for the place. Clay Hill Church squatted atop a hill, cursed with clay that turned into something like overripe bananas when it rained. The slick grey and pink gook—we called it pipe clay— clung to your shoes until it became too heavy to walk. The only trees surviving on that lunar-looking ridge were a few scrubby Blackjack oaks, covered with willowy grey beards of Spanish Moss. It being a desolate place in a remote and lonely nook, one might be forgiven for thinking it God-forsaken.

In fact, it was anything but. What happened inside that clapboard frame house on Sundays was little short of miraculous. A beaten-down little crew of rag-tag nobodies gathered there to worship and praise the God who never forsook them.

Simple souls who often knew not what they would eat tomorrow, how they would pay their bills, or if they could dress their kids for school found rest and peace trusting in their all-sufficient Jehovah Ji-rah.

Despite deprivation, a hard-wired faith transfigured the tiny remnant of believers into worshipping saints gathered around the Lord's banquet table. They dreamed of a land beyond the sunset where skies are blue and hearts at rest. For a few brief hours, their burdens lifted. Soaring above circumstances, they turned tired eyes toward heaven. They lost themselves in worship as the Spirit came down to feed His lambs. Someone called it God's psychiatry, and its true professional shrinks would've had a hard time finding customers at Clay Hill.

Insofar as I know, Daddy was the only preacher ever to serve this tiny congregation. He was preaching there when I was born; when I was in grade school, middle and high school, college and graduate school; and when I married and moved to Tennessee.

As with many country churches, Clay Hill was mostly a one-family affair. The patriarch was a tall, powerful lumberjack called Boss Edwards. As in biblical times, the family patriarch made sure his whole family showed up on Sunday. So, Clay Hill was really half-church and half-family reunion as Brother Boss's blood relatives, nieces, nephews, cousins, in-laws, and possibly outlaws filed in to pay their respects to God and him, not necessarily in that order.

It was on a Saturday night in that dilapidated old house Jesus first spoke to my heart. Daddy was preaching and I daydreaming when suddenly I felt a powerful urging to ask the Lord's forgiveness. Too young to understand much about sin and guilt, I was nonetheless being drawn to the altar, as those good folks would say, "to get right with God."

Daddy was in mid-message, not even near an altar call, but the Holy Spirit was apparently making his own altar call. As soon as Daddy finished preaching and the opportunity came, I rushed up to the front weeping.

I was only seven years old, younger than the church normally accepted members, and people wondered if I was too young to realize what I was doing. Lucky for me, they didn't probe too deeply. With only a vague idea of the gospel, I couldn't have explained what songwriter Bill Gaither expressed so well:

> *He touched me, O, He touched me,*
> *And O, the joy that floods my soul,*
> *Something happened, and now I know,*
> *He touched me and made me whole.*[1]

So, they asked me a few simple questions about Jesus and what he did for us. I parroted back to them what little I'd managed to absorb, certainly not much theology.

The old patriarch, Brother Boss, came to my rescue. "We all see Brother Bennett's tears, and that's proof enough to me he's sincere. I move we welcome him into the arms of the church for baptism." End of discussion.

After the next Sunday's service, the tiny congregation gathered on the banks of Bogue Homa Creek. Daddy led me out into icy water and took me under—a cold day warmed by sacred memories.

To get to that lonely, old, wooden church took deliberate effort. Passage over those clay-slick roads in inclement weather was difficult. When it rained, driving a car uphill to the church was so risky folks parked along the roadside and hiked up the hill.

Out back of the old converted schoolhouse—and a respectable distance downhill—stood two ancient privies used by school kids in bygone years. Valentines, cupid arrows, and poems scrawled in crayon told of loves won and lost.

A rusty cast iron pump survived on top of Clay Hill, another holdover from school days. Some determined well digger penetrated hundreds of feet down through near-impermeable clay before finding sand, gravel, and drinking water.

The only way to coax water from the pump was by priming it, pouring water into the contraption's mouth while pumping fast and furious. Every kid had to try it. But woe to the child who failed to refill the can with priming water for the next thirsty seeker.

The old, wooden, church rotted away, and people dispersed. Yet, their God who showed up there on Sundays is the Ancient of Days who does not fade away. Simple folk with such childlike faith are not soon forgotten. Such memories likely inspired this old classic:

> *There's a church in the valley by the wildwood,*
> *No lovelier place in the dale;*
> *No place is so dear to my childhood*
> *As the little brown church in the vale.*[2]

When Daddy let me tag along on his pastoral calls, my education truly began. Maybe he was trying to make a preacher out of me, or maybe he was just keeping me out of trouble.

Television was reaching into country homes by the 1940s. Those simple souls often didn't think to turn the tube off (or volume down) when their pastor called. Daytime soap operas, tame by today's standards, got pretty steamy.

This made for awkward moments. Once, sitting bedside with a sick lady, we were forced to watch intimate love scenes—or get up and leave without praying for her. Another seriously ill saint was watching the World Series. Daddy had to wait until the game was over before praying for him.

One lady was dying of cancer. The smell of death was overwhelming. Daddy held her hand as he prayed for her. Yet, her fevered eyes were glued to *Days of our Lives*. One could barely hear Daddy praying above her blaring TV. Seeing how frustrating this was to Daddy, I later asked him, "Why didn't you ask her to turn it off?"

He responded, "Oh, she didn't know any better, and I didn't want to hurt her feelings."

We visited a cousin, who was suffering the latter stages of diabetes. His fingers and one leg had been amputated. His wife had left him.

His children were married and gone. Dirty clothes were heaped on the floor.

"Who's taking care of you?" Daddy asked.

"My sister comes when she can," he answered bravely. Daddy read from *Psalms* and prayed for him. As we said goodbye, Daddy's eyes grew moist. A dying man, almost blind, crippled, and ill-nourished, had been left alone in a decaying old house. Even as a kid following Daddy on his pastoral calls, I saw how tragic and cruel life can be.

Some pastoral visits were X-rated. Dad was asked by a deacon in his Pascagoula church to visit a retired dock worker who regaled us with ribald teamster jokes. I recall how uncomfortable Daddy looked until the sick man paused long enough for us to pray for him and leave. Later, he warned me severely against repeating crude jokes.

One of Daddy's church prospects lived on a farm with enticing fish ponds. The preacher's boy was allowed to fish for bream and bass while Daddy fished for souls. I remember thinking, "Who has the better deal?"

Did that man find peace with God? We can't say for sure, but isn't letting a kid fish in your pond like giving a cup of cold water to one of the least of these?

Invasion of the Holy Wasps

What can steal a kid's attention from God? How about stinging wasps buzzing around in a sanctuary?

Clay Hill Church was located so far back in the woods the electric company hadn't found it. The dilapidated old building was once a school house. So, instead of sitting in pews, we hunkered down in oak desks to worship. Running my fingers under a desktop one day, I felt the underside covered with well-chewed gum kids had hidden and then forgotten.

Since it was unheated, the drafty old place couldn't be used in cold weather. So, members volunteered their homes for winter services. After one particularly cold winter, when we went to clean and reopen the church for spring services, we ran into a problem.

When we unlocked the doors and opened the windows to air the place out, we found that the ceiling was covered with wasps: red wasps, black dirt-dabbers, Guinea wasps, hornets, and yellow jackets—all God's stinging and buzzing cousins. Since it was a cold spring day, they were still hibernating or too frozen to move, but Daddy knew when it warmed up and they began awakening, we'd be in trouble.

How to get rid of them? Everyone had a surefire remedy. Spraying with insecticide to kill them was ruled out for fear it could exterminate us. Someone vouched for burning sulfur-soaked rags inside the building. So, we collected large metal buckets, filled them with sulfur and old clothes, and set them all over the sanctuary.

Firing up the smoke bombs, we backed out, closing doors and windows. Of course, we watched through the windows as sulfur fumes began saturating the room. As the ceiling filled with rancid smoke, our invaders came to life, zooming around like fighter planes strafed by enemy fire. One by one, they buzzed out and fell to the floor. Finally, it was safe to go back into the sanctuary and sweep up the casualties.

But that's not the end of the story. We left the building closed that Saturday night and returned Sunday morning for services. Only a few of our stinging brethren had survived, and those had pasted themselves on the ceiling. So, we went ahead with the service.

Maybe our hallelujah singing revived them, or maybe it was the warm sunlight streaming in those windows? They slowly began crawling around on the ceiling, kicking out their heels, washing their faces, and coming to life.

As Daddy took to the pulpit for his message, my eyes were glued on a few thawed-out, smoke-crazed wasps now circling, dipping, and diving. The preacher bravely ignored them, pressing on with his sermon. It's a shame to admit it, but I was secretly hoping for a direct hit.

The Lord must've been watching over him because Daddy finished his sermon without being stung. It may have been a great message, but who knows? A mean little boy was betting on the wasps and lost.

Running Trap Lines

I'll never forget the day Daddy decided I was big enough to run trap lines with him. He set his traps in Bear Branch, Mill Creek, Beaver Dam, and streams within walking distance, checking them every day—a circuit of ten miles. Wearing wading boots, the preacher took a burlap sack to stuff his varmints in. He set his traps in shallow water where mink and fur-bearers hunt for food.

On a typical day he would bring home mink, otter, beaver, fox, or raccoon. Less desirable in the fur trade were skunks, weasels, opossums, and bobcats. Yet, even their hides yielded a few bucks. Daddy skinned them all, nailed their raw hides to our smokehouse wall, and then sold his hides to the highest bidder.

"Take my hammer and this box of tacks," Daddy told me one day. "You're big enough to start helping me cure these pelts."

That may not sound like a promotion, but it was a big deal for a kid itching to grow up and cut mamma's apron strings. I was going to be helping my Daddy, thank you.

The first coonskin I stretched out and nailed to the smokehouse wall looked pitiful, but Daddy knew my balloon was flat and needed air. "It's not bad for your first job" was as far as he stretched the truth.

Raw varmint hides have a distinctive aroma, none of them pleasant. A male raccoon skin reeks of urine. A polecat hide is the worst. Mink pelts emit a sweet smelling musk. Since mink fur was highly prized, the preacher didn't mind.

"Smells like money," he joked.

So that he could get back into his fields by noon, Daddy ran his trap lines beginning at daylight, walking at such a fast pace I was soon gasping. Kindly, he slowed down long enough for me to catch my breath and then took off through the woods, with me straining to keep up. When we reached a stream, Daddy waded in shallow water along the bank to keep from leaving his human scent—that would have warned varmints to avoid his traps.

His traps were so well hidden one could be looking directly at the spot without seeing them. One by one, we began collecting the night's catch. Sensing I was eager to help, he gave me the burlap bag to carry.

After a while, the varmints grew too heavy for me, so he took over. As we tended trap lines, Daddy entertained me with childhood stories:

> "Grandpa took me to town with him one day to buy supplies. As we were riding down the street in his buggy, grandpa leaned over to me and said, 'Ira, do you see that man crossing the street in front of us? There's a man the Lord hates.' That got my attention.
>
> 'Why does the Lord hate that man, Grandpa?' I asked.
>
> 'Well, my Bible says the Lord hates a proud look. Check him out.'
>
> When I looked back at the man, his nose was lifted high in the air, like he was looking down on everyone he met. Grandpa enjoyed his little joke— and gave me something to think about."

I always suspected Daddy was practicing his sermons on me, telling his favorite *Bible* stories like what happened when some mean boys made fun of Elisha, mocking and calling him baldy. God's prophet cursed them in the name of the Lord, and two female bears came out of the woods and killed them.

"Think twice, son, before you mock or make fun of your elders!"

Out on the trap lines, the preacher gave me heavy doses of parables and how Jesus outsmarted the Pharisees with wisdom that sent them slinking off in shame.

"How come Jesus always answered their questions with another question?" I asked.

"What kind of question is that?" the preacher replied.

Running traps with him one day, I asked Daddy why he never joined the Ku Klux Klan. I'd heard of cross burnings by mysterious men in white sheets. They sounded dangerously exciting, but I knew Daddy had a low opinion of them. I needed to know why. The preacher was short on education but gifted with what country folks call common horse-sense. I knew his advice could be trusted.

"Why are you asking?' Daddy came back at me, sensing a budding interest on my part.

"Someone told me they take wife-beaters out and whip them." Daddy waited for me to go on. He wanted to know how much I knew.

"And men too sorry and low-down to work and feed their family, they tar and feather them don't they? And deadbeats who gamble and drink until the grocery money's gone, don't they drag 'em out, beat 'em up, and warn 'em to straighten up or die?" Daddy was silent for a long time. Finally, he spoke.

"Son, it's a dangerous business when folks take the law into their own hands. Just because they wear white hoods don't mean they're doing God's work. Sometimes, the ones doing the beating are worse than their victims. Sometimes, they pick on someone because they have a grudge against him. Sometimes, their violence is fanned by hatred or prejudice. Be sure you think about what I'm telling you. Think about it long and hard before doing something you'll later regret".

That ended my infatuation with the KKK. For an impressionable kid, this one-on-one time with Daddy was all-important. He was sharing a legacy of integrity. Coming from a loving parent, this bonding time was a sacred gift. The preacher failed miserably, however, when he tried to teach me to become self-sufficient.

Honey Without Walmart

Daddy was amazingly resourceful in keeping food on our table. Honey was a good example. Even in this land of plenty, our milk and honey didn't arrive in bottles or on our doorsteps every morning.

Daddy grew up in Mississippi's backwoods where the towering trees had never been harvested. Wild honey bees thrived in those swampy hardwoods, making their hives in hollow trees. The trick was to find those hidden honey pots and then play Smokey the Bear by helping yourself.

Daddy learned how to watch a single bee collecting nectar, follow it through fields and woods, eventually returning to its hive. Marking the spot, he would return with smoke billows, axe, crosscut saw, and dishpans for convincing the bees to share their honey.

He tried to show me his tricks. We went out into his pasture one day where bees were feeding on clover blossoms. He picked one out:

"Here's the lady we're going to follow."

We watched her as she collected her sugary juice and then lifted into the air, heading home.

"We mustn't get so close we spook her but keep near enough we don't lose sight of her."

She'd lost me long ago. I was simply following Daddy. Into the woods she went, with us in pursuit. I was huffing and puffing, ready to give up when Daddy yelled, "Here they are!"

Racing up, I see streams of bees buzzing in and out of a hole in a hardwood tree.

"You see how easy it is!" Daddy bragged.

The color and taste of wild honey depends on the seasonal flowers the bees are feeding on. We were convinced wild honey is tastier than farm-raised honey.

I vowed to become a tracker, but my bees never cooperated. They managed to give me the slip every time. Having failed as a woodsman, I made up for it by eating more wild honey.

Bee colonies separate in the spring, with a queen bee eloping with hundreds of worker bees to form new hives. As they search for a new home, the queen alights on a limb and is covered with her loyal followers. Daddy would gently cut off a limb with the queen and her new family and then gingerly transplant the swarm into a new home he'd prepared for them.

In the spring, the bees went to work filling their new homes with honey. The preacher quietly collected dishpans full of honeycombs, leaving enough for the newborns to feed on. Using a wire mesh veil, long sleeves, and a smoke billows, he was seldom stung.

Unfairly, the bees took exception to me, going out of their way to single me out. Bees can smell a person who's afraid of them, and it makes them nervous. I must've been leaking fear. After being oft stung, I left the beekeeping to Daddy.

Mr. Russell, who farmed the land next to ours, robbed his bees with no protection. He wore short sleeved shirts. The bees covered his hands and arms while he gently removed the top of the hive and lifted out their precious honeycombs.

"Don't you get stung?" I asked.

"It doesn't hurt much, and, besides, it heals my rheumatism." OK.

Yes, the little boogers discriminated against me terribly. May they never qualify for a government grant!

Our ancestors were a sturdy lot, surviving without paychecks. Against all odds, they existed by hunting and fishing, gathering nuts, fruit, and roots from the woods, raising their own meat, and growing their own vegetables. They found the world full of promises but no guarantees. Realizing Uncle Sugar's not holding out a safety net to catch him when he falls takes away a man's crutch. He must make it on his own. He learns to work hard and trust in God. Our ancestors got it.

Learning From Hard Knocks

Do you remember thinking you'd never grow up? My siblings had all flown the coop. Living free, calling their own shots, having a ball. Life seemed so unfair!

A boy was playing by a fireplace near his momma and daddy. Would he ever grow up, he wondered? After dinner, Daddy was reading the *Bible*. Momma was nodding off in her rocking chair. Above the fireplace, a heavy log served as a mantle. The mantle towered above him as the boy romped near the fire.

"I can't wait 'til I'm as tall as that mantle!" he complained to no one in particular. Daddy lifted off his reading glasses; watching the boy stretch to touch the mantle. Even on tiptoes, the mantle was a good foot above the child. The preacher responded, "Well, it'll happen sooner than you think."

Fast forward two or three years, and the same kid is playing near the fireplace while Daddy is absorbed in *King James*. Suddenly, the boy stands up, cracking his head against that mantle. Going into a tailspin, he's groaning and complaining.

"I thought you couldn't wait to grow as tall as that mantle!" teases Daddy. He and Momma enjoy a good laugh, and the boy learns from one of those hard bumps that life often teaches.

The preacher allowed himself one vice: chewing tobacco. In his overalls bib, he kept a plug of his beloved Apple Sun Cured chewing tobacco. If Old Pete, his cantankerous mule, behaved himself, Daddy sometimes cut off a tiny bite for him to taste.

Oh, how good that Apple Sun Cured tobacco smelled! Daddy squirreled it away in his dresser drawer. When he wasn't watching, I'd slip around, open that forbidden drawer, and sniff the rich aroma.

One day Daddy cut off a plug to chew. Yielding to temptation, I screwed up my courage to ask, "May I try it?" The preacher cut off another plug and handed it to me. He watched in amusement as I stuffed it in my mouth, chewing and tasting the sweet juice.

Now, Daddy could've said no. He could've warned me against swallowing the juice. Instead, he let nature take its course. Soon, I grew terribly nauseated. Hot saliva flooded my mouth, threatening to empty my stomach.

"What's the problem?" Daddy wanted to know. After that, he never needed to hide his tobacco.

A Neighbor Steals His Land

Our farm consisted of eighty acres of black fertile soil. Later when the owner failed to pay his taxes Daddy bought a third forty-acre plot.

Not being able to pay one's taxes was common following the Depression. So, Daddy went to the courthouse, paid the back taxes, and was given a Quit Claim Deed. Years later, a neighbor looking through county records discovered Daddy had neglected to convert his Quit Claim Deed to a regular deed.

Seizing this opportunity, the scalawag signed an affidavit swearing the land was unclaimed, knowing Daddy had fenced it and was paying the taxes. When Daddy told the tax assessor of the false affidavit, a court date was set to hear the case. On the day of the hearing, Daddy failed to show up. The swindling neighbor's lawyer convinced the judge to award the land to his client.

The man was a highly respected member of our community. One day he drove up to our house to make peace with Daddy. Momma refused to let him come inside so Daddy went out and sat in his car to talk.

He claimed it was all a misunderstanding. Daddy knew better but let him have his say. When they parted, he even shook the scoundrel's hand. Momma was furious, but Daddy explained, "The Lord wants us to live in peace with our neighbors." He believed God settles all accounts, and he slept well at night.

Hero worship of Daddy made me wonder if God was calling me to be a preacher. One night, I almost heard that call. Two carloads of people arrived from Daddy's church in Mobile. Momma had invited them out to the farm to visit and enjoy a home cooked country meal. After dinner, they gathered in our parlor for singing and worship. Then, they passed the hat for the preacher.

As the hat filled with dollar bills, one of the deacons had a fine idea—or so it seemed to me. "I think Brother Bennett's going to be a preacher. Let's pass the hat again for him." Digging into his pocket, he came out with a handful of change. Others tossed in quarters, dimes, nickels and pennies. It was almost enough to make one hear the Lord calling!

Daddy took me aside later to make it clear that God's call to ministry was a sacred trust, not to be influenced by a hatful of money. Though Daddy didn't put me in the pulpit to preach, he let me ride the Greyhound bus and travel with him.

Circuit Riding on Greyhound

Daddy was without a car until I was in high school. When I was old enough to ride the Greyhound bus, he often took me on his weekend preaching trips.

Daddy served Alabama churches in and around Mobile, including Prichard, Chritten, and Semmes. By catching a bus in mid-afternoon, we'd arrive in Mobile before dinner. A deacon would be waiting at the bus stop to take us home for dinner.

When we reached Mobile one Saturday afternoon, Brother and Sister Rachael were waiting to take us home with them for dinner. After the meal, we sat out on their cool screened-in porch talking God stuff.

Then, Brother Rachael did a strange thing. He reached in his pocket and pulled out a nickel, "Brother Bennett, take this to the end of our street, and wait on the corner. Pretty soon you'll hear a bell ringing. A van will pull up and stop. Go to the open window, and hand the driver this nickel. He has a surprise for you."

So, the country boy did as he was told. The man handed me a double-dip vanilla ice cream cone, the first one I'd ever tasted. Dying and waking up in heaven would've hardly been more thrilling.

After dinner, we piled in the deacon's car, heading for Saturday night church services. After church, we'd stay overnight with the same family who met us at the bus stop. After Sunday services, the church ladies spread their potluck dishes on tables underneath the giant evergreen oaks for a time of food and fellowship. They called it "Dinner on the Ground."

After eating and fellowshipping, it was time to catch the bus home. Back in the country, Daddy donned his overalls or trapping boots until next weekend.

The most colorful character we traveled with was Brother Banks, one of Daddy's frequent preaching companions. We called him the preaching judge. Elder Banks was a retired judge. A lanky man with shaggy silver hair, Brother Banks came with a repertoire of lawyer jokes.

Brother Banks and Daddy rode circuit together, responding to invitations to preach at local churches. When I was old enough to go with them, the judge sometimes convinced Daddy to bring me along. Sitting in the back seat, I enjoyed their bantering and warm friendship. Some of the judge's lawyer jokes were too colorful to suit Daddy's taste, but he tolerated them out of respect, warning me not to repeat them.

One Saturday afternoon, we went fishing with the pastor of a church where they were to preach that night. This pastor was a well-known bass fisherman, who carved his own lures.

He guided us to a bass-filled lake and loaned us his boat, fishing rods, reels, and lures. We were expecting great things, but an East wind kicked up, tossing us up and down the lake. We came back empty-handed.

Recalling the story of Jesus showing the disciples where to cast their nets, Judge Banks remarked, "We sure needed His help today didn't we? No, on second thought, even Jesus couldn't catch bass with an East wind blowing!"

Daddy dreamed of pioneering a new church. One day, opportunity knocked on our farmhouse door.

A carload of folks had driven out to the farm to see Daddy. They were from Pascagoula and Moss Point, towns on Mississippi's gulf coast. Looking to start up a church, they asked Daddy if he would pray about helping them.

Daddy had already been praying for a new ministry opportunity. Convinced this was God's answer, he gladly accepted their invitation.

They found a Masonic Lodge to rent, notified friends and family, and held their first service the following Sunday. After a year or so in their rented quarters, the young church built a permanent house of worship in Pascagoula.

One Saturday night after church services, Deacon Hollis's son took me out on the town. He was into drag racing on city streets. Unfortunately for him, the police had been alerted. They clocked us going through a red light at 90 MPH. They were not quick enough to stop him but took his license number. We came home after midnight and went to bed thinking we'd eluded them. Then, his father's telephone rang.

It was the police. The deacon woke us up and hauled us down to the police station. The police booked the deacon's son for reckless driving and warned me about the company I was keeping.

Brother Hollis must've felt compassion for me—he didn't tell Daddy. Nonetheless, it was a sobering lesson to think of the shame we caused an innocent father—and the risks we foolishly took of killing someone or being killed.

One of Daddy's deacons (not that one) pulled strings to get me a summer job at Ingalls Shipyard in Pascagoula when I graduated from high school. Because I was saving money for college, the family let me live with them rent free.

Crawling through steel hulls of warships under construction, we installed copper gas lines. Summer heat was stifling inside the belly of those destroyers. Humongous electric fans kept us from being overcome by heat stroke.

The work was miserable but paid well. I was grateful for the opportunity. Sister Faulkner (my host family) fed me and did my laundry. By their kind hospitality, I saved enough to pay tuition for the first year of college. Thanks, dear friends, for giving the preacher's boy a break.

Before packing off to college, the school-of-hard-knocks had more lessons to be endured. Every time the preacher was called away from home, trouble sneaked in our back door.

The Preacher's Bull

Daddy bought a young bull of great promise. A pure-blood Shorthorn, he would hopefully upgrade our beef cattle herd by doing what bulls do best. We pampered and petted him until he grew so gentle cousin Clem and I began to get ideas. One weekend when Daddy was away preaching, we decided to break him to ride.

It was early spring, and Momma's garden had been freshly disked for planting. We decided this soft ground would be a perfect spot for bull-busting. So, we borrowed ropes from Daddy's stable, tying one around the young bull's middle and another around his neck. Together, we led him out for training.

Clem held him while I mounted, locked my legs around his body, and twisted my hands under the rope around his middle. When Clem let go, the bull went wild, quickly bucking me off. Landing in the soft dirt unhurt, I climbed back on. After several more unsuccessful attempts to hang on, Clem climbed on while I held the ropes. He fared no better, but we were having great fun.

Gradually, the bull began to tire, bucking less and more weakly until finally he gave up. We rode him around the garden and out to the house to show Momma. Sadly, she did not share our triumph.

"What's your Daddy going to say?" she warned. This was a new and disturbing thought. Sure enough, her concern was well founded. What we counted as a great victory turned into near tragedy.

Next morning, the yearling bull was sick. Apparently, he'd become so overheated and overwrought, pneumonia had set in. There was nothing to do but wait for Daddy to come home and confess our sins. He took one look at the bull and the mess we'd made in Momma's garden. Then, Daddy did what fathers down through the ages have done to "bring up a child in the way he should go." The preacher was not a disciple of Dr. Spock.

The good news is the young bull survived. However, our careers as bull-busters were over. Pains of childhood began morphing into agonies of adolescence.

The Devil Made Us Do It!

We learned from the preacher that laughter is a solvent for tough times, a balm for bumps and bruises. Humor helped him navigate when his compass failed, but he drew the line at friskiness or frivolity at the dinner table or the church door.

Sisters Iris and Geraldine were often rebuked for tittering at the table. Iris could merely look at Gerry and make her crack-up. She reveled in using her tickle power to get Gerry in trouble.

Knowing the preacher didn't tolerate foolishness at the table made it doubly tempting. In fact, the madder he grew, the harder it was for the girls to control their tickle-box. Meals were missed when one or the other, sometimes both, was banished from the table.

We were constantly in danger of calling down lightning by our unbridled horseplay. As much as we feared Daddy's wrath, the temptations often proved too strong to resist.

I'll never forget my first communion. Always a sacred rite, it was even more solemn on the one Sunday each year when a foot-washing ceremony was added. As a child, my feet were so ticklish I couldn't bear anyone touching them. Of course, when they discovered this, my sisters took turns holding me down and tickling my feet.

When I joined the church, I was expected to wash a brother's feet and then let him wash mine. You can imagine what a danger this posed. The prospect was frightening. I knew it would be impossible to get through the service without making a scene. Lord forgive me, I pretended to be sick that Sunday.

Have you been in places or situations where you couldn't laugh? (I need some empathy here.) Didn't that make it almost impossible to control?

"I was in Sunday school," recalls my buddy John. "A bashful boy was reading aloud to our class. 'Great crowds are following Jesus around the Sea of Galilee to see his miracles and hear his teachings. And the multitudes came down to the water,' says the scripture.

Unfortunately, the boy's pronunciation wasn't perfect so it came out like this: 'And the mule tides came down to the water.'"

On another memorable day, the preacher was reading an *Old Testament* story of the Lord coming down to fight for Israel and rout their enemies: "And God's foes were fleeing." Unfortunately, his tongue got tangled, and it came out, "And God's fleas were flowing."

You see the problem? Learning when not to laugh was like walking a tightrope—without a net. The results were often disastrous. Surely, the Devil was having a field day!

Coffee Breaks

Southerners relish their coffee breaks like polar bears enjoy their icebergs. Daddy was no exception. Next to his time alone with God, coffee breaks came in a close second. Making a fresh pot of coffee was the first thing he did in the morning. After a quick first cup, he rushed out to do barnyard chores, returning for breakfast with coffee. He then worked in the field until mid-morning, at which time he took another coffee break. Iced tea for lunch was followed by a mid-afternoon coffee break. After supper, Momma brewed a fresh pot that she and Daddy sipped until bedtime.

"Coffee never keeps me awake at night—unless I've left some in the pot," he joked.

The preacher drank his hot coffee country-style, pouring it into a saucer to cool and then slurping it down loudly. When I tried it, Momma grabbed my saucer. "Just because I married a yokel doesn't mean I'm raising one."

Running from Daddy

One day, sister Geraldine and I were playing outside when she did something to upset me. Sisters know just what to do to get your goat, right? I've long forgotten what she did, but I rose to the bait, screaming out at her a most uncharitable name. Big mistake! Daddy was down in his peach orchard and overheard our little tiff.

"Bennett, I think you better come over here a minute," he called. Oh, how those words chilled my naughty little bones. I'd been busted. Gerry was gloating.

It seemed like a mile, trudging over to Daddy, who was still pruning his peach trees. Approaching, I noticed he'd cut off a slender branch and was preparing it just for me. This was too much. I wheeled around and bolted the other way.

"Don't you run from me!" he yelled. I ran faster. There was just one problem: my legs were shorter than his. From somewhere behind me, I heard him take off after me.

Sensing big time disaster, I revved it up to the last notch, but it was not enough; Daddy was closing in fast. I pulled out the last straw in my bag, the old dead possum trick, falling down and pretending to be dead.

Daddy lifted me up by the strap of my little overalls and began using his peach switch. Naturally, I bellowed and pleaded to no avail. The teaching moment continued until Daddy lost the will to go on. Then, he dropped the switch and held me in his arms.

"Son, believe me that hurt me more than it did you." "Doubtful," I'm thinking but wisely kept my mouth shut.

"But I had no choice. You called your sister a bad name and then ran from me to avoid your punishment. Have you learned your lesson?"

"Yes, Sir!" It was the first and last time I ran from Daddy. I can't say it was the last time I fought with my sister, but I never did it when Poppa Bear was within earshot.

Now, if the preacher was severe with me, he truly hardened his heart against the Boll Weevil.

Boll Weevils and Scuppernongs

Goliath never made it to Mississippi, but the Preacher faced his own giants. Cotton was his big cash crop. It was also the weevil's gourmet meal ticket.

Momma bought our school clothes with the first bale of cotton Daddy ginned every September. Daddy took what was left to pay off his bills where he'd bought animal feed, fertilizer, and farm supplies on credit.

So, when boll weevils descended like a plague, it struck fear into the hearts of every soul with a cotton patch. The ugly little boogers put many out of business by eating the buds, blossoms, and bolls off their cotton plants.

The preacher went out and bought a machine-gun-looking contraption to wage war. It was a hand-cranked duster he strapped on his back and filled with a deadly poison called arsenic of lead.

I can still see him walking fast between two cotton rows with that evil-looking machine fogging out a cloud of poison. The duster sported forked tubes, so by walking between two rows of cotton, he was dusting two rows at a time. Sometimes, his duster would be throwing out such a cloud of fog we could see nothing except the preacher's legs and feet churning up and down those rows.

This was before it was known that arsenic is a deadly pesticide that causes cancer. Daddy wore long sleeved shirts, gloves, face mask, and breathing filter. Still, when he came out of the field, he looked like a bumblebee that's been wallowing in pollen. His whole body was yellow with arsenic dust. Besieged farmers were taking a terrible risk, but they had no choice. For all the danger it posed, arsenic saved our cotton crops from ruin.

The preacher had a world of friends but few enemies until the boll weevil came hopping along. Smaller than a watermelon seed, looking like the old movie star Jimmy Durante, a weevil's snout is almost as long as his brownish black body.

Daddy was told his weevils were a gift from Mexico. Cousin Fishing Jimmy heard it from a hobo who heard it in a Bogalusa honky-tonk:

> *De boll weevil is a little black bug*
> *f'um Mexico dey say,*
> *He came to try dis Texas soil*
> *An' thought he'd better stay.*
> *CHORUS: A-lookin' for a home,*
> *Jes a-lookin' for a home.*[3]

Fishing Jimmy said the sneaky pests backpedaled across the Rio Grande into Texas around 1890. Into blazing dry fields they marched, did this first wave of immigrants.

Feasting in West Texas cotton fields, they thrived in that weevil heaven. By this time, lawmen had conquered Billy the Kid and a host of pretty-faced gunslingers. The good citizens of Texas now turned their blazing six-guns on the boll weevil, rhetorically speaking. Rounding up all buffalo left on the plains, they spooked them into a stampede. The young and virile boll weevils, their ears to the ground, felt the earth shaking and wisely beat it across the state line into Louisiana. Of course, no elderly or lazy teenage weevils made it to the border, being ground into Texas sand by a thousand thundering hooves.

The invaders found Louisiana even less hospitable. Local folks called Cajuns scooped them up in crawfish nets, battered them with Tabasco sauce, and then French-fried them as a side dish. This was too much for the boll weevils. A remnant escaped, hiding on the banks of the Mississippi River in trash cans and outdoor privies.

When Big Muddy swelled over her banks next spring, the discouraged survivors hopped on dead limbs, floating leaves, and debris, dog-paddling their way across. Crawling ashore, they found Utopia—thousands of acres of delicious cotton in the Mississippi delta. Home at last!

And that, according to Fishing Jimmy, is how Mississippi became the Hospitality State. Thank you, Gomez!

For every affliction suffered under those blazing summer suns, the good Lord sent a blessing. Or so the preacher claimed. Maybe God felt so bad about the boll weevils, He gifted Southerners with Scuppernongs. Scuppernongs keep more kids down on the farm than a mother's love. Of course, watermelons and strawberries won our hearts, too, but nothing compares with stuffing mouthfuls of those delectable grape-like clusters into your mouth until juice dribbles down your chin.

Only in Dixie does one find scuppernongs growing on arbors a kid can walk under—plucking them off the vines, cramming them into their mouths, crushing them, and swallowing quickly before the sweet nectar overflows and bubbles out.

Daddy planted his scuppernongs in low bottomlands he called branch-heads, below his fields in the edge of the woods. The dense foliage under scuppernong arbors offers a welcome shade from hot fields. Like a mirage in the desert, we couldn't wait to take a rest break so we could stand under the vines, popping scuppernongs in our mouths until the preacher called us back to work.

Years later, we learned our new home in Maryland is the northernmost region where Scuppernongs can be grown. God had not abandoned us. When our grandkids were old enough to enjoy scuppernongs, we built them an arbor. Recently, one of those wide-eyed scuppernong eaters, now grown up and enrolled in college, called from his campus.

"Guess what, Peeps?" (Peeps is his pet name for me) "I just went to the grocery store here in North Carolina and found scuppernongs!" No doubt his education is complete.

Competing With Daddy

In those growing-up years when boys need a role model, Daddy rode forth in shining armor. Watching his every move, I decided he could do no wrong. He became my gold standard.

True, he was merely a country preacher, a self-educated dirt farmer. A humble man, he truly thought others better than himself. He called his best friend "Mister Russell" and said "Sir" and "Ma'am" to his neighbors.

The sun rose and the moon set in my Daddy. I tried to imitate his deep baritone voice, his rollicking laugh, and his every manner. When I was a teenager, this infantile worship morphed into competition. I wondered if I'd ever best him at anything. My heart told me the preacher would always be faster, stronger, smarter, and in every way better than I.

So, it became super-important to outdo him at something, anything to prove my manhood. Of course, Daddy caught on to my juvenile schemes.

"Do you seriously think you can outdo your Daddy?" he teased. So, he enjoyed our little competition, and he always came out on top.

The preacher had picked 300 pounds of cotton one day in the fertile Mississippi delta. On my 16th birthday I decided to test Daddy's record.

September 22 promised to become a furnace. Up jumped the sun and slapped the Devil's wife. It was one of those long sultry days when the vernal equinox can't decide to let go of the sun, when touching a car door burns one's hand or walking barefoot across a blacktop road blisters your feet, when gravel roads turn into ribbons of dust and dirt devils dance at the slightest breeze, when birds sit on telephone lines lifting their wings to cool overheated bodies, when buzzards ride air currents, sniffing for a free meal, or sit in dead treetops with drooping heads and stricken hearts, when pigs seek relief in water-filled mud holes, when dogs crawl under front porches and cats slink inside shady corn cribs, when doodlebugs peek out from a hole in the ground, then close their trap-doors and cry.

But for a boy determined to outdo his Daddy, it was fine cotton-picking weather. So, I bounded out of bed and into the field at dawn. By the time Momma called us in for breakfast, I'd picked 40 pounds.

Wolfing down her hot biscuits, eggs, and bacon, I hurried back to the field, picking furiously with both hands, dragging a six-foot-long cotton sack behind me. By noon, I'd picked and weighed-in 150 pounds, on target to become the new champion.

My hopes were soaring, never having beaten Daddy at anything. This was big. What a great way to celebrate becoming a man—to leave my father in the dust. Of course, Daddy knew what was going on in my fevered little brain, how this crazy dare had mushroomed into a do-or-die dream. He must've been wonderfully amused.

How was this going to end? Would I have to eat crow and once again acknowledge the preacher's superiority, like those countless times he'd trounced me fishing, hunting, playing games, or working in the fields?

Knowing how badly a boy wants to beat his Daddy, the preacher egged me on with good-natured gloating. True, he was always one step ahead, and it rattled my nerves. Today, though, I had a fighting chance.

Came noontime, Momma made me sit at the table long enough to gobble down her cornbread and field peas, cooked with fatback, washing it down with raw milk. After lunch, Daddy and our cotton pickers took a break to cool off and let their food settle. Not me. No siesta was worth risking failure. Back in the field before they finished eating, I was feeling invincible.

But Old Man Sun was going to have his say. Before mid-afternoon, thermometers leapt well above 100. It was a day the sun stood still—Joshua must've still been praying. Sweat was rolling down our foreheads, into our eyes, burning and blinding us. We couldn't drink enough water to stay hydrated. I was losing salt, slowing down, and watching everyone head for the nearest shade tree yet too stubborn and too dumb to know I couldn't last much longer.

"Come on, son, your face is beet-red; let's go down to the spring and cool off before you have sunstroke," Daddy was gently tapping me on the shoulder. That's when it dawned on me that beating Daddy wasn't all-important. He was protecting me because he loved me; that made my silly game seem petty.

Yet, I still wasn't ready to admit defeat. Late afternoon came and went; the sinking sun loomed large and red in the sky and finally dropped beyond the horizon. I kept picking. Everyone left to weigh in their cotton. I stubbornly kept going until it was getting too dark to see.

Finally, Daddy came out and said, "Son, it's time to come home; you couldn't see a snake if he crawled on top of you." That got my attention.

Did I win? No and yes. I'd picked 275 pounds. It was not enough to beat Daddy, but strangely I felt good about it. I'd won my father's respect, and he'd shown how much he loved me. What could be more important than that?

Years later, I finally realized my lifelong dream of outdoing Daddy. When it happened, would you believe it was bittersweet? With Dot and our young daughters, Linda, Jan, and Talisa, I was living in Oak Ridge, Tennessee. One day, I found a fishing lure that looked promising and mailed it home to Daddy. The first time he tossed it in a river he caught a four pound bass.

"I'm thinking, this is going to be a winner," he recalled. He never caught another fish with that lure.

Months later, we came home for a visit; Daddy and I went fishing in our favorite farm pond.

"Here, try my new lure," Daddy urged. On the first cast, a bass struck it. Same thing happened next time. After catching several fish, I handed it back to Daddy.

"Give it a try," I said. He'd been watching me cast and retrieve it. He tossed the same lure using the same jerky-twitchy motions to attract a bass. No luck. Finally he gave up, handing it back to me. When I tossed it out again, the same thing happened; bass began striking it.

Somehow, it just didn't seem right. After all those years of admiring the preacher, he would always be my ideal. It brings little joy *ever* to outdo your hero.

A Dream Comes True

Someone has said every boy needs to hear three things from his father: "Son, I love you;" "Son, you're good at what you do;" "Son, I'm proud of you."

Maybe it's in our DNA, this burning passion to please our father, to win his respect and admiration. Certainly, I was no exception. If I'd only known, my father's love wasn't performance-based. It flowed freely out of his gentle heart. Like God's love for us, we don't have to earn it. He loves us because that's His nature. In fact, He created us for companionship, to be with Him forever. Before Daddy died, a small miracle helped me put this puzzle together.

Trent Lott, then a Congressman and soon to be Leader of the United States Senate, was fighting an uphill battle to keep the Federal Government from burying high-level nuclear wastes (HLW) in a salt dome under the town of Richton, MS.

The town was in Mr. Lott's voting district and near our farm. In fact, Daddy often trapped in Beaver Dam Creek which the Feds planned to confiscate as part of the HLW repository. Ten thousand residents would lose their homes and be relocated. Citizens were frightened, desperate, and angry.

Since I was working at the Nuclear Regulatory Commission, Mr. Lott asked me to join his staff as Congress was drafting laws to control HLW disposal. When he and his friends in Congress were successful in steering the waste away from Mississippi, the people were jubilant.

Soon afterward, the Congressman was speaking to a crowd of grateful citizens in Petal, MS. He knew my father was in the audience.

Trent pointed the preacher out to the crowd and then went out of his way to shamelessly magnify my role in keeping nuclear waste out of the nearby salt dome. Daddy called me that very night.

"If you'd been here today," he declared, "People would've elected you mayor!"

Soon after that funny episode, the preacher was called home, but not before he'd given me those three gifts every boy needs from his Father.

J. Bennett Easterling

PART III

A BOYHOOD TO DREAM OF

About falling in love with a pig, a dog, a team of log-hauling oxen, and bellowing bullfrogs, but barely surviving a pack of bloodhounds and the preacher's devil-mule.

J. Bennett Easterling

A Boy and a Dog

Pup was the dog every boy needs: a Black and Tan Coonhound, a gift from friends. We named him Little Pup. After he grew up, that ingenious name no longer fit. So, we came up with one even more creative: Old Pup.

Pup was a bosom buddy to whoever tossed a biscuit his way. He was *my* constant companion. One day, my sister, Edith, took us back in the woods looking for Honeysuckle and Sweet Shrubs—wildflowers to plant into our yard.

At Bear Branch, as we were crossing over a foot log, Little Pup fell into the swollen stream. I thought he was a goner. Without thinking, I leaped off the log to save him—a bad idea since I couldn't swim a lick.

Edith grabbed the back of my shirttail just as I leaped, dragging me back onto the log. Little Pup dog-paddled out, shaking himself off, happy and ready to roll. Nobody had told me puppies come into the world knowing how to swim.

Pup knew Daddy was his master, but I was his buddy. He loved our whole family, but his heart belonged to me. We ate and slept together—doing chores, going to the mailbox, playing hide-and-seek or toss and fetch.

Little Pup could soon outrun me. He loved our racing contests. He learned to STOP and GO on command. Looking up at me for the GO, he'd blast off. When he was almost out of sight I'd yell STOP! He'd wait for me to catch up so we could do it again.

When he was bigger, I taught Pup to dance, putting his front feet on my chest for a lively tango. But when I kissed him on the nose and he licked me in the mouth, my sister Geraldine lost it. She had a point. After all these years, I can still almost smell that hound dog's halitosis.

One day, Pup followed me out to the barnyard to feed our chickens. Knowing he wanted to please me, I took advantage of his loyalty by ordering him to eat corn. He looked up at me as if to say, "You don't really mean that, do you?"

Of course, dogs don't eat corn. Pup certainly knew it. Nonetheless, I shelled some grains out on the ground and insisted, "Pup, eat that corn!"

He pretended to eat it—just because I said so. That wasn't good enough, though. I got down on all fours, pointed to the corn, and demanded in my most severe kid voice, "Pup, eat that corn!" God bless him, he did it!

Pup hated possums, but he loved to hunt them. He roamed the woods with us at night, following his nose until he picked up a fresh possum scent. Howling with delight, he'd begin trailing the possum until he would catch up with it and run it up into a tree. His bark turned into a deep-throated call, "Come on guys, here he is!"

When we shined the headlight up in the tree; two bright eyes were often looking down at us. Pup circled the tree faster and faster. If the possum was on a low limb, we'd see his face, even his white teeth, grinning down at us. If the tree was small, we'd shake the possum down, proudly presenting it to Daddy, who skinned and sold varmint hides to fur buyers.

Pup became obsessed with possums. At night, he'd pace back and forth begging us to go possum hunting. If he couldn't get a taker, Pup roamed the woods alone. He'd tree a possum and then circle the tree, barking until someone came to claim his prize. If no one showed up, Pup stayed there all night, baying at the moon. At daylight, if the possum still had not come down, Pup would finally come home, disappointed. "Where were you?" he seemed to be chastising us.

On warm summer nights with our bedroom windows open, we'd hear Pup down in the woods, yelping forlornly for us to come get a possum he'd treed. Sometimes, even Daddy didn't have the heart to ignore him. We'd fire up the carbide lamp and head out, following Pup's hopeful barking.

Sometimes, he'd have a surprise waiting for us—an unhappy raccoon up the tree. A raccoon skin might bring ten bucks—quite a windfall for a hard-pressed preacher with eight mouths to feed.

Pup dearly loved hunting squirrels, and he was particular about his hunting companions, preferring to hunt with Daddy or me. A brother-in-law Pup refused to hunt with turned out to be quite a rascal. Momma joked that Pup knew a bad egg when he smelled it!

Pup never tired of playing our "tick game." Tick powders were unheard of on the farm. If they existed, only people with money could afford them. So, we used home remedies to get rid of fleas and ticks. Dog ticks are so tiny they're hard to see until they gorge themselves with blood, becoming the size of butterbeans. Then, we'd pick them off for Pup to attack, kill, and eat. Pup was never happier than when we were helping him get revenge on those tormenting ticks.

Pup didn't know about Adam and Eve's encounter with the serpent, but he inherited a woman's disdain for snakes. He attacked every one he ran across, grabbing them in their mid-section, slinging them, and popping the life out of them. All this time the snakes were viciously striking him. After these fight-till-death battles, Pup's face sometimes swelled up twice its normal size. He'd lie around for days near death while the venom raged. Taking him to a doctor was out of the question. "No vets for pets" was a hard fact of life on the farm.

So, we'd rub him down with liniment, telling him what a good snake killer he was, coaxing him back to the world of the living. Sooner or later he'd recover—ready to sling the guts out of the next snake unlucky enough to cross his path.

Pup was a Romeo, disappearing for days at a time, falling in love and making puppies. We never met any of his romantic interests. We'd simply wait for him and welcome him back home. Years passed, but Pup never lost his zeal for romance. One day, he left home and didn't return for a long time. When he did, he'd been in a fight with a younger or stronger dog. He was chewed up and mauled beyond recovery.

We washed off his wounds and gave him a bowl of cool water. He couldn't raise his head so we opened his mouth and squeezed out a wet bath cloth, giving him a few drops to cool his fevered tongue.

Momma brought out a soft blanket for him to lie on. We moved him out of the hot sun to the shade of a Tung oil tree outside Momma's kitchen window so she could watch. Soaking his wounds with Pine Orem ointment to keep him comfortable, the preacher patched him up to stop the bleeding.

As Pup lay dying, Daddy and I dragged a couple of lawn chairs out to the shade of that Tung tree to be near him. Watching his life ebb away, we talked of the good times he'd given us. Pup couldn't understand what we were saying, but seemed to sense our breaking hearts.

Daddy reminisced of raccoons and possums Pup helped him get when he desperately needed a few dollars to pay grocery bills. I reminded Daddy of the day Little Pup fell off a foot log into Bear Branch and how I was diving in to save him when Edith grabbed me by the collar.

We laughed together about Pup's eating habits. Docile by nature, he tolerated no interference when eating. Interlopers risked a mauling if they tried to steal a bite. We dared not mess with him while he was wolfing down his vittles. Though Pup loved me like a blood brother, he had one limit: "Don't touch my plate!"

This was hard for a kid to understand, but Pup had his reasons. Hungry cats were lurking nearby, dashing in to grab any unguarded scrap. Other dogs belonging to our farm workers were watching and waiting. Momma's free range chickens were looking to steal a bite. So, when we dropped food in his bowl, he gulped it down fast, glancing side-to-side, growling furiously at any intruder.

I'd tease him while he ate, pretending to take his bowl away, but I dared not touch him until he finished. Food is serious stuff, and over the years I came to appreciate Pup's no-nonsense rules.

Yep, Pup had his priorities: "Nobody trifles with my food." It's become one of my guiding principles.

Pup seemed to know we were hanging out there just for him, sharing those last moments. He looked up at us with his soft brown eyes, feebly wagged his tail, trying to say, "I love you guys."

Time stood still. For a long while, we stayed beside him. Daddy fanned our old wounded warrior with his turtle shell hat to keep the blowflies off.

Gradually Pup's breathing grew softer. It was time to say goodbye. He gave us one last look of loving appreciation and quietly slipped away.

Daddy saw me sobbing. I was ashamed until I glanced over and saw tears in his eyes. Momma came out to join us. We stood over his body in a little circle as Daddy said a prayer.

The preacher said God had given us a faithful friend. We stood there with a thousand memories washing over us, reliving the joys. Then, Daddy made me go inside while he dug a hole and buried him.

Those of you who've loved and been loved by a special pet will understand: Such a bond is never broken. A beloved companion passes on, his faithful heart stops beating, but in our memory's eye we still see and touch him.

Oh, for those halcyon days when love flowed so freely!

A Tale of True Love

Bell was not meant to be a pet. She was merely a Britney Spaniel with a bugling bark that sounded like a clear ringing bell—hence, her name. She shared a kennel with other hunting dogs, but that was about to change.

Dogs were almost as important to Daddy as his mule. True, mules helped keep bread on the table, but what's bread without meat? That's where his dogs earned their keep.

Church mouse poor, yes, but we were rich in dogs. Canines helped us hunt wild game for food. Bird dogs, squirrel dogs, rabbit chasers, deer hounds, all did their share. The preacher also used them to hunt mink and other valuable fur-bearing animals.

This one sweet female dog named Bell won our hearts. She was so eager to please and thought she was human. The preacher trained her to hunt mink. Bell had a terrific nose to sniff out a mink's scent and trail it to a hollow log or hole in the ground where Daddy could capture it.

While poor folks were rebounding from the Great Depression, scrounging for nickels and dimes, rich divas still demanded their stoles and fur coats. A premium mink hide was worth a week's wages. To a hard-pressed preacher with six kids, Bell's uncanny nose for mink made her Daddy's special meal ticket.

Word spread about his superstar mink dog. Neighbors and strangers began showing up, wanting to buy her. Daddy wouldn't hear of it.

Making sure she wasn't kidnapped by envious hunters, Daddy took Bell out of the kennel at night, bringing her in to sleep on our screened-in back porch. Of course, we kids fell in love with her. Despite Daddy's strict rules against such folly, we secretly adopted her as our very own pet.

All this attention didn't spoil her sweet nature; she remained as gentle as a kitten. Bell was happy with the world, her smile-train going 24/7. We snitched goodies from the table, slipping them to her. Momma didn't care for dogs, but Bell won her over by easing up to her rocking chair and nuzzling her little chin on her lap. Momma stitched together a soft quilt-pallet for Bell to sleep on.

She loved to play "keep away." We circled round her, tossing a rubber ball just over her head. Sometimes, we'd play until Momma called supper or until it became too dark to see the ball.

She loved us more than she loved her canine family. When anyone stepped out of the house, Bell abandoned the other hounds to play with us. If we were working in the garden, she tagged along at our heels.

One day a stranger drove up and offered Daddy an incredible price for Bell. This time, Daddy blinked. Times were so hard he felt compelled to sell her. We couldn't have been more devastated if he'd agreed to sell one of us into slavery.

Daddy tried to reason with us. Bills were piling up. Hard times force hard choices. We were having none of it. Even Momma refused to speak to him for days. Maybe if we shunned him, (we thought) Daddy's heart would soften. Or maybe his conscience would rise up in revolt. Maybe the buyer would change his mind—or forget where we lived.

We begged and pleaded. I tried bargaining with God, promising to become a missionary in darkest Africa, eating monkeys and grubs, saving lost souls.

Too soon our black day dawned. The heartless buyer showed up with a steel crate in the back of his pickup. He paid Daddy $75 in cold cash, claimed our Bell, loaded her in that prison cell, and drove away. We watched Bell until she vanished out of sight. The whole bunch of us bawled for a long time.

Our house was like a morgue without Bell. Momma hid her pallet so we wouldn't see it and be crushed every time we passed the back porch.

Her new owner lived so far away we never expected to see Bell again. However, about a month later when Daddy went out one morning to feed the dogs, Bell almost knocked him down, leaping into his arms. That crazy dog was smiling again, wagging her tail, in a frenzy of joy to be home.

"Boy, I'm glad that's over and I'm back where I belong," she was telling us, "Back to my family!"

We kids took turns hugging and kissing her. We got out her favorite rubber ball and played keep away. All this time Daddy was looking like he'd swallowed a blow fly. Finally, he called us in and told us the worst possible news. He tried to do it gently.

"You know we're a Christian family. So, we must do the right thing—no matter how bad it hurts." That's all we kids heard, but we knew what was coming next.

"We have to call the man and tell him Bell is here. I know how much it grieves you. It breaks my heart, too, but we have no choice."

A few days later the man showed up to take Bell away from us again. This time we let Daddy do the dirty work. Momma took us kids to the back of the house so we wouldn't have to tell her goodbye again.

Daddy called to sweet Bell, took her in his arms and gently laid her in the man's cage. When he came back inside, tears were in his eyes. So, we wept and grieved anew. It was like going to her funeral twice.

We were still mourning a month later when Bell arose from the grave. When Daddy went out to feed the dogs on a cold December morning, Bell leaped on his back in a fit of joy. We begged Daddy not to send her away again. He seemed to be weakening or at least hesitating.

"Let's see what happens," was all we could get out of him.

A few days later, he went to see the man who bought her. Daddy told the man how much the whole family loved Bell and how this was breaking our hearts.

"I don't have the money to buy her back," Daddy told him. "But would it be possible to work something out so we could send you a few dollars until you're satisfied?"

That's when our miracle appeared. Daddy said the man heard his pitiful story quietly. When he finally spoke, he told Daddy he'd been doing a lot of soul-searching.

"You can have your dog back, and you don't owe me a cent. I knew when I came to get her last time it wasn't right." The man continued, "That's a wonderful dog. She helped me earn more money than I paid you for her. I would never put her or your family through that again." He reached out to shake Daddy's hand.

"Somebody once told me you'll never regret doing the right thing. I guess this is your lucky day."

That's how Daddy got his superstar back. For us kids, it was the best Christmas ever. Our beloved Bell had survived her Babylonian captivity. Jerusalem never looked so good!

Daisy the Blue Ribbon Pig

We brought her home on a cold December day, cradled in my arms. Mr. Russell, our neighbor, chauffeured us in his old pickup truck. Daddy rode shotgun.

Daisy (my new pig) and I squeezed in between them. Freshly weaned from her mother, the frightened little thing soon nestled down in my lap, wrapped in a warm blanket.

One look at that precious little porker was all it took. Daisy didn't need a caretaker; she needed a mother. Embracing my surrogate duty, I opened my heart, adopting her with all the passion of a lovesick boy.

She came into the world hungry, a trait she never outgrew. She weighed four pounds when we hooked up, 640 when we parted. But we're getting ahead of the story.

Daisy was a gift from the Sears Roebuck Pig Chain, a charitable group helping 4-H Club farm kids learn to raise and care for their animals. Such thoughts never troubled Daisy. She was sure she'd adopted us.

To get Daisy, I promised to properly feed and groom her, to breed her to a registered male when she came of age, then donate a female pig from her first litter back to another kid to keep the chain going. We also pledged to enter her in livestock shows to compete with her peer pigs.

So, Daisy came to live with us. For months, I'd dreamed of her arrival. Daddy helped me saw and nail together a little log pen to keep her. We stocked up on Purina Pig Chow to mix with her corn and wheat shorts. The 4-H Club pig owners bible commanded we give our new porker a healthy start.

Desperate to be a good parent, I doubled her meals. This double-dipping later proved to be a problem. At the time, however, Daisy thought it a stroke of genius.

Worried she would be terrified without her mother, I talked Momma into letting me keep Daisy in a cardboard box beside my bed that first night. Sure enough, she couldn't settle down. Her squealing and pleading became too painful to ignore.

I slipped out of bed, picked her up out of the box, and made us a pallet on the floor. After a warm milk nightcap, she cuddled against me on our pallet and slept soundly.

Is it any wonder why boys love pigs? Go to the fair, and watch the pigs. Pigs love dirt. Boys love dirt. A boy is simply a pig at heart. Sadly, moms refuse to give dirt a chance.

Our pastor took his two grandsons to the fair. The boys loved the rabbits, the calves, the lambs, but when they came to the pigs they were electrified. They watched in wonder as caretakers hosed their blue ribbon piglets off, air brushed and dried them. As soon as they were spotless, the precious little things went looking for a mud hole. Soon, they were happy pigs again.

Next morning, Momma found Daisy and me sleeping together on the bedroom floor. She laid down the law, "I will not have two pigs living in my house."

Callous and cruel was Mom's ultimatum, beyond a doubt. Nevertheless, baby Daisy was banished. Momma meant well, but she clearly didn't understand love at first sight.

"I'll never forsake you!" I vowed.

Daisy didn't take it personally. In fact, she loved her new log pen, going to work immediately, rooting up its dirt floor. Next night, we bedded down in her new digs. She curled up against my chest and was soon asleep. I wasn't so lucky. Momma's throwaway blanket over a bed of pine straw worked okay for Daisy, but those pine needles kept sticking and poking me.

Hungry fleas moved in on us. Hoot owls organized a concert. A barnyard full of hogs, cows, and a mule were loudly celebrating Daisy's arrival. About midnight, a cold wind kicked up, chilling my bones. This convinced me that Daisy would be just fine alone.

I slipped out of her stall and headed inside. A warm mattress and blankets never felt so good. I'd barely dozed off when Daddy shook me awake. "Daisy's ready for her breakfast."

I hadn't understood this to be my responsibility. Breakfast was always hot and ready when I awoke. My, how the world had changed! It was barely daylight, and I'm making breakfast for a hog.

We trained every day to get ready for Daisy's first show. She learned to follow me, stand at attention, turn around on cue, and roll over on her side when her belly was scratched. Each time she responded correctly, she was rewarded with food. Daisy caught on quickly: more tricks, more food. We became best friends as she worshipfully followed me around the barnyard.

In due time, we entered Daisy in the South Mississippi Livestock Show where she won the prize of Reserve Grand Champion.

This satisfied my obligation to 4-H Club, ending her show days. Daisy and I enjoyed our fleeting moment in the spotlight. She adored the children brave enough to reach over into her stall, rub her back, or scratch her ears. She and I shared corn dogs, fried dough, and cotton candy. I might've taken her on the carnival rides were it not for higher up spoilsports.

Germ conscious health experts at fairs today are taking away most of the fun for kids—forbidding them to touch the animals. Do-gooders have managed to shut down petting zoos where kids can touch and play with them. Pet parades may be the next casualty.

Now that Daisy's glory days were over, she could relax and enjoy being a pig. She loved acorns. When I came home from school she'd be waiting. I'd let her out of her pen, and off we'd go hunting. Daisy's nose was our guide; she could smell an acorn for a mile!

Friends were amazed that Daisy preferred my company to her four-footed cousins. They never discovered our secret: keeping peanuts and goodies in my pockets won Daisy's love and loyalty.

Daisy was fast growing into a lovely young lady. Soon, it was time to find her a suitable mate. We went back to see the man who owned her mother. He'd bought a champion boar, offering him for stud services. Daddy and Mr. Russell helped me watch Daisy for signs she was ready to become a mom. When that day arrived; we loaded Daisy back into Mr. Russell's truck and took her over for a rendezvous.

Foregoing courtship, they got right down to making piglets. The facts of life are learned early on a farm. So, none of this surprised me. Daisy, my baby, was eager to make babies.

My 4-H Club advisor said we should weigh Daisy. A sow weighing more than 500 pounds tends to squash her newborns when she lies down to let them suckle. The scales told us we had a problem; Daisy now weighed nearly 600 pounds. Daddy and I built a birthing pen to allow her piglets to scoot out of the way when she lay down on her side to suckle them. When the big day came, Daisy gave us nine little clones of herself. When visitors came, she proudly showed them off.

When her babies were eight weeks old, we sent word to my 4-H Club sponsor. Soon, a boy came to claim his pig. We let him choose his pick of the litter. Daisy said her goodbyes, and another kid went home on top of the world. The Sears Pig Chain would go on.

This all happened long ago in a faraway place. Yet, neither years nor miles can separate us from those we love. Yes, I do still dream of Daisy, and in those dreams, I'm still 10 years old, squeezed in between

Daddy and Mr. Russell in his pickup truck, holding that little red piglet in my arms.

Bonding with Daisy, his blue
ribbon pig

The Preacher's Mule

"He's got the Devil in him!" even Daddy said of his mule. Ole Pete was the nickname we saddled on him. He would've won a "meanest mule" contest hands down. Daddy never apologized for bringing Pete home. The way he saw it, he needed a plow mule real bad, and Pete came real cheap. A kindly neighbor sold Pete to Daddy for bottom dollar. When Ole Pete came to live with us, we understood why our neighbor was so obliging. He must've been abused as a colt. There's no other way to explain his malicious heart. We knew nothing of Ole Pete's ancestry, but my older brothers often remarked on his parentage.

When Ole Pete moved in, my life forever changed. We could've been buddies, but Ole Pete had no sense of humor. I wasn't mean to him unless you count slipping up from behind to poke him with a stick or sneaking up while he was asleep to yell, "Giddy Up!"

Like a wounded bull elephant, he never forgot my pranks. No, sir, he was not about to forgive. He could smell me coming. Once he was asleep when I slipped into the barnyard, but when I started tiptoeing to his stable, hoping to surprise him, he picked up my scent.

Ole Pete jumped to his feet, fully alert, daring me to approach. He laid back those big donkey ears, warning me, "I don't trust you—and you'd better not trust me!"

He started snorting and carrying on like a crazed water buffalo. He would've exploded through his stall doors if I'd gone one step further. I shot out of there.

Not that he was more congenial with Daddy. In fact, he made the preacher's life miserable. When Daddy first put collar and bridle on him, Pete reared up and tried to paw him. When Daddy poured feed into his trough, he tried to bite or kick him.

He was half-wild and half-crazy. When the preacher began training him to plow, he bolted and ran away with the whole rig. What a great home video that would've made: Pete roaring down the lane, the plow kicking up dust behind him, Daddy chasing after him, screaming dark threats. (I didn't suggest this to the preacher.)

Daddy's feet could barely keep up with his ornery plow mule/racehorse. After pulling a heavy plow all morning, Pete tired and slowed to a normal walking pace. For the rest of the afternoon, Pete behaved himself. Next morning when Daddy hitched him up, it was off to the races again.

With Pete stalking my every move, barnyard chores became hazardous. He shifted to the back of his stall while I came to feed him. Pretending he was unaware of me, he would wait until I leaned down to pour his oats. Suddenly, he would lunge, trying to slam me against the stable wall. Yes, the old guy seemed Satan-possessed. A cousin swore that a mule bit off his grandfather's ear. Without a doubt, Ole Pete would've loved to mutilate mine. It paid to tread softly and stay alert. Pete and I finally learned to tolerate each other, but I kept my guard up, knowing he was only biding his time, waiting to ambush me.

A frisky mule kicked my school buddy in the head when he went out into a pasture to bridle him. When he awoke in the hospital, his first question was: "Daddy, did you shoot the mule?"

Pete would've rejoiced to see my blood flowing and was no doubt scheming to kick my brains out. Ole Pete was an equal opportunity hater: cows, pigs, and dogs. He ignored chickens, possibly deeming them low-life creatures beneath his contempt. Once, a pig wandered into his stable. Pete bit off his tail and chewed it up. Maybe it left a bitter aftertaste; after that, he never attacked our hogs.

Attacking Laws and Dogs

The preacher kept our cows in a separate pasture to keep them safe from Old Pete. Unfortunately, someone left a gate open one day, and the cows escaped. Pete bolted out behind them, chasing the terrified herd. We watched helplessly as the stampeding cows took off with Pete charging after them like a heat-seeking missile. They thundered down our country lane, Pete smelling blood. No way were those cows going to win that race.

Pete was gaining on them as they swung around the bend out of sight. The preacher jumped in my brother's old Plymouth, stomping the accelerator and chasing after them. When he caught up with them, Ole Pete had raced past the whole herd until he caught the lead cow. He attacked her, pawing her to the ground. When Daddy arrived on the scene, Mrs. Russell was standing by the fallen cow, shaking her broom at Ole Pete to keep him from killing the poor thing.

The brave lady had heard cows bellowing, looked out to see Pete biting, kicking, and mauling them. Knowing he was insane, she ignored the danger to herself, grabbed her broom, and rushed out to beat him off. By sheer force of anger, that gentle lady confronted the beast, holding him off until Daddy arrived.

Our beloved hound dog Pup also became a near-victim of Ole Pete's ire. Pup was following us across the pasture one day when Pete intercepted him, getting between him and Daddy. Pete lowered his head until his eyes leveled with Pup's. Snorting and sniffing, he pawed ground. Pup sensed he was in trouble even before Pete charged. Daddy knew Pup was in danger, but he was too far away to stop it. Screaming out threats, all he could do was watch the drama unfold.

Pete closed in for the kill. At first, Pup tried to outrun him, but Pete was too fast. On the first charge, Pup scooted out of range as the demon donkey lunged at him. As Ole Pete turned and raced back, Pup started circling and darting just enough to outmaneuver the crazed mule, keeping barely a step ahead. Looking back at Pete, the little dog was growling bravely even as he raced to save his life. Daddy finally grabbed a stout tree limb and rushed up to beat Pete off.

But, Pete was the preacher's mule—and the preacher had no choice but to keep him. When you're a one-horse farmer without a horse; you take what you can get.

So far as I know, despite the Preacher's long conversations with his uncircumcised mule, Pete was never converted. So it went: Ole Pete taking liberties and trying Daddy's soul. Never did Daddy give up on a human being—nor did he give up on Ole Pete. Momma told Daddy, "Maybe the Lord sent that mule from hell to test and try you."

Ole Pete pulled the preacher's plow many years. Yet, even Momma didn't cry when years later Daddy bought a tractor and loaded Pete on the soap factory truck.

Chased by Bloodhounds

What could be more terrifying to a kid? Cousin Cecil and I lived for those times we could play together. His father was Daddy's brother. Both were preachers—as was Cecil years later. Cecil grew up in bush country near Jayess, a tiny Mississippi community 25 miles from the Louisiana line.

Uncle Oscar and Daddy sometimes traveled together, team-preaching at rural churches. This gave Cecil and me opportunities to roam the woods, looking for high adventure. Four years older, Cecil assumed the mantle of ringleader.

Once while playing in piney woods, we heard a pack of dogs chasing something. Cecil remembered that a cook at a nearby tuberculosis sanitarium had gone crazy carving up and killing two patients with a butcher knife and escaping before he was caught.

"They're probably on his trail," Cecil warned. "Let's get out of here fast. You know what bloodhounds do to a person when they overtake him." I had no clue what those savage animals do to their prey, but it didn't sound healthy.

Cecil's mind was churning. "There's an old abandoned road near here that will take us to Pearl River," he remembered. "If we reach it before they catch us, we'll swim across." It sounded risky.

"You know that's what escaped convicts do. They swim across rivers to elude the hounds," Cecil confided as we dashed for the river. I didn't know that, either, but it made perfect sense.

"The bloodhounds can't smell us once we get across. They'll just rush up to the river bank and then circle around howling until they give up."

Cecil was now in full flight, but my short legs were no match for his. With heart pounding and side aching, I was lagging behind. Cecil saw me petering out, so he slowed down and circled back.

"I'm not going to leave you. [Cecil sounded just like Jesus.] Just run as fast as you can. I'll hang back with you. Look for sticks we can pick up to fight them off."

It struck me as doubtful that two kids could beat off a pack of fierce bloodhounds. Still, as we ran, I began looking for a weapon.

"We'll stand back-to-back and fight them off 'til help comes. We're blood brothers, aren't we? " I wasn't about to argue.

"They're coming closer!" Cecil whispered. "Can't you run any faster?" By now my lungs were screaming, but I vowed to try. Finally, Cecil stopped to listen. "Sounds like we outran them—and we're close to the river. Can you swim?"

This thought struck new terror in my heart. "Not a big river. I can barely dog-paddle," I admitted.

"Don't worry. I know a shallow place we can wade across." His bravado failed to bolster my quaking heart.

"But I don't hear the bloodhounds anymore," I protested. "Why do we have to cross the river?" Cecil rolled his eyes, looking at me like an exasperated teacher glaring at the class dummy.

"You sure don't know much about bloodhounds, do you?" I acknowledged the obvious.

"When they stop howling, it means they're closing in on their victim. They've probably already seen us so we have to skedaddle." Finally, we reached the river.

"Follow me," Cecil ordered and waded in. Soon, the water was up to my bellybutton and getting deeper.

"Jump on my back!" Cecil yelled, grabbing my hand and swinging me up on his shoulders.

"Everybody should have a cousin like Cecil," I'm thinking. Bravely, he crossed the dangerous river, leading me to safety. The dogs had long since stopped barking, but Cecil rebuked my rising spirits.

"Don't let them fool you. They're still over there looking for us."

The sun was sinking fast, reminding me it was dinner time.

"What do we do now?" I pleaded with Cecil, knowing full well that my hero would think of something. Sure enough, he did not disappoint.

"Simple. You know bloodhounds have to eat at sundown." I let that one slide, not wanting Cecil to know what a clueless greenhorn he was dealing with.

"Now, when we get home, don't tell anybody about this," Cecil cautioned. "We're not supposed to be crossing the river, but I had to do it to keep you safe." We took a blood oath to keep our secret.

"A blood oath is like swearing on a stack of Bibles," Cecil explained.

So, for 50 years we guarded our lips, never breathing a word about how close we came to being torn apart by bloodhounds. I suppose, though, it's okay to tell it now.

Momma's Indian Cling Peaches

Momma was in her front porch swing, peeling peaches. Not just any old peaches, her famous Indian Clings. These unique peaches reveal a deep rosy flesh when peeled. Her half-gallon jars of dessert Clings won blue ribbons at the county fair.

Daddy had picked a bushel of tree-ripened fruit for Momma to pickle. Momma had her jobs, Daddy his. Today, Daddy was letting me skip work in the field to help Momma.

Rheumatism and high blood pressure spared Momma from field work. Once, she was paralyzed—never expected to walk again. Two more children were born since then; now Momma's health was fragile.

So, slaving in the hot sun was left to Daddy and his crew of squabbling serfs. Daddy was head honcho of his fields; Momma held sway over everything else. We kids belonged to both work crews. Boredom we knew not. Oh, how we would've loved to be bored!

Sometimes, they both needed us at the same time. So, they divvied us up. Daddy took the big ones, Momma the culls. Guess who got me?

But, wßhy complain? While they swatted mosquitoes and dodged dog flies, Momma and I hunkered down on our front porch under the shade of a big wisteria vine.

Momma believed I was her gift from God to help her get over Hobert, a child who died before I was born. So, we enjoyed a special bond.

She loved her tea roses. We worked side-by-side, tenderly feeding them with chicken droppings. Responding magnificently, the roses produced saucer-sized blossoms.

Her Home Demonstration Club ladies begged for cuttings. They didn't know it, but they would've had to take Momma's chicken droppings home with their cuttings to equal her jumbo roses.

Momma swung back and forth in her wooden swing, peeling her lovely Indian Clings, dropping them whole into a bowl of water at her side. Her paring knife moved swiftly. I was enjoying the show, awaiting orders.

"Bring me two more buckets of water." I grabbed two milk pails and headed downhill to a hand pump. This was our water source for drinking, cooking, washing dishes, and mopping floors.

Pumping and fetching water seemed like a full-time job. I never understood why one family needed so much water. When the buckets were filled, I lugged them back uphill. Momma emptied the cold water into a large pressure cooker on top of her wood stove.

When the water began to steam, she poured her peeled peaches into the pressure cooker, adding heaping cups of sugar. While the peaches were bubbling, Momma scalded a dozen wide-mouth jars. With her ladle, she filled each jar with the scalded peaches and juice. Caps and lids were screwed on. Then, she submerged her jars into the steaming pot to let them boil inside the cooker.

Sweat beads ran down her forehead as Momma worked over her jars and pots. She dabbed her red face with a flowered apron she'd cut out and sewn from a Purina pig-feed bag.

Momma's religion was not so severe as to ban all make-up, but she used it modestly. "I don't want to look like an old shrew, but I'm not painting myself up like a circus horse, either".

Momma had that graceful female magic— doing a dozen things at once. While her peaches were cooking, she'd be making lumberjack-sized lunches for Daddy and his field crew.

Slightly overweight, Momma wore a few extra pounds well. Or so it seemed to adoring eyes. Her dark brown hair was long and American Indian straight, pulled back into a bun that never varied. Nor should it, for this was Momma.

Highlighting her face, smiling brown eyes lit up whenever a loved one came into view. Just now, she was staring so intently at the simmering pot she didn't notice I'd slipped up behind her. Or so I was thinking.

"Don't try to slip up on me," she snapped playfully. "And don't play near the stove; that boiling water will scald your hide off!" As she hovered over the wood stove, Momma was so beautiful—not worldly gorgeous but inside beautiful.

"Honey, your momma's old and ugly," she once kidded me. I cried until she took it back.

She fretted that a hairy mole on her chin was growing larger. To those who loved her, that silly mole mattered not a bit. Instead of thinking it unsightly, we kids teased Momma because it bobbed up and down when she laughed, and Momma laughed often. She enjoyed every funny story we brought home.

Momma was not outwardly religious; that was Daddy's department. Rather, she had internal serenity. She was not a bumper sticker type. She didn't sew Bible verses on her aprons. Yet, she quietly showed us what makes moms so special: a selfless love and devotion.

She never completed high school yet insisted that all her children do so. She fiercely guarded our school days, keeping us in school when other parents were keeping their kids home to pick cotton, and she was chief cheerleader when one of hers left for college.

"Well, don't stand there gawking! Get me more jars!" The orders were gruff but spoken with love. She didn't expect much from a seven-year-old but knew I wanted to help. She called for more spices. Soon, the smell of cloves filled the air.

Momma could be stubborn. When she married Daddy, she was a Missionary Baptist devoted to both home and foreign missions. Daddy, a Primitive Baptist, was dead-set against missions, convinced they were a brainchild of the Roman Catholics.

When Daddy was ordained, he hoped Momma would come over to his side. Nothing doing! She stuck to her guns, insisting on attending her own church. She even invited her pastor and visiting evangelists for meals. We kids expected Daddy to pick a doctrinal argument with Momma's preachers, but he treated them as honored guests.

When Momma had dinner guests, she laid on quite a spread. So, we kids looked forward to entertaining her preachers. Once, when two evangelists kept refilling their plates, I asked them, "Don't you need to loosen your belts?" The preachers thought it was hilarious, but Momma gave me a look to melt Siberia.

Momma was full of warnings and advice: "Don't go fanning around in that night air; you'll catch your death of pneumonia". Or when I sassed her: "Somebody's gettin' too big for their britches. Maybe your Daddy would like to hear about this."

The aroma of bubbling peaches and spices was filling the kitchen. Momma stood watch over them. "How will you know when they're done?"

"If you can tell time, I'll show you," she teased. "When the big hand gets to 12, they'll be ready."

Indian Clings were bubbling in their spices on top of Momma's stove. Oh, that aroma, I can still smell them! Soon, she was lifting her precious jars out of the cooker with tongs, one at a time, placing them on cooling racks. She grasped each jar with a drying cloth. Holding lid and cap, she tightened each one by hand.

"Now, let's go out to the swing and listen," Momma whispered.

"What are we listening for, Momma?" She was enjoying her little game.

"Just come along and be quiet!" she teased.

So, we went outside to the porch swing. A wisteria vine shaded us from a merciless sun, perfuming our world with fragrant lavender blossoms. From this wooden swing, Momma surveyed her lovely garden of giant tea roses and spring flowers. Her blood-red Easter lilies vied with yellow daffodils and purple tulips. We drank deeply from God's rainbow of colors. Later, her crepe myrtles, zinnias and marigolds would extend the show into late summer.

Far out in the fields, I saw my siblings leaning on their hoes, wiping their brows, hating me for lollygagging in the cool shade with Momma while they were boiling in the sun.

All was quiet for what seemed like eons. Suddenly, a pop exploded from the kitchen. "What was that, Momma?" She was looking wise but giving nothing away.

"Just keep listening." Another loud pop rings out, then another.

Momma grinned mysteriously. "It's the lids sealing themselves. When they pop, it means they're airtight. Germs can't get in to spoil them. It means our job's done—and we did it right." Momma was so smart. All was right with the world.

Snorting Catepillars

To pay our bills, Daddy sometimes sold his pine and hardwood timber, hiring a neighbor with giant oxen to drag the logs out of swampy bogs. Yoked together, these powerful brutes huffed and puffed in and out of wet places no log truck could go.

They put on an awesome show, 12 or 14 of them hitched together in pairs, straining to snake a huge log out of standing water or seemingly impossible muck. Yet, those ferocious looking beasts were so gentle their owner let us kids come up and pet them while they were eating or resting. Mr. Conway's "live, snorting caterpillars" were eventually replaced by gas-and-oil-driven machines, but the sights, sounds, and smells of those huge muscled animals straining in humid swamps live on.

Possibly sensing that his oxen teams were on the way out, Mr. Conway jumped into local politics and was elected to our Board of Supervisors. He made sure his voters' private lanes, connecting us to public roads, were well maintained, scraped and graveled. Such help was sorely needed when heavy thunderstorms flooded roads, cutting people off, isolating them until the high water receded. When my Grandfather Bill Easterling died in 1949, his minister was cut-off by high water and could not get across the river to preach his funeral. *(Excerpt from the church newsletter: "Funeral services were conducted by Elder O.R. Mozingo, as our other pastor, Elder C.N. Ware, was not able to be there on account of high water.")*

Famous for his brown scuppernongs, Mr. Conway—ever the politician—invited friends and neighbors to come help themselves. By taking good care of his voters, Mr. Conway never worried about being re-elected.

Chasing Rainbows

If you see a rainbow in the sky and rush to where it touches the ground, you'll find a pot of gold. What kid has not been teased with this legend? But who has been so gullible as to try it? Yep, my greedy little eyes glazed over at the thought of that glittering pot.

One day in a lonely field opportunity knocked. A rain cloud passed over, and the sun's reflection created a brilliant multicolored rainbow, so bright both arcs seemed to be touching the ground. Racing off toward the nearest end, I willed myself not to give up or tire out. Soon, I was breathing hard; my side began cramping. Still, I refused to quit. That pot of gold was beckoning: on across Daddy's cotton fields, over pasture fences, down into the woods, across a creek. Watching the rainbow, I almost panicked when it began fading. Yet, I was no closer. Nagging doubts raised their ugly heads.

"What if this is a trick? What if my sisters are watching and laughing their heads off? If it's so easy, why didn't they find it?" As the last rays of that rainbow faded, my dream also dimmed and died.

"But one of these days," a stubborn voice whispered, "When I'm bigger and faster, who knows?"

Tasting Bullfrogs

Southern wetlands are blessed with noisy but tasty bullfrogs. In hard times, poor folks resort to frog-gigging. Daddy made his gigs by straightening out big fish hooks, then wiring them to the end of a cane pole. Using a carbide headlamp at night, he'd find their eyes reflecting in the edge of ponds and streams. When I was old enough to follow him, Daddy let me carry the burlap sack he used to carry the bullfrogs.

When he'd gathered enough for a meal, we brought them home. Daddy cleaned them, handing them over to Momma. She rolled them in flour with salt and pepper, frying them in hog lard.

The secret to frying frog legs is using a covered skillet. Why? Often the nerves in their severed legs haven't gotten the message. Momma learned to grab the frog legs fast, throw them into her hot skillet, popping a lid on quickly before they jumped out. We all gathered in the kitchen to watch Momma do her thing.

Years later, Dot and I were treated to bullfrog legs at a fancy restaurant on the Mississippi River levee in Natchez. Alas, we didn't get to see how the chef kept them from jumping out of his pan.

Wearing Sister's Panties and Sleeping With Momma

Sisters Iris and Geraldine were out in the garden digging new potatoes and picking English peas. Momma was washing my clothes. I was maybe three years old.

With nothing to wear, I was ordered to stay home. Facing such a disaster, I pitched a hissy fit, crying and carrying on. So, she handed me a pair of Geraldine's step-ins.

I was mortified but determined not to be left out. Burning with shame, I put on those pink panties and wore them out to the garden. Seeing how embarrassed I was, they pretended everything was perfectly normal. Aren't sisters wonderful?

We never knew what it was to have one's own bed. Since I was the baby, I slept with Momma until I began sleeping crossways, kicking her in my sleep.

Momma was crippled with rheumatism, screaming out when anything bumped her. "It feels like someone's stabbing me in the back with a butcher knife" was the way she put it. When Daddy heard her crying out in her sleep, he figured out what was happening. So, moving me over into his bed, Daddy laid down the law:

"You're to stay on your side. Don't get crossways—and don't you dare start kicking me."

I was afraid to go to sleep, but Daddy's threats registered in my little subconscious brain. My buckaroo days were over.

Churning Butter And Frying Donuts

Momma sits over a two-gallon clay urn, half-dozing, churning raw milk into butter. Up and down her ancient wooden paddle goes, mixing and churning creamy milk. Soft chunks of butter begin floating to the top.

She skims off the floating butter, pressing it into a wooden mold, but not before filling a saucer for us to eat with her hot buttermilk biscuits, fig preserves, eggs, and bacon for breakfast. Could life get better?

We lived so far out in the sticks we felt like Robinson Crusoe. Few people owned a car, so getting to town wasn't easy. On Saturdays, someone drove an old school bus to Hattiesburg for country folks to go shopping.

One Saturday on her birthday, Momma left Ray and Geraldine in charge and caught the bus to town. Knowing she'd be gone for the day, they decided to surprise her by frying donuts.

"You read the recipe. I'll measure and mix the ingredients," Gerry told Ray. With their having zero experience, this idea was highly ambitious. Things were going well, though, until Ray stumbled on an unfamiliar word.

"What's shortening?" he asked.

"Beats me," Gerry confessed. "It must not be important." (Country folks in those days used rendered hog fat called lard.)

So, Ray and Gerry mixed their no-shortening donuts and then fried them on top of the stove. Can you guess how they turned out?

When we threw them out in the back yard even Ole Pup, after sniffing them, wrinkled up his nose and yowled. Well, it's good intentions that count, right?

Born to Sing?

Bo Didley, a Mississippi home boy, is credited with inventing Rock 'N' Roll music. He went on to win hearts in England and around the world.

The king of Rock 'N' Roll, Elvis Presley, was born just up the road in Tupelo. Blues legend, B.B. King, sprung from Bena, Mississippi, born of Delta sharecroppers. Bobbie Gentry whose haunting ballad "Ode to Billy Joe" made her famous came from poverty-stricken Chickasaw, Mississippi, near the Tallahatchie Bridge of which she sang. Native son, Willie Dixon, wrote "Hoochie Coochie Man," achieving instant fame when it was recorded by rhythm-and-blues musician, Muddy Waters.

Hollywood stars, gospel and soul singers, and a rainbow of musicians count Mississippi as their birthplace. Blues artists found their voice in Mississippi's cotton fields or churches.

Being preachers, Daddy and Uncle Oscar took their singing seriously. A third brother, Uncle W.J., was gifted with a rumbling bass voice.

Their sister Della owned a piano, inviting us over to her place on Sundays after church where they entertained family and friends. Southern churches joined together on Fifth Sundays—those months having an extra Sunday— to sing and visit together.

We kids were fascinated by the harmonizing of our uncles. They sounded like those deep- throated croakers that serenaded us at night after big spring rains. Someone dubbed them the "Baptist Bullfrogs."

Springing from such musical roots, one might think every mud-caked kid of the cotton fields could sing. Wrong. Daddy even sent me to music school to learn to read shaped notes. I couldn't carry a tune in a basket. My parents and grandparents sang; so did sisters, brothers and cousins.

People turn their heads in church when I try to sing—until my wife nudges me gently in the ribs to knock it off. At family birthdays, I try to join in without being heard. Everyone bears a cross, right?

Waiting for Christmas

It seemed like we kids spent the whole year waiting for Christmas. Our thrill of thrills was roaming the woods to find a perfect tree. Choices were limited to pine, cedar, or holly since by December all the others had shed their leaves.

This ritual involved Momma and every sibling, plus lots of arguing, yelling and screaming.

"Look at this one!"

"Come on, that's a Charlie Brown tree!"

"Oh my goodness, this one's perfect!"

Momma was referee, judge and jury. When she rendered her verdict, one of us chopped it down with Daddy's hatchet. Then, we took turns dragging it home.

Daddy never joined our tree-hunting parties. Maybe, he was too busy keeping us out of the poor house, knowing he couldn't afford to put presents under the tree.

No matter. We were transported to Alaska every year by decking our tree with icicles and spraying it with fake snow, and Santa sometimes found a way to surprise us.

Then Iris would impersonate Andy Williams, singing "I'm Dreaming of a White Christmas."

That dream seldom comes to pass in the Deep South, but when it snowed at Christmas, we knew Jesus was smiling. Momma would send us rushing outdoors before the snow melted to scoop it up in bowls while she mixed milk, eggs and vanilla extract for a rare treat—snow ice cream. Momma also helped us make holiday goodies—fudge, divinity, peanut and pecan brittle, hickory nut bread, and her famous fruitcake soaked in Ray's homemade possum grape wine.

> *Precious memories, how they linger,*
> *How they ever flood my soul*
> *In the stillness of the midnight,*
> *Precious sacred scenes unfold.*[1]

J. Bennett Easterling

PART IV

COLORFUL CHARACTERS

Of cotton pickers, crazies, fortune tellers,
Mormons, Choctaws, and Gypsies

The Courtneys

After my siblings escaped the farm, Daddy hired local farm workers to help us. That's how we came to know the Courtneys.

You've already met Bones, the patriarch whose beloved dog was killed by a rattlesnake. His family included his wife, Margie, young adult, live-at-home children, Hattie Mae and C Bell, and son Lee Roy, soon to be a teenager.

The Courtneys rented a tin roof shack not far from us, hiring themselves out to local farmers. They became Daddy's go-to field hands. He paid them by the hour to help work his 80 acres.

One of the preacher's labor-intensive crops was Tung nuts. A native of China, Tung trees thrive in the semi-tropic South. Tung nuts, after harvesting, are taken to processing plants where they're crushed. A poisonous, putrid-smelling oil is extracted for quick-drying varnishes, paints, and waterproofing. Cows and hogs refuse to eat the foul smelling nuts so the preacher planted Tung trees in his pastures. As Tung nuts ripen they fall on the ground and are left to dry. Workers with bushel baskets crawl around gathering them. Without the Courtneys' help, we would've been overwhelmed.

When Daddy asked, the Courtneys came running. At least, Bones was willing—and his vote was the only one that counted.

Blacks sometimes disrespected one of their own by calling him a "nigger" but were rightly offended if a white did so. Unfortunately, I didn't yet understand this. One day, as we crawled on the ground, gathering Tung nuts, Hattie Mae complained, "This makes me feel like a slave!" Without realizing the trap I was stepping in, I agreed, "Yep, Daddy has us all working like Niggers!"

Hattie Mae exploded, "Big Ben, how dare you talk like that? I'm telling your Daddy on you. Didn't your Momma teach you no manners?" I was crestfallen that I'd hurt her. Surprisingly, Bones came to my rescue.

"Settle down, young lady," he told her. "You know Big Ben didn't mean to insult us." Then he gently explained, "That's a bad word—like us calling you a honky." They were too kind to rat me out to the preacher, but I learned an embarrassing lesson.

Bones was the hardest working plowman I ever saw. Like legends of black field workers he made hard work bearable with a repertoire of Negro spirituals and long forgotten folk songs:

> *Sometimes I plow my old grey horse,*
> *Other times I plow old muley,*
> *Soon's I get this cotton crop by,*
> *I'm gwine home to Juley.* [1]

Momma once set me up in business and put me on the road selling Blair Household Products. This may have been her idea to get me out of the house. She helped me order supplies by mail and load them in my bicycle basket. Then, I'd take off peddling up and down the dusty roads hawking them door to door.

Bones and Margie were my best customers. Margie bought spices, flavoring, pie filling mix and household products. Bones kept coming back for my perfumed toilet water.

"What do you do with all those bottles of cologne?' I asked him.

"I gives 'em to the church sisters."

Despite the taboo against blacks and whites socializing in the post-depression South, his son, Lee Roy, and I wrestled and played as we helped Momma take care of her prize roses. We became secret buddies.

Yet, our friendship was complicated by prevailing times and customs. This was before the Supreme Court forced an end to segregation. So, Lee Roy went to all-black schools, worshipped at an all-black church, sat with his black friends in the movie balconies, ate at separate lunch counters, drank from separate water fountains, rode in the back of the bus. We'd never heard of civil rights or forced busing or Bull O'Conner's dogs or bull whips. We were just a couple of fun-loving boys. So, when we found ourselves alone, we played stick ball, threw rocks and corn cobs, wrestled, and challenged each other to barefoot races. Nonetheless, we knew not to cross certain lines. I dared not invite him for a pallet party. He knew not to invite me to his birthday celebrations.

Lee Roy drank sassafras tea made from roots dug out of the woods. A born entrepreneur, he earned a little money doing odd jobs like polishing shoes and digging graves for whites.

"Gimme a 6-ft tall man," he boasted, "an' I'll dig 'is grave in dis red clay and hav' 'im buried in three shakes of a lamb's tail." I never witnessed it, but that's what Lee Roy claimed. Could've been his sassafras tea talking.

Lee Roy was happy-go-lucky with big-time personality. Whatever kid stuff I suggested, his response was, "Count me in."

He lived by Mark Twain's motto: "Admit a mistake freely. It throws those in authority off-guard and allows you to commit many more." [2]

Bones had given Lee Roy an old banjo. He learned to pick it passably well, regaling us with forgotten songs like this one:

> *Old Joe Clark had a yellow cat,*
> *She would neither sing nor pray,*
> *She stuck her head in the buttermilk jar*
> *And washed her sins away.*
> *Old Joe Clark had a dog*
> *As blind as he could be.*
> *Ran a redbug 'round a stump*
> *And a coon up a holler tree.* [3]

Like most blacks in that time and place, Lee Roy believed in "hants." Since he was two years older and I was clueless, Lee Roy undertook to educate me.

"Ghouls is bad dudes what wanna kill folks. Witches and goblins, dey don't hang round 'cept at Halloween. We talkin' 'bout Hants here. Hants be dead spirits come back to torment dey enemies," he explained.

"Mostly dey hangs out in graveyards and old houses. Mos' of 'em you finds 'em where somebody done got murdered." Lee Roy claimed he could call up dead relatives.

"I'll prove it to you," he boasted, reading my doubts.

"All I haffa do is say gutinhimmerstein [phonetic spelling], and the spook comes arunnin'. His spirit gonna sneak into my body—or maybe yours—and talk wif us."

Well, what's a kid to do? I knew the preacher would be upset if he found out –and this sounded spooky, but the thrill would be worth it.

"It gotta be on a full moon," Lee Roy went on. "Ain't no hants gonna come back 'til de moon's full."

So, we waited for the firmaments to align themselves. Sure enough, on the next full moon, we met at Prospect graveyard after dark.

"Is you ready?" he asked as we tiptoed into the deserted cemetery.

"You bet! Let's do it." That's me trying to sound bold.

Lee Roy began circling an old sunken grave, moaning "gutinhimmerstein" and calling "Aunt Doodlebug, come up!"

Lee Roy had told me her tragic story. Aunt Doodlebug left her dinner cooking on the stove one day, disappeared, and was never seen again. When volunteers gave up searching for her body, a funeral was given, using an empty casket.

"But I's called her back. She don't likes it, but she allas comes," Lee Roy claimed.

So, he went on chanting and calling until hope faded. I didn't know whether to be disappointed or relieved. When I suggested we give up and go home, Lee Roy screamed, "She's acoming—here she is!"

Suddenly, Lee Roy's voice was commandeered. Now it belonged to Doodlebug. She shrieked hideously at being disturbed, barking like a marine drill sergeant.

"Who you got wif you?" she demanded. "How come you messin' wif me, yanking me up outta dis grave, showing no respect?"

No answer. Lee Roy had lost his tongue.

She clawed at a tombstone. "I oughta jerk this slab up and whack you boys up sidda head!"

"We meant no harm," I managed to croak.

"Dis ain't even my boneyard. Why you bring me up in de white foks burying place?"

I'm ready to bolt.

"Come on Lee Roy; help me out here," I'm silently pleading.

Lee Roy finds his tongue: "I brung a frien wit me. Why you mad at us? It's mighty cold down there, ain't it?"

"Hush yo rattlin on. Dis ain't no social visit. You coming wif anuther dead cat for me to baptize?"

"No'um, I ain't got no dead cat this time."

"Is dis white child a heathen?"

"No'um, he be a preacher's boy."

"A preacher's boy! Do he tote a Bible round, thumpin' hit?"

"No'em. He jus like you and me."

"Jus like us? He sho look pale to me!"

His dead aunt's ghost turns on me.

"You got any cats, boy?"

"Yes'um. A tom, a momma, and five kittens."

"Did I ax you how many?"

"No'um"

"Do dey eat outta spoons?"

"No'um."

"Do dey talk?"

"No'um."

"Do dey eat rats?"

"Yes'um."

"Is dey cannibals?"

"No'um."

"Is dey Presbyterians?"

"No'um."

"Will dey go to heaven when dey die?"

"I don't know, ma'am."

"Well, le's hope so. I sho nuff don't wants 'em down in dis hole wif me."

My trial by fire is suddenly over. Doodlebug turns back on Lee Roy, both of them talking out of the same mouth.

"You think I likes being jerked up just to talk to dis white boy?"

"Auntie, we meant no harm."

"No harm, you say? Think again. Don't you ever drag me up to talk to no preacher's boy," she screamed. "I'm gwine back down, and iffin you mess wif me again, y'all gonna be plenty sorry!"

Muttering vile threats, Doodlebug takes leave of Lee Roy's body as quickly as she possessed it. Lee Roy melts to the ground, shaking violently, holding his throat.

Petrified, I don't know if he's dying or recovering. Finally, he begins to come around. His voice is weak, but it's the old Lee Roy.

"Well, I told ya. Now what ya say ?"

I was too stunned to say doodlum-squat. Even today, after so many years, memory says it was quite a show.

Did Lee Roy call up his dead aunt, or was he hoodwinking me? I'm not sure I want to know the answer. At any rate, it was a foolish game. Maybe the good Lord protected us because we were young and ignorant. The topic was never mentioned again by Lee Roy or me, and you can be sure we didn't tell the preacher we'd been dilly-dallying with dead folks.

The Courtneys were enjoying an ice cream social one day when I happened by. We both knew blacks and whites were not allowed to eat together in the segregated South of those days. Yet, they offered me a bowl of homemade vanilla ice cream made with Pet milk. Well, the day was blistering hot, and nobody was around to yell at me. Sitting in the shade of a giant oak tree, I consumed a goodly portion of their hand-cranked ice cream. Nothing ever tasted better.

Bones belonged to a Spirit-filled Pentecostal church where meetings grew loud and lively. (Pagans called them kneeling, bowing, moaning, shouting Holy Rollers.) Their preachers hurled lightning strikes down the aisles like rolling pins.

"Peter and Paul didn't have nutten on our guys," Bones declared. "When we gets wound up an' de Spirit takes wing, watch out! Sinners hear thunder a-rumbling and hell-hounds a-barking. Dey see visions of bleedin' moons an' fallin' stars, coffins bustin' open, an' sinners climbing out weeping an' cryin' like a mammaless child."

Bones told this story:

> "One night in church my C Bell and her best
> girlfriend got slain in de Spirit and fell on de floor.
> Later C Bell's husband come into de service drink-
> ing and raising a ruckus.. 'Where my wife?, he
> demands. Somebody point to de floor. "Who dat
> under dat blanket wit C Bell?' he screams. Me and
> another deacon ease him outside and order was
> restored."

Margie helped Momma with ironing. In turn, Momma paid her
with clothes we'd outgrown. Momma's hand-me-downs must've
seemed like slim pickings to Margie. We're talking about patched
shirts and dresses, holey socks, and see-thru undies.

Marjorie was boneyard poor yet held on to her dignity like a
drowning man clings to a floating chunk. She decided Momma's sec-
ond-hand clothes weren't worth her efforts. One day, Momma sent
word by my sister Geraldine,

"Tell Margie I have some clothes for her if she'll come and help
me." No response. Again Momma sent word asking for help. Nothing.

"When you see her kids, ask 'em if they told Margie what I said,"
Momma ordered Geraldine. So Gerry tried again. "Did you tell your
momma what my momma said?" she asked. This time the answer
came.

"Yes 'um" they assured her.

"And what did she say?" Gerry pressed.

"She just said [barnyard word deleted], and that's all she said." Case
closed.

Bones was a great teaser. Once he told me, "The best time I ever had
was the night after my first wife died. The ladies of the church came
for her wake and stayed all night. Oh, what a comfort they were—and
they loved the cologne you sold me!"

People in those days held all night wakes when someone died. The deceased would be decked out in their Sunday best, laid in a coffin, and kept in their own home until burial. The church ladies took turns keeping watch during the night—a vigil of singing, socializing, retelling fond memories of the deceased, and praying over the body.

Some believed that a person's soul hangs around a dead body until it's buried. Loved ones often came to watch over the spirit of the departed until it was released to travel on to its final destination.

Neighbors and friends dropped by during the night to pay respects. Some dragged their terrified children up to the open casket for a final viewing. Menfolk mostly sat on the front porch or outside on lawn chairs and swings sharing memories, dozing, sipping coffee or whiskey.

Late one night, Bones and Margie drove up to our house and called for Daddy. When he went out, they told him Bones had tasted too much wine. They fought. Margie pelted him with rotten eggs. They'd never really been married—just living together. They wanted to make things right—and would Daddy marry them?

He did it on the spot. When a deacon questioned him, Daddy explained, "When people decide to do the right thing, why not help them? Besides, I was thinking of their kids."

Daddy thought the world of the Courtneys, and they loved the preacher. Years later, Bones was stricken with cancer. As the disease progressed, he was in great pain. He asked Daddy to come pray for him, to help him make peace with the Lord.

"Preacher, I'm scared I'm not going to heaven. I've done so many bad things. Do you think the Lord will forgive me?"

Bones had indeed made his share of mistakes and carried a load of regrets, but he'd always faced life with courage. This was possibly his first time to fear anything. Daddy knew our old friend didn't need any more burdens to carry. So, he tried to put his mind at ease.

"Are you sorry for your sins and have you asked the Lord to forgive you?"

"Preacher, I do it every day." That was just what Daddy wanted to hear.

"Well, Bones, you can rest in peace. The good book says that's all the Lord requires of us."

Daddy urged him to use his last days to pray for his family. Bones asked for one last favor.

"Will you come and give me my morphine shots?" Who could refuse such a mercy?

"His dried-out skin was tough as shoe leather," Daddy lamented. As his body wasted away, it grew harder to penetrate with a needle. I didn't want to hurt him."

In torment, Bones begged Daddy to go ahead. "Just do it."

"I had to press with my whole weight on the needle," Daddy recalled. "It was one of the saddest things I ever had to do." God mercifully took Bones home a few days later.

He died peacefully. Life's most important question had been answered. Who could ask for more? With a hatful of memories, we said goodbye to a faithful friend.

Grandpa Bill Goes Crazy

Daddy kept people laughing in good times and not so good. When he laughed, it was so loud and raucous it scared the cats off our back porch. He looked for good in people, but when he couldn't find it, he'd find the ridiculous. A streak of humor helped him cope.

"You have a weird sense of humor!" says my wife, Dot. I blame it on the preacher and his father. Grandpa Bill entertained us with hilarious tales. If we think about it, maybe God gets a kick out of creating folks who can laugh at life.

Grandpa Bill told this story on himself: "Once during a time of stress, I suffered a breakdown. My mind flitted back and forth. Family worried about me. But I must've been relatively harmless; they didn't ship me off to the nuthouse. Instead, they guarded me at home. Grandma ruled the roost, keeping our kids in line.

Ira, my oldest son, was big enough to take over my field work. So, I stayed in bed, ate, and slept. Not a bad deal, right?

A sorry good-for-nothing skunk lived down the road apiece. He was a thorn in my side, always causing trouble. He hears I've flipped my lid, so he comes to see the crazy old goat, nosing around where he had no business.

By then I'm coming to my senses—and I know what he's up to. He wants to check me out, see how loony the old coot is, so he can go tell his buddies and have a good laugh, but I'm ready for him. He comes in all smiles, asking Grandma if he can see me.

"Of course," she says, leading him back to my bedroom.

I've mangled my hair, torn my undershirt to shreds. I'm retching and sniffing, lying on my bed in a fetal position, wild-eyed as a marsh hare.

'Oh Bill, I'm so glad to see you,' he gushes. 'All of us are so sorry to hear of your troubles! Tell me how you're feeling.'

He's about to get his money's worth. I'm foaming at the mouth, growling like a cur dog. Muttering nonsense, I'm beating my chest, rolling my eyes, screaming. By this time, he's forgotten his Good Samaritan act. He's glancing toward the back door, looking for a quick exit.

I spring out of bed and grab his hand as if to shake it. I spin him around, kick him soundly in the rear, heaping insults on him and yelling insanely, 'I know why you came, you lowdown son-of-a-gun, and if you ever darken my door again, you better have your will ready. Your widow's going to need it!'

I followed him to my front gate, ranting and raving, throwing dirt at him. Well, he got the show he came for—and I greatly enjoyed his visit."

Uncle Harry, the Gypsy

Mississippi tongues were wagging when Aunt Daisy up and married a gypsy. True to his ancestry, Uncle Harry had no roots but drifted hither and yon telling fortunes for a silver dollar. Momma worried that he'd drag her sister and their babies through hell on earth. How could they go to school? How would she know where they were or what was happening to them?

Daddy was suspicious of Uncle Harry because God warns his people not to have anything to do with mediums, soothsayers, and those who divine the future.

"If you want to know something, ask Me," God says.

Nonetheless, it didn't take Uncle Harry long to win us kids over. On his first visit, he arrived with a bag full of silver dollars. Emptying them out on the kitchen table, he invited us to play with them. We'd never seen so much money.

Uncle Harry handed Geraldine and me a shiny silver dollar to keep. Our eyes must've grown big as the coins. Sister Iris was a teenager so he felt embarrassed to offer her one. Not wanting her to be slighted, I asked, "What about Iris?" He chuckled and shoved one across the table to her.

We kids were thrilled to have a "rich uncle." Momma was not so easily persuaded. She watched him like a momma bear watches coyotes circling her cubs, remembering the old wives' tale: *Gypsies kidnap children, selling them to carnivals and circuses!*

What did this dark nomadic man do when he wasn't cheating widows out of their silver dollars? Did he lie, cheat, and steal everything not nailed to the floor? So, Momma worried. She was not alone. Two generations ago, mistrust of such vagabond wanderers was near unanimous.

"The Gypsies are coming!" alarmed mothers screamed as they frantically ran to gather up their babies and lock the doors. Where such stories came from is anybody's guess. A frightened boy told this harrowing tale:

"One night I crawled to the top of a hill overlooking a Gypsy camp. I watched them singing and dancing around their campfire. Suddenly, a young girl's high-pitched scream stopped the music cold. Then, I saw a man dragging her into his tent."

The terrified spy bolted home and breathlessly reported, "The Gypsies just stole another kid!" The boy's parents, suspecting he'd seen a dad disciplining his child, ignored the eye witness report.

Yet, a day came when Momma's fears proved valid. Aunt Daisy and Uncle Harry began dropping their "young'uns" off with kinfolks so she could drift with him, telling fortunes.

One summer day, they left their six and eight-year-old boys to spend the weekend with us. We heard nothing else from them until the next spring!

The eight-year-old was a miniature Uncle Harry, dark of skin with black hair and mesmerizing eyes. The other little guy was blue-eyed and blond, a spitting image of Aunt Daisy. They showed up, barefooted and in rags. We fell in love with them but grieved to see the little fellows heartbroken and homesick for their mom.

Sure enough, they'd already picked up bad habits. Both were budding little kleptomaniacs. The older one stole my pearl-handled pocketknife (the one that protected me from the Great Eagle) the first night. But they were sweet kids, just lost and trying to cope. Momma laid down the law so I reluctantly shared my toys.

When school started back in September, Momma used her egg money to buy them shoes and school clothes. We cousins took them to school with us on the bus and brought them back home.

And so it went. Day after day, they climbed off our school bus and raced all the way home to see if their parents had come for them.

They'd sit watching Momma fix breakfast. The little one loved fried eggs but hadn't quite learned the difference between eggs and the pan they were fried in. When Momma asked him what he wanted for breakfast, he would pipe up, "Some egg pans!"

I was too young to understand the trauma of being abandoned. Momma and Daddy showered them with love. That long fall and winter spent under the preacher's roof may have been God's special provision for them. They certainly had opportunity to become part of a loving family. The preacher drilled into them a sense of right and wrong. Momma helped them with their homework. They soaked up all our love and attention.

Finally, on a warm day next spring, Aunt Daisy showed up without Uncle Harry to claim her kids. I recall Momma taking her into a back bedroom, locking the door, and having *a long private talk.*

By then, the little guys had stolen our hearts. So much so that I gave the older one the little pocketknife he'd stolen from me that first night.

Aunt Daisy moved to Mobile but never came back to visit so we lost track of the boys. As long as Momma lived, she never stopped praying for them. What happened to Uncle Harry? Nobody seems to know. Maybe, he's still telling fortunes for silver dollars.

Another Fortune Teller

It was a blossom-fragrant spring day, perfect for hunting and gathering those delectable little wild apples, called May-haws.

Teenage sisters, Iris and Geraldine, were also looking for romance, but would they let me go on their little safari? They knew I'd embarrass them if they were lucky enough to meet up with boys, but Momma insisted so they reluctantly agreed to let me tag along.

May-haws, a wild fruit found in waterlogged swamps of the Deep South, are prized by local folks for jams and jellies. The juicy red fruit, about the size of crab apples, ripens in late spring, hence the name May-haws.

So, milk pails and syrup buckets in hand, off we trooped in search of May-haws and boys. Across Bear Branch and through the woods we tramped with high hopes. Soon, we came out on a gravel road and headed toward a May-haw thicket.

Hiking cross-country, we were passing the home of "Uncle Ely," an eccentric man said to be a fortune teller. The old gentleman was working in his garden.

"Would you lovely ladies like to have your fortunes told?" he called to Iris and Geraldine. He ignored me because a boy apparently has no fortune.

My sisters knew the preacher frowned on palm-readers or anything having to do with the occult. They were, however, yearning for adventure, and this was too good an opportunity to pass up.

So, Iris dropped her milk pail and offered up her palm. "Oh, what's this? I see a husband, three, no four little ones running around!"

Taking Geraldine's palm, he frowned. "This is going to be difficult; things are dark—but wait—now it's coming clear. Today will be a big day for you. Before the sun sets, you girls will meet two tall handsome young men, and they'll offer you a ride home."

The girls, giggling and turning beet red, thanked him, and we took our leave. Soon, we came to a May-haw bog. The trees were loaded with ripe fruit. A spring rain had flooded the swamp. The trees were standing in knee-deep water.

We waded into the pond, shaking the slender trees. Ruby red May-haws fell into the water and floated. It was easy as pie to scoop them up. Soon, our pails were full.

Emerging out of the bog, we'd barely started toward home when Geraldine and Iris's miracle happened. A spiffy car was speeding toward us. The driver slowed down; two local hot-dogs were out for a spin.

"How about a ride home?" they asked the girls.

"You're going the wrong way." they protested half-heartedly.

"Not anymore!" the boys laughed as they spun the car around.

You know how this is going to end, right? The sun was hot; the girls were thirsty; the guys were offering us ice cold drinks. Maybe, they'd bribe little brother to keep his mouth shut.

Piling into the car with them, we took off. As we passed the old fortune teller's house he was standing in his garden, leaning on a hoe. When he saw who it was, he dropped his hoe, started laughing and clapping his hands. "I told you so!" was written all over his face.

A little birdie told the preacher. Of course, he fussed at the girls for playing footsie with the Devil, but he must've been smiling at the coincidence.

Cousin Arthur Hears a Voice

Arthur was a wizened little man with rawhide skin, weathered from a wandering life. His darting black eyes never rested. He was once married, but his wife disappeared without a trace. Rumors circulated, but nothing came of them.

He was Daddy's cousin. Nobody else in his family would have anything to do with him. I suppose because Daddy was a preacher, he didn't feel like disowning him.

Cousin Arthur drifted through life by leaping on slow moving railroad boxcars for a free ride. Every spring, he showed up at our doorstep for hot meals and a bed. Momma didn't have the heart to refuse him.

When he wasn't bumming a bed or meal, Cousin Arthur lived in culverts, makeshift cardboard lean-tos, or any dry place he could crawl under. People tolerated him as a harmless hobo. A colorful character was he, spinning ghost stories that curled our toes. Evenings after dinner, he and Dad stepped out to our front porch to visit and talk man stuff, but Daddy was no match for Cousin Arthur when it came to hair-raising yarns like this one:

> "I was raising a thousand fryers to sell. When they were almost ready for market, thieves cut through my wire chicken house one night and took every last one. My dog didn't bark so I figured it was somebody we knew. When I told my neighbor about it, he said, 'I know who did it—and I know something else. When they pull off a job like this, they post someone nearby with a rifle. His orders are to shoot to kill. Just thank God you didn't wake up and go out there.'"

Cousin Arthur regaled us with stories of strange people and enchanting places, thrilling us with "true-so-help-me-God" encounters with grisly ghosts and graveyards. Soon, he had all us kids under his spell. To us, he was a world traveler and authority on everything. Dad doubted some of Arthur's tales but treated him kindly.

While we kids thrilled to see him coming, Momma dreaded his vagabond visits. She had a point. He reeked of urine. Body odors rode the air around him, stomach-churning smells. Being a bachelor hobo, he refused to bathe.

Momma declared him too dirty and smelly to sleep inside. So, she fixed him a pallet on our screened back porch. After a big country breakfast next morning, Cousin Arthur would bid us goodbye, sling his replenished knapsack over his shoulder, and amble off down our country lane.

It always saddened us to see him shuffling down the road into unknown dangers. We kids watched until his head disappeared over the horizon.

I knew what my next orders from Momma would be:

"Take Cousin Arthur's pallet out in the back yard and burn it." I knew better than to protest, but it pained me to see Momma taking such a harsh view of Cousin Arthur's hygiene habits.

One day Cousin Arthur sent word that he was in jail. He needed Daddy to come pray for him. There in a prison cell, Cousin Arthur unloaded his woes to the preacher:

"In my travels I met a widow, married her and moved into her place. Quit my nomadic ways. Soon she became ill. Doctors couldn't help her. One day, she went down to her cellar to get something. Fell and broke her back. I heard her screaming, rushed down, and found her in terrible pain. That's when I heard a voice. God told me, 'Arthur, you must stop her suffering.' So, I obeyed the Voice. Took my claw hammer and put the poor thing out of her misery. Ira, you believe me, don't you?"

Daddy chose his words carefully, "Cousin Arthur, I don't doubt you heard a voice, but I don't think it came from God." Remembering the rumors about his first wife, Daddy prayed for him and left grieving.

Threatening calls prompted jailers to shift their prisoner to a secret place. Arthur dropped out of sight. Later, we learned he'd been convicted of murder. He served time in Parchman, Mississippi's notorious State Penitentiary. One Christmas, the Governor gave holiday passes to trustworthy prisoners. Arthur went home to spend Christmas with his family and never returned.

A search was made. His body was found bound with chains in a river near the deceased widow's home. The widow's two sons were charged with the murder; a jury refused to convict them. Somewhere along life's journey, our wandering cousin veered horribly off-course and lost his way. How could such a thing happen? Only God knows. Looks like the rest of us will have to wait to find out.

Mad Dog Killer No More

On a brighter note, not all who wander off into darkness stay there. Bobby Jim Tatum was a bad dude. He was the Ku Klux Klan's most feared hit man in those troubled times after segregation was outlawed and Mississippi was fighting court orders to integrate.

In Mobile, where my Daddy preached, Bobby Jim as a teenager came under the influence of hatemongers who convinced him that civil rights activists were being manipulated by a Jewish-communist plot to destroy America. He was willing to die to stop them. It's a miracle he's alive today.

He teamed up with KKK Imperial Wizard Sam Bowers who masterminded their terrorist campaign from Laurel, Mississippi. The FBI thinks Bowers masterminded nine murders and at least three hundred bombings, beatings, and burnings. Known as the Mad Dog Killer, Tatum hid in a safe house in the mountains of North Carolina, slipping out at night to strike his victims. His modus operandi was so secretive few of his blood brothers, fellow Klansmen, even knew his name.

He zealously joined in the fray, firebombing black churches and Jewish homes and synagogues, gunning down a policeman, and matching wits with detectives and the FBI. In one night-rider attack, he machine-gunned the home of a black woman. Flosie Lindsey's six-year-old niece was wounded, narrowly escaping death.

Willing to resort to anything to stop the killings, terrified Jews paid two KKK informants $50,000 to set up a death trap. Working with the FBI, Meridian city police ambushed Tatum as he was placing a dynamite bomb to kill a Jewish leader. A small army of lawmen opened fire with high-powered rifles and shotguns loaded with buckshot.

A pretty young elementary teacher, night-riding with Tatum, was shot to death. Tatum body was riddled with buckshot and high-powered military-style rifle bullets. Almost blown away, somehow he survived and was convicted and sent to Parchman, one of the nation's toughest prisons.

Landing in a maximum-security unit known as Little Alcatraz, Tatum was slammed into a cell on death row. Soon, he ingratiated himself with wardens and was made a trusty in the prison hospital. Right away, he began plotting to escape.

With the help of two other prisoners, he masterminded a sensational jail break. Again, one of his night riding buddies, bribed by the police, sold him out and led a squad of troopers in helicopters and squad cars to their hideout. One of his partners was shot to death. Tatum surrendered alive, still determined to escape and return to the killing fields.

This time, Parchman lived up to its reputation. Imprisoned in a fortress of concrete, brick, and steel, he was watched night and day by guards who dreamed of killing him. Slowly, the Mad Dog Bomber came to realize that this time there would be no escape.

He fell into a deep funk, feeding his bitterness with Adolph Hitler's *Mein Kampf* and racist hate literature. After a long season of living in a hell of his own making, Tatum finally turned to the *Bible* he had abandoned.

One day reading in the *New Testament*, he was shocked to hear Jesus asking, For what is a man profited if he shall gain the whole world, and lose his own soul? [4] Here is what Tommy told a reporter:

> "It just exploded in my mind and heart, and I realized I had been doing precisely that. I got on my knees in that cell and just gave my life to Christ and asked him to come in. I didn't even know that He wanted it, but I said, 'Lord, I've ruined my life, but if you want it, I'll just give it to you completely. Here it is.'" [5]

Legendary FBI Director J. Edgar Hoover was rightly suspicious. He sent some of his guys to see if Tatum was playing another con game. They came away convinced he was born-again. Slowly, he began to win over skeptics who feared his change of heart was simply another ploy to get out of jail. Even some of the detectives, cops, Blacks, and Jews he wanted to kill came to visit him in Parchman. They found a new man, ashamed of his past, determined to win them back with kindness and love.

When Jewish lawyer, Al Binder, visited him in jail, Tatum drew him a map of the man's own house—one he'd prepared for a nightrider attack and murder. After peppering him with questions for three hours, Binder was satisfied he was dealing with a new human being. He agreed to help Tatum if he pledged to use his freedom to fight anti-Semitism.

Later, Tatum applied to Duke University, Rutgers College and the University of Mississippi and was accepted by all three. He spent two years at Ole Miss, making straight A's, studying the classics, Greek and the *New Testament*—and writing a book, *Conversion of a Klansman*.

More than 40 years have passed since God found Bobby Jim in a prison cell. Since then, he's told thousands of the Lord's love and mercy, taught at religious colleges, and served in church leadership positions.

"Today, Bobby Jim is one of the kindest, humblest, most loving men you'd ever want to meet," says his friend, Englishman Paul Yates. They say a leopard can't change his spots. But Bobby Jim will tell you this, Jesus can—and he does it every day.

> *It is no secret what God can do.*
> *What He's done for others, he'll do for you.*
> *With arms wide open, he'll welcome you;*
> *It is no secret what God can do.*[6]

Mr. Charley's Violin

Two miles from our farm as the crow flies lived a couple Daddy and Momma dearly loved. Mister Charley and Miss Corinne's children were grownup and gone. So, they made a big deal over me.

"Just look at those big brown eyes," Corrine gushed. I was old enough to be embarrassed by her attention yet enjoy it.

Charley's wild hair and moustache made him a Mark Twain lookalike. A natural storyteller, he entertained with wild gestures and hilarious mimicking. Charley smiled easily, lighting up a room when he entered. His white hair gave him the air of a village elder.

In the spring, Momma and I hiked through the woods to visit them. Sometimes, we picked wild plums for Corinne along the way.

They often insisted we stay for lunch. While she and Momma talk-ed girl stuff, Charley took me in tow. With his dog, Roan, we trekked down to Spring Branch to fish.

Charley rigged our cane poles while I dug for grubs and earth-worms. Red-Belly perch and catfish loved our worms.

When we'd caught enough for Corrine's iron skillet, we hit the trail back for lunch. Sawing logs and man-handling them out of piney woods left Charley's back permanently bent. Yet, his steps were still spry, his hand-carved hickory walking stick ready to whack a snake.

Charley was famous for growing "good-enough-to-die-for" purple scuppernongs, training his vines on an enormous latticed arbor. His purple scuppernongs were so scrumptious neighbors marked their calendars to remind themselves when they ripened.

Friends brought milk pails to help themselves. Charley and I stood underneath the arbor, popping the sweet balls in our mouth, crushing them and swallowing the heavenly nectar.

Charley and Corrine lived off their orchards and garden—plus hunting and fishing, picking wild berries, fruits, and nuts. Despite liv-ing on desperation's doorstep, they were happy.

One day Corinne asked Momma if I could spend the night with them. Knowing they missed their grown-up kids, Mom agreed. They treated me to home-grown popcorn; letting me stay up long past bed-time as Charley took me around the world with his violin.

Corinne laid a pallet on the floor for me. It was my first night away from home, but I slept unafraid, knowing Mr. Charley's shotgun was hanging over my head, resting on two nails driven into his bedroom wall.

Charley was a survivalist. Like many settlers harassed by torna-does sweeping in from the Gulf, he and Corrine walked their floors at night, watching out their windows as lightning flashed and thunder rumbled. Charlie believed the good Lord helps those who help them-selves.

"We prayed, but I also kept digging."

Charlie dug a storm shelter in a hillside facing their cottage, a place to run from tornadoes. Here he kept a hurricane lamp, cots, five-gal-lon jugs of water, and cans of food— plus a bushel of sweet potatoes.

Charley treated me to a tour. Inside by flickering kerosene lamp, he told of horrific storms they'd escaped by fleeing to the shelter.

Charlie also used the dark storm cellar as a stage for spine-tingling tales like this one:

"One night Roan woke us up barking out at the barn. Something was attacking our chickens. I grabbed my shotgun and flashlight, rushing out in nothing but my pajama top. As I bent over to shine my flashlight in the henhouse, Roan slipped up from behind, nuzzling my bare rear with his cold nose. I shot two chickens off their roost and scared the others half to death. Never found the attacker."

Now Charley was on a roll: "Corrine and I were fattening this pig we'd named Jowl. She's stuffing him with scraps from the kitchen table. Any leftover milk I'm mixing with wheat shorts. Jowl's supposed to be our next meal ticket.

One morning he's missing. Some lowdown thief slipped in and grabbed him while we slept. I grabbed my shotgun and called Roan. He picks up the bad guy's scent, and we dash off after him. The thief's carrying Jowl in a burlap sack, but the pig's so heavy the guy sits down every few minutes to rest. Soon, we see him running through the swamp.

'Sick'em, Roan!' I yell, and he lunges after the guy, ripping a hole in his pants.

I sting his backside with a load of birdshot. He drops Jowl, high-tailing it off through the woods. I'm too tired to carry the pig so Roan helps me herd him back home."

The pride of Charley's life was a beautifully carved and polished violin he'd bought during the Depression. Preacher McCardle, a traveling evangelist hard up on his luck, sold it to him for one dollar. Charley taught himself to play and was soon serenading young lovers at local dances. Country parties in those days were called "frolics."

Charley sawed logs all week, knocking off at noon on Saturday. Rushing home, he'd shave, bathe, put on his party clothes, and head for his next frolic.

Being a devout man, Charley began wondering how the Lord might use him.

"I knew I should be giving my talents to God."

He picked up a church hymnal and taught himself the popular hymns. His lively melodies became a featured attraction at church socials, political, and community affairs.

Years passed. Charley sits in an old rocking chair on his front porch, reliving his glory days. Entertaining a kid with his beloved violin; in his mind's eye he's a strapping lumberjack again.

"My violin got me into some high places and some low ones," he jokes.

Daddy said it was true; he and Momma danced to Charley's music when they were "courting."

Preacher McCardle convinced Charley his instrument was a rare Stradivarius, handcrafted by the famous Italian violin maker. Charlie knew the old fiddle could be worth a fortune. But it was also the pride of his impoverished life, his magical traveling companion.

"Money can't buy my best friend," vowed Charlie.

Still, the possibility that it might be priceless, added to his love affair. He found himself handling it more carefully, polishing it more tenderly. His cherished violin spoke of centuries past, of classical orchestras, of Rome, Paris, and Constantinople.

He never found out if his old friend was a Stradivarius—but his dream lived on. When Charley came to the end of his playing days, he passed his precious violin on to a fellow music lover.

It's exciting to think that somewhere out there in the great American backcountry; another country bumpkin may be playing a multi-million dollar Stradivarius. May Charley's beloved old keepsake endure for a thousand years, enthralling dancers and dreamers yet unborn.

Granny Was a Choctaw

Having "mixed blood" sadly was a disgrace in the United States in the early 1900s. So, it was a hush-hush topic that my maternal grandmother was half American Indian. How the family thought they could keep it a secret is beyond me. Granny had penetrating black eyes, high cheekbones, straight black hair, and distinctive red skin.

Choctaw Indians were the aboriginal residents of Daddy's land. Our farm was littered with their arrowheads, rock knives, grinding stones, and other relics.

Granny's sister, great-aunt Dora, could've passed for a full-blooded Native American. Yet, it was never spoken of in our family—except in whispers.

When Granny was still a young wife, her husband suffered a mental breakdown, spending the next two decades in an insane asylum. During the Great Depression, Granny was left to raise a son and four girls on their small farm.

When Grandpa landed in the cuckoo's nest, Granny was on her own except for God and Government commodities. Not one to wait for Santa to climb down her chimney, Granny hitched up a mule and planted a garden to feed her fatherless kids. When they grew big enough to help, she put them to work in the fields.

Plowing a mule, heavy work even for a man, she raised cotton, corn, and vegetables. Twice a month, a friend drove her to New Augusta, the county seat, where Uncle Sam doled out food commodities to destitute families.

Dried beans, flour, rice, sugar, salt and cured pork meant her kids would not go to bed hungry. (Does anyone remember how terrible that reconstituted grapefruit juice tasted?)

Granny taught her only son to hunt and fish—not for sport but to feed her little brood. Quail, venison, squirrel, and wild turkey were plentiful. Catfish were frequent guests at Granny's table.

Once, a greedy neighbor tried to cheat Granny out of her small farm. He hired a buddy to re-survey his property lines. Not surprisingly, they claimed Granny's lines were wrong. He came to give Granny the bad news, telling her his men would be moving her fence. Granny

knew little of surveyors or lawyers but she knew right from wrong—
and when she was being cheated.

Granny was normally a sweet soul, but, Lordy!, when someone got
her dander up, she could cuss off a Billy goat's whiskers, singe a bald
man's toupee, and cause black-eyed peas to sprout in a pressure cooker. The scheming thief left with his ears burning.

When the crew showed up to move her fence, Granny was waiting. She grabbed her husband's shotgun, meeting them at the property
line.

"I'll shoot the first sorry polecat that touches my fence," she warned.
The crew loaded up their tools and left.

My sister, Edith, tells of Granny fishing in the Tallahala River one
day during deer rutting season. As Granny fished from a homemade
canoe, a buck deer swimming across the river to escape from hunters
threatened to collide with her boat. She began yelling at him, slapping
her paddle in the water to frighten him off. He paid her no attention
but kept on coming. Desperate, Granny stood up in her boat, clubbing
him over the head to beat him off. That's Edith's story, and she's sticking with it!

Years later, my American Indian heritage proved to be a blessing when I was sent from Washington to powwow with tribal leaders
about nuclear waste. At first, they were highly suspicious of a white
man from Washington. They'd heard the old lie too many times: "I'm
from the Government and I'm here to help you." However, when I told
them about Granny their hearts softened. Affectionately, they dubbed
me "Gentle Ben" and welcomed me into their tribal councils and cultural celebrations. The Yakima Tribe in Washington State even invited
me to be their honored guest at their annual Festival of First Fruits, a
sacred ceremony they've been observing for centuries.

Visiting with these gentle folks and listening to their life stories,
I remembered how Granny fought her own battles of loneliness and
deprivation. Granny was my calling card to their world. She opened
my soul to these remarkable people.

A deer was feeding in our yard when I went out to pick up the
Washington Post this morning. Granny's heart would've skipped a
beat. A grey fox was trailing a rabbit in the fresh snow outside our win-

dow one wintry morn. Granny would've been rooting for the bunny. In a creek out behind our Maryland home, beavers dammed up Crabb's Branch, creating a small lake attracting mallards and Canadian Geese. Granny would've grabbed her bonnet and hurried out to watch. At sunset, thousands of crows fill the sky, making their way home to roost. Granny would've thrilled to hear them calling.

President Abraham Lincoln once said, "I understand how one can look out on human nature and have doubts about the Creator, but I cannot understand how a man can look up into the heavens on a starry night and say there is no God." Granny's love of nature convinced us that, indeed, the heavens are declaring the majesty of God.

Granny taught us to see beauty in a sweet gum ball, a wild turkey, and a red corncob. A wrinkled old lady was she, with a heart full of wisdom. Thank you, Granny!

Grandpa Stevens

Momma's Daddy lost his mind when he was a young husband with a loving wife and kids. One day he was a doting father and husband, then without warning his mind went off track, traveling unfettered into time and space. He wasn't abusive or dangerous but too sick to function normally. Granny had no choice but to have him committed to an asylum for the insane. He spent the next twenty years there.

"I was just a shirt-tail girl when they came to get him," Momma recalled.

By the time he regained his sanity, Momma and the rest of his children were grown and married. His wife had survived the Great Depression and raised his family. They had nothing left to give each other.

"I'd forgotten what he looked like," Momma said of her missing father. So, the family built Grandpa Stevens a log cabin with a dirt floor in the piney woods where he lived out the rest of his days.

He cooked on a fireplace. The only memory I have of him is when he walked through the woods to visit us. He was toting a dead possum. He asked Momma to cook it for him. So, she took out her big cast iron skillet, laid the possum in the center, surrounding it with sweet pota-toes. How scrumptious that baking possum smelled!

Grandpa loved collards with hot pepper sauce, so Momma also in-dulged him with fresh collard greens and crackling cornbread. When his meal was ready, Momma sat Grandpa down at the table to eat alone.

To Momma's horror, I asked Grandpa if I could taste his possum. He took me up in his lap where he and I enjoyed a gourmet possum saturated with sweet potatoes.

It breaks my heart to think how people treated Grandpa when he finally left the asylum and came walking up the road one day to his long-lost home. They were not being intentionally mean. They just didn't know any better.

Folks knew next to nothing about mental illness in those days. In-stead of rushing to help victims, even their own families felt shamed and disgraced. They kept it hush-hush, swept it under the rug.

They acted like Grandpa was to blame, like he enjoyed going cra-zy—lollygagging there in the Whitfield State Hospital for the Insane, excusing himself while they suffered through the Great Depression. They blamed him for ruining the family name—for besmirching our reputation. How tragic his own loved ones couldn't see Grandpa sim-ply as a damaged, recovering human being trying to carry two cross-es—his insanity and their shame!

I'd like to dig Grandpa up and talk to him. "Grandpa, we love you. We know now you couldn't help being sick. We know you didn't run out on your babies."

I'd tell him how great Momma turned out: how she sacrificed to make a better life for her kids, how honest she was, and how hard she worked. I'd tell him she got her wonderful qualities from him. I'd hug Grandpa Stevens for giving us such a loving Momma—and I'd thank him for sharing his possum with me.

Granny Herring

She was technically my brother-in-law R.J.'s grandmother, but Granny Herring belonged to kids everywhere. She lived alone in a tottering log house that was straining to survive the next strong wind.

A sweetly devout little lady with two warts, she dipped snuff from a tin can and smoked a corncob pipe. Tiny and frail, Granny H. looked like the next whirlwind might blow her to Kansas. Her shriveled skin was the color of the preacher's tobacco juice. With a bemused smile, she constantly nodded her head from side to side. This endearing trait had all the kids nodding along with her.

When her figs began to ripen, Granny H. sat in a rocking chair on her back porch, plunking rocks at hungry marauding blue jays. Her weapon was a slingshot made from a forked stick, two strips of automobile inner tube, and a leather shoe tongue cradle. The big bossy jays were stealing her ripe figs—darting in with loud bullying squawks to scare off rival mockingbirds and redbirds. "They'll gobble up the whole bunch if I don't throw the fear of God in 'em."

It's doubtful she ever killed one, but, gracious, how they fussed! After a few moments of pitched battle, they'd retreat and wait for Granny to take a coffee break.

One day she admitted she could no longer see the jaybirds. She handed me her slingshot with a bucket of rocks. "Let's see if you can knock their tail feathers off. They're laughing at me."

My aim wasn't much better, but Granny whooped and clapped her boney old hands every time my rock sent a thief into panic.

Figs the birds didn't steal, she picked in syrup buckets with a wire bail, cooking them down into thick preserves on top of her wood stove. In a big wooden dough pan, she mixed up buttermilk biscuits so good they caused dogs to bay and sinners to repent.

Her kitchen was separated from her main house, connected by a covered walkway. Her pine lumber floors were pitted with rotted-out knot holes the rats used to play hide-and-seek with Whiskers, a brindle tom cat.

Granny doted on her cats. She made them talk to us. Whiskers could recite *John* 3:16. One mewed the *Lord's Prayer*. One predicted the weather and could tell the color of your shirt. When we finally caught on that Granny Herring was throwing her voice into the cats, we were sorely disappointed.

Granny H. passed the winter sitting by her fireplace, an ancient cane rocking chair her creaking companion. Whoever built her house left wide cracks in the wooden floor. She used these cracks to spit her snuff juice between the boards. Nobody could visit without staying for "a quick cup of coffee." She kept a pot of the potent stuff by her fireplace.

When family visited, she grabbed her fire poker, raked a pile of red-hot coals out from under the blazing logs, and set her coffeepot on the live coals. She used chicory in her coffee, making it so strong only those with galvanized stomachs could swallow it.

Kids loved her ghost stories. Granny would pile a couple of logs in her open fireplace and throw cushions on the floor for little ones. Soon, her wide-eyed fans were caught up in worlds of ghouls and goblins. Years passed, and, well, you know the story. Everybody got so busy. No one had time to visit.

She kept her wire spectacles on the mantle above the fireplace. Here she spent her last years happily reading her *Bible* and dime store romances, rocking, sipping her chicory coffee, and dozing.

One day R.J. knocked on her door. "What's going on?" she asked him, puffing on her corncob pipe.

"Granny, Iris just bought a new washing machine that does it all. It rolls around the house, gathering up our dirty clothes. Then, it washes and dries them. Then, it sorts and folds them and returns them to the closets." Granny H. was beside herself.

"I thought I'd heard it all, but this takes the cake. What will they think of next?" She told everyone about Iris' new washing machine. When she found out R.J. was pulling her leg, he was in big trouble!

Now, Granny H. has been gone for many years; memories of her are fading. Yet, in our mind's eye she still dozes by her fireplace with a faded *Bible*, spectacles on her nose, waiting for someone to stop by for a quick cup of coffee.

Our Mormon Cousins

The Chicken Littles were clucking when someone in Daddy's family up and did the unthinkable. She married a Mormon.

After moving off to Utah with her new husband, Cousin Cleo with her clan returned every few years to visit her Mississippi relatives. During these reunions they tried to convert Daddy. He relished opportunities to debate theology.

As I mentioned earlier, Daddy was a Primitive Baptist preacher as was his Uncle Luther and brother, Oscar. Like Presbyterians, the Hard-shells, as some called them, saw divine providence in every puff of wind. Like Abraham Lincoln, they made much of God's sovereignty.

"God's in charge, and I'm okay with that" was Daddy's credo. Not a popular theology—then or now.

"Folks have trouble letting God be God," the preacher liked to argue. "It sticks in their craw, gets under their skin, and reminds them they don't have the last word."

Our Mormon cousins didn't know what to do with Daddy. They couldn't convert him, and they certainly were not buying what he was selling.

Daddy feared they were going straight to hell. They were convinced that only Mormons go to heaven. The preacher quoted scripture to them, speaking of the resurrected Lord, "...with your blood you purchased men for God from every tribe and language and people and nation."[7]

To us kids, our Utah cousins were royal visitors. Gossip circulated that some of their disowned sects still practiced polygamy. Just the possibility made our eyes bug out like saucers.

We loved to see them coming because they always showed up with treats. For us, the candies and goodies topped all religious differences.

After supper, adults gathered round our fireplace to swap tales and talk God stuff. Their friendly arguments lasted far into the night. We kids hoped in vain for fisticuffs. When no punches were thrown, we nodded off to sleep.

Of their attempts to convert him, Daddy kidded them with this scripture, "...ye compass sea and land to make one proselyte; and when he is made, ye make him twofold more the child of hell than your-selves." [8]

No one ever won these good-natured debates or changed anyone's mind. As for us, we loved our cousins and always rejoiced to see them coming.

Both sides were convinced theirs was the only true version of Christianity. Could it be God's screen is just a tad wider than ours, that when we get to heaven, both sides of the family may be genuinely sur-prised to see "lost" relatives who've somehow made it past Saint Peter?

Daddy's Best Friend

After working in the fields, doing his barnyard chores, and eating supper, Daddy loved to sit with his best friend, Mr. Russell, swapping tales.

We kids were their silent partners and mesmerized fans. On steamy summer evenings, we retreated to our front porch to catch a cool breeze. In winter, we hovered around an open fireplace, warming one side while freezing the other. When Mr. Russell didn't show up at our place, we strolled down our country lane to his house.

The Russells had migrated from Mississippi's Kemper County near Philadelphia, a once-grand antebellum town whose reputation was smeared when Klansmen murdered Emit Till, a black youth, for whis-tling at a white woman and then buried him in an earthen dam.

The Russells settled on a large track of land next to us. Having lived near the Choctaw Indian Reservation, Mr. Russell's stories often featured those colorful neighbors with their animated gestures and dialect.

> "One day I took my friend, Sunnyface, fishing,"
> he recalled. "He caught a nice-sized bass, put it on a
> string, and hung it up in a tree near the river. Soon,
> I caught a little one and decided to play a joke on
> my buddy. So, while Sunnyface watched his fishing
> poles, I slipped back into the woods, took his fish
> down, and swapped it for my little one.

When we were ready to go home, Sunnyface
goes to the tree where he left his fish. I'm watching him, pinching myself to keep from laughing out
loud. As he reaches up to take his fish out of the
tree, Sunnyface stops dead still, trying to figure out
what happened. He sees me watching him. Sunnyface shrugs his shoulder disgustedly and exclaims,
'Ha! Him shrunk!'

When I 'fessed up and handed him back his fish,
Sunnyface enjoyed the joke on himself. 'My friend
made a funny!' he told his wife."

Mr. Russell took me fishing with him on Leaf River, a tributary of
the Pascagoula River that empties into the Gulf of Mexico. Driving
his truck down a logger's trail, we penetrated deep into thick swamp.
Parking his truck, we climbed down the river bank and were soon
catching hand-sized bream (sunfish), bass, and catfish. Returning to
his truck as night was falling, we found a stranger waiting in the cab.

"Do you think he has a gun?" I asked.

Mr. Russell ignored my question, walked up, and opened the cab
door. A drunk fell out on the ground. Without hesitating, Mr. Russell
bent down, picked him up and put him back in the truck.

"Can you tell us where you live?" Mr. Russell asked. He mumbled
something unintelligible. So, we propped him up between us in the
cab. Mr. Russell put the truck in reverse and backed out of the woods
to the main road. We began stopping at each house, asking, "Do you
know this guy?" Soon, we found someone who knew him and where
he lived.

Driving up to a rusty trailer that looked abandoned except for
starving cats and a bedraggled cur dog, we honked the horn. Kids ran
out of the woods, surrounding our truck.

"Is your mom home?" we asked. Instead of answering, they ran
into the trailer, slamming the door. The man's wife charged out of the
house. Seeing her drunken husband, she began hurling wondrous
words of abuse upon him, grabbed him roughly by the collar, and
dragged him into the trailer. "Well, looks like our job's done, and hers

is just beginning," Mr. Russell joked as we climbed back in his truck, heading home.

He managed a large cattle spread owned by a wealthy absentee landlord who showed up monthly to collect his profits. One day, Mr. Russell found a mixed shepherd puppy for sale on a nearby farm. He brought him home and trained him to herd cattle. Shep became his constant companion. As soon as Mr. Russell started toward his truck, Shep would leap into the cab ready to work. When raising cattle in fenced pastures, ranchers rotate their herds from one field to another to keep them from overgrazing the grass. As cattle feed in one pasture, the grass is growing and replenishing itself in the next one. Shep became a marvelous helper, anticipating Mr. Russell's every move, rounding up strays, moving cattle from one pasture to another. Shep looked like Lassie, the famous canine movie star. He became the fastest dog we'd ever seen.

Mr. Russell taught Shep to hunt squirrels. He became a useful hunting dog but was so fast he often frustrated us by catching squirrels on the ground before we could get a shot at them.

"Maybe I'll start leaving my gun at home," Mr. Russell joked. "Or maybe I'll just tell Shep how many squirrels we need for supper and send him out by himself!"

One day we watched in awe as Shep chased a red fox squirrel, overtaking him just as he jumped into a pine tree. Shep leaped 6-8 feet into the air and took that squirrel off the tree before he could scamper out of reach.

When Mr. Russell drove into town to buy supplies, Shep rode shotgun in the cab. Naturally, he was so proud of his dog he couldn't resist bragging about him, telling everyone how good Shep was in herding cattle—plus the fastest and smartest squirrel dog.

Then one day—maybe the darkest day of Mr. Russell's life—Shep disappeared; vanished without a trace. Everyone knew how much his dog meant to Mr. Russell. The shocked community joined in searching for him.

We looked high and low, asking everyone we saw. Kids made signs and nailed them to trees along country roads. Mr. Russell's preacher prayed and appealed from the pulpit for help.

We cried, suffered nightmares, and dreamed of finding Shep. We followed every lead: someone thought they might've seen him over at such and such a place. No luck.

Days dragged on, became weeks, then months. Hope flagged, but Mr. Russell refused to give up. "If he's alive and not locked up, he'll find his way home."

When we passed his house after Shep vanished, Mr. Russell would often be sitting on his front porch, watching up and down the highway. That front porch was the very spot where Shep had waited for him day and night. Now, he waited for Shep.

Mr. Russell seemed to grow older suddenly. He'd be half-asleep in his rocking chair, smoking one of his hand-rolled Prince Albert cigarettes, lost in memories. Sadly, Mr. Russell never found Shep or learned what happened to him; he also never got over missing him or longing for his return.

On a happier note, Mr. Russell later bought a young Shorthorn bull of the highest bloodline—registered and pedigreed out of championship stock. He brought him home and named him Noble.

He should have named him Sampson for he grew up to be a mighty man of valor. Mr. Russell generously shared Noble's stud services with Daddy and other neighbors to breed their cows, upgrading the quality of our herds.

It worked like this: when a cow came in heat (note for city folks: her hormones telling her, "It's time to become a mother"), we loaded her in the back of a truck and took her to Mr. Russell's pasture. Noble took it from there. When the romancing was over, the mom-to-be was loaded up and taken home.

Noble seemed to like this arrangement, but when the ladies didn't visit for a while, Noble decided to call on them. By this time Noble was so enormous that fences must've looked like spider webs or match sticks. He'd simply lower his head, push a fence post down, and walk over it.

Mr. Russell tried everything to contain him, even stringing up an electric fence to shock and deter him—no luck. When Noble got that gleam in his eye, it was, "Mañana, see ya later."

One day, Noble came calling on our cows uninvited, so Daddy decided to toll him into his mule stable with food. Noble gladly came in to enjoy a free meal.

Meanwhile, Daddy took a steel railroad rod and reinforced the stall door. As soon as Noble ate his fill, he lowered his head against the heavy oak door and pushed. The steel rod doubled like a horseshoe, and Noble resumed his rendezvous with bovine ladies.

Daddy kept the steel rod for show and tell. I suspect he and Mr. Russell were secretly proud of Noble's zeal and single-minded dedication to duty. They began calling him Houdini.

Farming can be a lonely life. Daddy and Mr. Russell enjoyed each other's company. From the time the Russells moved down from Kemper County to the farm next to us, he and Daddy hooked up as best buddies.

Daddy showed him his favorite fishing spots and hunting grounds. Mr. Russell was a self-made mechanic, blacksmith, electrician, and handy man. We were convinced he could fix anything. He helped Daddy keep our tractor and farm equipment running. In turn, we shared fruit from Daddy's orchards.

Neighbor helped neighbor to survive hard times, a character trait ingrained in those good-hearted people. Castrating their young bulls and boars was a joint project. Dehorning their cattle, worming and branding them were also done on the "buddy system." When it came time to take them to market, the two buddies corralled them, loaded them in a cattle truck, and hauled them to stockyards to sell at auction.

I enjoyed sitting in the auction house as stock handlers opened the gates, animals to be sold bursting into the arena below. A fast-talking auctioneer would begin barking out his spiel, buyers yelling their bids. Someone winked, nodded, or tugged his ear; a ring man saw him and shouted to the auctioneer.

"We've got a 30 here," the auctioneer would shout to the crowd, "Someone give me 35."

Back and forth it went so fast I could barely follow the action. Suddenly, the auctioneer would bang his gavel, point to the highest bidder and yell, "Sold to Mr. X for 40 cents a pound!"

As those animals were prodded, poked, and driven out of the arena, cowhands drove in a new bunch. The auctioneer would slug down a swallow of coffee and begin his yelling, coaxing, and singsong act again.

The bidders matched his fever pitch with their own show of lung power. It was so exciting to a wide-eyed kid that I decided on the spot to become a professional auctioneer. That dream soon faded because I could never talk fast enough.

Rats were an ever-present nuisance, destroying bushels of grain and costing us dearly. Daddy and Mr. Russell lay awake at night, trying to outsmart them. They tried D-Con and all kinds of poisons to exterminate them. They raised hordes of cats, feeding them in the barn in hopes they would add critter protein to their diets. They thanked us by curling up asleep in the hayloft while the rats frolicked and played.

We tried slingshots, but they were inaccurate— the rats were too fast for us. We set traps; they stole the bait. Oh, the tricks they played on us! Then Mr. Russell heard of a new 22-caliber bullet, filled with tiny lead beads, smaller than birdshot. He bought two boxes and gave one to Daddy. They had some success with their new "rat shot" cartridges.

One day, Mr. Russell was stalking rats in his barn when he spied his daughter coming outside to hang her washing on a clothesline. Knowing the tiny shot would not penetrate her thick jeans; he slipped up behind Opal and blasted away at her behind as she bent over to take wet clothes out of a hamper.

She screamed in horror and fled to her mother, who roared out of her den like a momma sow, coming to rescue a squealing pig. Mr. Russell claimed no harm came of it, but, he didn't try it again.

Mr. Russell's friendship was a special gift to Daddy. He also proved to be a worthy mentor and Dutch uncle to me. Big and strong with a generous heart, he belonged to the Free Masons, often dropping his own work to go help a brother.

Tough and resourceful, he thrived by an I-can-do-anything attitude. True story: He carried a pair of heavy wire pliers in his overalls. I watched dumbfounded one day as he reached into his rear pocket for those pliers, jerked out a jaw tooth that was decayed and aching, and then went back to digging postholes.

"A crowbar and a claw hammer will take care of 90% of a man's problems," he vowed. Mr. Russell, you're nominated to this kid's Hall of Fame.

Miss Edith Strikes Again

Speaking in her loud teacher's voice, Miss Edith overwhelms a room full of people just by entering it. Widely traveled, she insists on educating family and friends about all the exotic places she visited.

On her 90th birthday her daughters took her to China, where she scaled the Great Wall and came home brimming with Chinese culture and armloads of ceramic Terra Cotta Warriors.

A voracious reader, Miss Edith regaled us with detailed book reports on all the exciting-to-her marvels she encountered in the library.

Her politics bordered on the extreme. Political correctness was as foreign to her as a blue Martian. Yet, she was such a tour-de-force that for every person she offended, she made a dozen new fans.

We have a saying in the family, "Edith was born a teacher and will die teaching." Blessed with a big heart, she cared deeply about people—their pains and problems. For 94 years, she devoted most of her life to people needing a helping hand.

She's a larger-than-life character. At class reunions, her former students regale each other with Miss Edith stories. Some of their favorites include the following:

> One day she grew concerned that one of her students had become distracted. His grades were suffering. At noon, she walked across the street from school to pick up a sandwich when she noticed a familiar looking car parked on the sidewalk. A man was waiting inside. She recognized him as the distracted boy's father. On impulse, Miss Edith walked up to the car and knocked on the window. When the man lowered it, she said, "Excuse me, sir, but I think you're the father of one of my children." The

poor fellow turned white, looking like a deer caught
in a car's headlights. When she realized she had sent
the wrong message, Miss Edith tried to explain, but
the man was so shell-shocked by then, she decided
the best thing to do was beat a fast retreat.

Always a whirlwind of activity, the dust had no chance to settle
around her. One day, Miss Edith complained to her doctor of a nagging stomach ache. He decided to do some routine tests, handing her
a kit for taking stool samples.

A few days earlier, she'd gone to Sears to buy new drip pans for
the top of her stove. The new pans failed to fit. So, since the labora-
tory and Sears were in the same direction, it seemed logical to kill two
birds with one stone. Grabbing grocery bags and dropping the items
in them, she was on her way.

Miss Edith dropped off her very personal specimen bag at the lab
first and then went on to Sears. You know where this is going, right?

At Sears, something told her to look in the bag before handing it to
the clerk. She discovered the mix-up and averted a dreadful outcome.
When she got home, her phone was ringing. It's the lab: "Miss Edith, I
think you left us the wrong specimen."

The hysterical nurse urges her to report to an emergency room immediately if that was a true specimen she'd left with them. "Just hold
that bag," she told the lady, explaining the mix-up at Sears. "I'll be right
over to exchange it," she promised, apologizing profusely.

"Don't worry about it," the lady told her. "People here are enjoying
your little mistake—and I haven't even told them yet that you left your
stool specimens at Sears! You've made our day."

Miss Edith was reminiscing.

"What's that I smell? It's a cold frosty December
morning at school. That big long room that served
as library, study hall, and English class is warming
up. As temperatures rise, it heats up a skunk odor
clinging to the brogan shoes of one of my country
boys. Evidently, the previous night's hunting foray
had been successful for one of my scholars.

Then, we had another problem one day when a rat trap went off while I was teaching Shakespeare's Macbeth. It popped like a pistol shot, and the captured rat began his death squeals. Rats had been seen scampering along the walls but there certainly hadn't been any orders to trap them during English class. I strongly suspected the author of these tales and his cronies. The great white hunters had struck again—not for monetary gain but to sabotage our study of Macbeth and create a little excitement. Of course, the rat must be removed then and there, requiring the aid of every brave male. The girls were standing in their chairs, squealing louder than the rat."

Since retiring decades ago, she works out at a local Wellness Center and signs up for nearly every class offered at nearby University of Southern Mississippi's continuing education program. If this is not enough for one her age, she volunteers as a friendly visitor at two local hospitals.

After teaching children nearly half a century and counseling with hundreds of parents, Miss Edith knows more people than a politician. As soon as she enters a hospital room, she begins asking about a patient's family. Soon she connects with someone she's taught or known—or someone who knows someone she's known. By digging into family trees, she finds connections to nearly all the folks she goes to comfort.

She's never happier than when mentoring a needy child, buying school clothes for them, or connecting jobless people with someone who can give them a job—or hiring them until they can get back on their feet.

Once she paid off a wayward nephew's traffic fines to get his driver's license restored. She persuaded two nieces who'd dropped out of college to go back to school, even paying their tuition. She's been known to pay taxes, utility, and doctor bills for needy kin.

Countless lives have been touched by this remarkable lady. I don't know if heaven works this way, but maybe when she gets there, all those she helped will line up to thank her. Or, maybe, Jesus will simply hug her and say, "That's what I meant."

Asked the secret of her longevity Miss Edith teases, "There are still a few people I haven't aggravated enough yet".

She has outlived all her enemies except one—the sands of time. We all try to ignore it, but Grandfather Time will not be denied. Our days with this remarkable lady are slipping away. When that time comes, God's green earth will go on without her, but it won't be the same.

> *From this valley they say you are going,*
> *We will miss your bright eyes and sweet smile,*
> *For they say you are taking the sunshine*
> *That has brightened our pathways awhile.*[9]

Sister Edith, on left, taught all her five siblings in high school: Bruce, Ray, Iris, Geraldine, author

Who Wants to be a Zillionaire?

Early on, I decided that my only chance of becoming filthy rich rested in Uncle Abie who owned a country store, selling groceries, clothes, and farm supplies, plus a sawmill and large tracts of timber in Mississippi and Louisiana. He dressed in suits and ties, drove fancy limos, and wore Old Spice shaving cologne. Uncle Abie was an honest-to-God entrepreneur. We were immensely proud of him.

"Your Uncle has the Midas touch," Momma told us, "Everything he touches turns to money." That was his sister, Aunt Della's, cue to chime in, "Yep, Abie's a modern-day Rumpelstiltskin. The man could take broom sage out of Ira's field and spin it into gold".

Maybe it was inevitable, with the rest of us living hand-to-mouth, that Uncle Abie's fame and fortune grew with every retelling until it became legendary. "You're going to take after your Uncle Abie,"Momma would say. In my wildest dreams, Daddy's well-to-do brother was always willing his estate to me. He took a liking to me, unintentionally fanning the flames. It seemed simply a matter of time.

Uncle Abie bred and trained hounds to hunt deer in river swamps and was an expert turkey hunter and fisherman—a role model for any star-struck ragamuffin.

He invited me to stay overnight with him and go fishing for white perch. He hunted on a private preserve where he organized grand hunting parties. He used a "pusher" to take his hunting dogs to one side of the swamp, positioning hunters on the opposite side. As his dogs jumped deer and they raced off in our direction, we were waiting.

At sunset, lucky hunters gathered at a butchering shed to prepare and divvy up their venison. So, my dreams of inheriting lands, lakes and riches blossomed and grew.

At his country store, Uncle Abie plied me with Baby Ruths, Butterfingers and Payday candy bars. In a glass showcase, he stocked something every kid adored—Jawbreakers. You may remember them as mouthwatering wads of bubblegum inside a rock-hard candy casing, more damaging to kids' molars than cracking hickory nuts with your teeth.

"Take anything you want," he insisted, waving his hand around a room, filled with treasures. I was too timid to do it, but the offer made my knees buckle.

Always on the look-out for things he could buy to sell in his store, Uncle Abie carried an oversized wallet stuffed with hundred dollar bills in his back pocket. The wallet was fastened to a chain looped into a wide leather belt. One day, riding shotgun in his truck as he drove, my curiosity got the better of me. "Aren't you afraid somebody will knock you in the head and rob you?" His reply shocked and shamed me. "Not really; the Good Lord watches over me."

When Momma heard that Uncle Abie and Aunt Nora were coming to visit, she flew into tailspins; cooking and cleaning for days. This was music to my ears, knowing Momma would be frying a heaping platter of chicken and making banana pudding, my favorite dessert.

Aunt Nora herself was quite formidable. Simply by being Uncle Abie's wife, she basked in his reflected glory. Tall with black hair and gorgeous long eyelashes, Aunt Nora was a regal personage. We marveled at her classy dresses and patent-leather shoes and purses. Even the simple clip she used to keep her lovely locks in a bun bespoke of royalty.

Being a Church of God Holiness believer, she wore no rouge or lipstick. Her majesty did not suffer. We watched her carriage, mesmerized at her elegance. To my sisters, in their hand-sewn Purina Pig Chow dresses, Aunt Nora looked like she'd just stepped out of Buckingham Palace.

Uncle Abie bought enormous tracks of timberland to supply his sawmill. After clear-cutting them of marketable trees, he bulldozed off the stumps, converting them into farms. His farms were so vast he used giant diesel tractors to plant and cultivate them.

To keep his tractors running full time, he bought a helicopter to service them in the field. Using shortwave headsets, the helicopter pilot serviced his tractor drivers. When a tractor broke down, the driver called the pilot and ordered a replacement part. The pilot flew to his supply shed, picked up the part, and delivered it. On-site repairs allowed his men to quickly get an idle tractor back into motion.

Reaching out to help his family, barely surviving on puny farms, Abie opened stores in two other dusty little Mississippi hamlets, Broom and Bendale. He hired a brother and his family to manage one of them and a sister and her family to run the other one. He offered to do the same for Daddy, but the preacher said, "I'd have felt like I'd be abandoning my calling".

All this bonding with Uncle Abie seemed to be improving my chances of inheriting a fortune. When it was just a matter of spelling my name right on the will—as so often happens—a fly fluttered and fell into the ointment. What my childish dreams had failed to take into account was that Uncle Abie had three wonderful daughters and a son, Billy Rufus.

So, it happened that Billy Rufus and I went to college together, and then he joined his father in business. He took pilot lessons to fly the helicopter. Uncle Abie soon retired. Billy Rufus took over my dream estate.

Meanwhile, Daddy was still preaching, farming, and trapping—barely scraping by. After painful soul-searching I finally yielded to fate: I'd never be a rich gentleman farmer.

Can't you imagine the good Lord shaking his head and chuckling?

Plain Folks

We survived by learning to laugh at ourselves. Here are outrageous sayings we used to cope with bruising reality:

- We're not the hoity-toities you read about in *The Help*. The only bankers we ever see are frowning guys in three-piece suits who come to foreclose on our farms.

- Highfalutin' society calls us rednecks and white trash. It makes no sense. "Our necks ain't no redder than yourn and we're not all white." Come to think of it, we do have a thing for white. We whitewash our worn-out tires to use for marigold and petunia beds. We hold funerals for our pets, burying them under white crosses in our back yards. We dress up in starched-and-ironed white shirts under our spanking new overalls, and, yes, white lightening was under many doorsteps.

- We hang hollow gourds on a pole in our yards so Purple Martins will come guard our hens from chicken hawks. A loaded squirrel gun under the Christmas tree means somebody loves us. As our teeth rot, we yank them out until all we have left is gums. No big deal, our chickens live longer because it takes us awhile to gum'em down.

- Nicknames often carry shame. We had two Oscars in our family. When one of them was a toddler in diapers, he was playing with a spoon. His mother discovered him eating something with that spoon that forever branded him as Spoon Oscar. The other one, a minister, we called Preaching Oscar.

- In bitter cold, we bring our dogs and cats inside at night, throw another quilt on the bed, and sleep in our socks and mittens. We doubt Neil Armstrong walked on the moon but can tell you a hound's bloodline back to his great granddaddy.

- We know the difference between pork rinds, pork chops, pork bellies, streak-o-lean, fatback, and cracklings.

- Fourth of July, we throw a young goat on top of worn-out bedsprings in the back yard. Men barbeque the goat all night, celebrating with roman candles and fireworks. Womenfolk "june around" inside, slow-cooking collard greens that we top off with hot pepper sauce and devour with heaping plates of cracklin' cornbread, washing it all down with sweet iced tea.

- Country fairs are enlivened by tobacco-spitting contests, ladies sack races, mule -pulling rodeos, horse racing and throwing eggs at politicians.

- A widow with a dozen hens and a cow is considered a good catch. Men are easier to come by. As they tell the ladies in Alaska, "Your odds are good, but your goods are odd."

- Mississippi was the last State to give up on Prohibition that made it illegal to cook your own hooch. Bootleggers, politicians, and preachers became odd bedfellows, keeping Prohibition alive for their own reasons.

- Moonshine stills sprung up in swamps like dandelions. When a new sheriff was elected, he often visited the stills, collected his bribes, and promised to look the other way. Sadly, lead-pipe distilled whiskey poisoned the pitiful alcoholics, drinking it. It drove people crazy, paralyzed them, and destroyed their nervous systems. It was common to see folks staggering, stumbling, and shuffling along, talking to themselves. Slowly, folks came to see Prohibition as an impossible dream; saw the illicit rot-gut whiskey destroying families. The preacher grieved over their corpses in funeral parlors, helped dig their graves and lower their coffins in the ground, hugged their widows and orphans, then went home and waited for the next tragedy. Reluctantly they were forced to try something else, so ended a noble experiment.

- Finally, we may fight like cats and dogs among ourselves, but we stand ready with crowbars and claw hammers to bring fire down on anyone threatening our kin!

PART V

CHILDHOOD MARVELS

The world is an exciting place for barefoot kids thrilled by ghosts, bicycles, tractors, pigs and rattlesnakes. Trouble arrives with a boy's first shotgun.

J. Bennett Easterling

Barefoot Troubadours

Going barefoot from Easter to Thanksgiving is to live on heaven's doorstep. We hated shoes and never wore them 'til Momma put her foot down. Running through the woods, whistling and blowing our juice-harps—how good does life get? Wearing shoes to a boy is like chewing with wooden teeth. It's worse 'n smoking grape vines or corn silks. We'd sooner wash our underwear in vinegar.

Barefoot kids are happy-go-lucky adventurers. Who ever heard of one committing hari-kari? Shoes start wars and destroy civilizations. Our favorite barefoot game was wedging corncobs between our toes to see how far we could sling-kick them. I never figured out why this didn't catch on. (Don't bother looking for it in *Guinness' Book of World Records*.)

We were a fraternity of loafers and no-accounts. We boasted about our fathers, argued over whose dog was best, and lamented our sisters. Our highest ambition was to scrounge a dime on Saturday to go to the movies to see Tom Mix, Roy Rogers or the Lone Ranger spewing hot bullets and bringing law and order to the Wild West.

The preacher never made us work in the field on Sundays. On Sunday afternoons, I'd wander off into the woods alone. Tiptoeing over quiet pine straw carpets, I'd find a secluded spot to lie down and gaze up into a cloudless sky, perfumed by blooming honeysuckle. Not a care in the world touched me there, lazing under a warm sun, watching songbirds flitting by, chirping to their mates.

Far in the distance a Rain crow is pleading for rain, a farmer's mule is braying, and someone's hen laid an egg and is sharing the good news. Freshly hatched spring frogs are peeping in the marshes. A bumblebee suspends himself motionless in the air above my head, wings twirling so fast my eyes cannot follow yet going nowhere. A whippoorwill is mourning softly. Two grey squirrels are fussing that an alien has invaded their domain.

My faithful friend, Pup, tracks me down and comes to lie with me in the straw. No word is spoken, yet Pup's tail is thumping the ground, telling me, "This was a great idea!" If Pup talked, he might quote Rudyard Kipling:

> "If you love me like I love you;
> What can life kill or death undo?"[1]

In such faraway worlds, a boy's imagination is boundless. An army caterpillar ventures upon my prone body, looks me over, trying to decide whether to crawl over or go around. I lay dead-still as he ascends the mountain, working his way across. When he's safely over, I take him tenderly in hand, dropping him back where he started—so he does it again and again. Pup must've read my mind—his tail-thumping picks up a beat. Overcome in this blessed state, conscience spoke to me about fibbing to Momma. Not that I enjoyed lying to her, but sometimes it seemed the only way to stay out of trouble. I knew it was wrong, though, and resolved to begin telling the truth even when it was sure to bring down scorching coals. I remained in this reformed state of grace until nearly sundown.

Sadly, summers vanished almost before they began. When the first hard frost fell, Momma called us inside, pointed to last winter's brogans, and uttered her chilling edit: "It's time to put 'em back on."

Hope died like bugs slammed with a flyswatter. Wet blankets of doom gripped our livers, settling in our bladders. That magical season when we'd glory-danced with nature was kaput. Too soon we were trudging back to school, condemned, and sentenced to a black season of dangling participles and multiplication tables. Could hope endure another long cold winter? If so, the butterflies might return.

Barefoot Troubadours L to R:
Geraldine, Iris, author

Haunting Stories & Tricks

"I can still scare you to death." Sister Iris was taunting me on my sixth birthday. This had worked for years, but her jig was up. I was onto her silly games. Falling for the bait, I proudly dared her to try. Dusk dark was creeping upon us as she took my hand and led me out behind the chicken-house.

"I'll be back in a jiffy," she promised, then vanished. I wait. When she failed to return, I noticed how dark it was getting.

A ghostly fig tree was hovering over me, its leaves so thick I couldn't tell if anything scary was hiding up there, likely to pounce like a snake, a spider, or rabid squirrel.

Where was Iris? Suddenly, an old woman appeared out of the gloom. She was trembling, clutching a crooked walking cane, dragging one foot behind her. She cackled out my name in a strange voice. Staggering closer, she clutched at me. I was out of there like greased lightning.

The old hag was fast on my trail, racing after me, whooping and cackling. I beat her to the back porch. Eluding her final lunge, I burst into the kitchen, slamming the door behind me. The evil wench banged the door, forced it open, and staggered into the kitchen.

Iris pulled off a black silk stocking she'd pulled over her head. I was hiding behind Momma, clinging to her skirt and trembling like a leaf. Iris was scolded soundly but not enough. And she couldn't stop smiling. Will I ever learn?

One day, Iris invited younger sister, Geraldine, to play blind man's bluff. So, Gerry blindfolded Iris and guided her around our backyard to touch and identify things. Then, it was Geraldine's turn. Knowing Iris loved to play tricks, Gerry was hesitant but went along with the game.

Wrapping the bandana securely so Gerry couldn't see anything, Iris led her around to familiar places, touching and naming things. Then, taking Gerry's hand, she placed it on a Sweet Gum tree. Pressing her hand hard to the tree bark, Iris forced it down the tree trunk into warm, slimy, wet ooze.

Gerry screamed, yanked off the blindfold to discover a tree trunk, covered with Army caterpillars. She'd crushed the creatures into slush, turning her hand green with slime. Momma scolded and shamed Iris but not nearly enough to satisfy Gerry.

Iris Gets Her Comeuppance

Iris was afraid of her own shadow. She tried to hide it by scaring us. So, we were not very sympathetic when the tide turned on her.

Newly married, she was away from home for the first time, living in a deserted farm house. Her husband worked nights; she was lonely and afraid. Isolated down a long lane, their drafty old house trembled as winter winds buffeted it. A dark hallway ran through the house.

Iris lay wide-eyed awake at night, listening to every creaky sound. Petrified, she dared not close her eyes. When R.J. came home at dawn, she finally got some sleep.

One night, cowering under heavy blankets, she heard a bumping sound like someone hobbling down the hall. She remembered seeing an old man with a walking cane, shuffling up and down the gravel road in front of their house.

In one horrifying moment, Iris figured it out. "That bumping is his walking stick. He knows I'm here alone—and this is not a friendly visit!"

The bumping grew louder. Then, he was outside her locked bedroom door. How strong is a hollow wooden door? Then, back down the hall—stopping, bumping along. Up and down, back and forth, he rambled.

"He's looking into every room to find where I'm hiding," she decided. Iris slipped quietly out of bed, grabbed a baseball bat, and hid behind the door. Shivering in her nightgown, she clutched her club and waited. She knew it was only a matter of time before he tired of his cat-and-mouse game.

"My only hope is to cold-cock him when he bursts through the door," she tells herself. Then, she remembered the old house is so isolated no one will hear her screaming. "Maybe I can knock 'im out and run for help before he recovers."

Iris kept talking to herself. The night dragged on. The bumping faded out, then came back. Afraid to move, she was cold, trembling with fear—so alone.

Finally, dawn broke. She heard R.J.'s car turn into the driveway. She heard him turn off the motor and get out. He came to the door, unlocked it, and tiptoed down the hall to their bedroom. Iris relaxed her grip on the bat, crept over, and opened the door.

She rushed into his arms, crying and telling him of her horrible ordeal. They searched the house, finding nothing. Outside, they noticed footprints all around the house, but not human footprints. They belong to a herd of cows grazing nearby.

Slowly, the truth dawned on both of them: A fine crop of winter wheat was growing on the south side of the house, protected from the wind. The cows discovered it. Grazing on the succulent grass, their horns were knocking against the house. The bumping Iris thought was the old man's cane was her neighbor's cows enjoying a picnic.

Iris confessed, "I was so scared I forgot to pray!"

Down at the Privy

Momma was a sport, often enjoying or at least tolerating our juvenile pranks, but this one crossed a boundary. It happened innocently enough. Two cousins, six- and seven-year-old girls, came with their mother to see their Aunt Mary (my mom).

While the adults visited, my cousins decided to play hide-and-seek. They invited me to join them. The game was going well when nature called. The girls excused themselves and ran down to the outhouse.

When they came out, I needed to go. When I opened the privy door, a surprise awaited. The girls had taken off their step-ins [panties] to sit on the round holes and forgotten to put them back on.

Seizing an opportunity for fun, I picked them up and tossed them down into the pit. When my cousins discovered their mistake, they ran back to the outhouse to get them, but, they'd mysteriously vanished. Of course, they knew who the culprit was—and soon so did Momma.

All's well that ends well, right? Wrong. This story did not end well.

Momma scorched my ears. Instead of turning me over to the preacher's wrath, she sat me down in a chair facing her; gave me one of those eyeball-to-eyeball long and painful talks for which moms are famous. I had broken their hearts, she said, two innocent girls who loved me. How sad it was to betray their trust, she said, staring at me like she was facing down Satan himself, making me squirm like a worm in hot sand. I still see her brown eyes flashing fire. How disappointed God who saw it all must be, she said. And surprised and disappointed and lots of other adjectives now mercifully lost to memory.

"Don't you think being kind and loyal to those who love you is better than playing mean tricks on them?" she asked.

The condemned bowed his head in shame-faced agreement. I don't recall all she said that day, but by the time Momma's righteous anger was exhausted, so was she.

How could such a foul deed be righted? There's only one thing to do, she said. Handing me two pairs of Gerry's panties in a brown paper bag, she barked out my marching orders:

"You take these to their house, hand them to their mother, and ask her if you may apologize to your cousins." Would Momma go with me? I pleaded, begging for mercy. The answer was no.

"You got into this devilment; now you must make up for it." She sent me off, brown bag in hand, to "do the right thing."

Why, oh why, Lord, is undoing bad stuff so hard?

Thrashed With a Cotton Stalk

In back of our cotton fields, a low-lying swamp emptied into a muddy stream. To visit our cousins, we walked a foot log across Bear Branch and then passed through a creepy swamp.

In her teens, Geraldine was a big 'fraidy-cat'. This made for wonderful opportunities. Poisonous cottonmouth moccasins and copperheads hid in this boggy swamp, but it wasn't snakes that struck terror in Gerry's heart. It was the "boogers" lurking there. Cousins told of seeing strange humanlike creatures covered with long hair.

"It's the Choctaw Indians come back as hants!" they warned. One of the hairy humanoids, they told us, "slipped up one night and stole a chicken right off our roost."

So, as Gerry and I passed through the spooky place to play with our cousins, I broke out singing at the top of my lungs to attract anything hiding there (ghosts, criminals, escapees from insane asylums, aliens, etc.). Gerry ran out of the dark swamp and waited on the hill.

"Keep your mouth shut on the way back, or I'll whip you with a cotton stalk," she threatened. Sure enough, on our way home, as we penetrated deep into the swamp, I began serenading her, calling for the boogers to "Come and get us!"

Gerry ran on through the spooky darkness and waited. When I arrived up in Daddy's field, she took a cotton switch and worked me over. I started bawling and threatening to tell Momma. Since I was wearing knee breeches, the switch left red marks on my bare legs. This could spell big trouble.

"Let's go by the store," she urged. Momma allowed each of us to spend a nickel for treats when we went to buy groceries. Gerry knew how to tempt me.

"If you promise not to tell, you can have my nickel and yours," she promised.

So, off we went. I bought an R.C. Cola and a Moon Pie, sat down on the grocery store steps, and, with her watching, greedily consumed them.

As soon as they were gone, I jumped up and ran all the way home to tell Momma and show her my red legs. When Geraldine told Momma what I had done to provoke her, Momma rendered her verdict: "You probably got what you deserved."

A Tractor and a Rattlesnake

Daddy finally traded his mule for a new tractor. I couldn't wait to get my hands on it. After much wheedling and begging, he let me drive it to haul sacks of cotton to the weigh-in station.

To drive that new tractor, I volunteered for all kinds of chores, meeting the postman, mailing Momma's cards or letters, picking up the daily *Hattiesburg American*, and—in case anyone remembered us—bringing home the mail.

Our mailbox was located a mile down a country lane, sitting out on the public road. I convinced Daddy his new tractor would get me back to the fields sooner.

One day as I drove past a dried-up frog pond, a granddaddy rattlesnake was slithering across the road. I revved up the tractor to catch him.

As the front wheels ran over him I slammed on the brakes so the big back wheels ground him into the loose gravel. When I looked back, it was plain he'd survived, was fighting mad, and looking for the enemy. What to do? I'd already given him my best shot.

I wasn't brave enough to hop off and confront him alone. Slamming the tractor in reverse, I backed up until one of the four-foot-high rear wheels pinned him down. As I was wondering what to do next, a truck came roaring along, dust billowing behind it. I stood up on the floorboard, waving the driver down. It was Mr. Hillman, my agriculture teacher. He'd been out buying cows.

Checking to make sure the rattlesnake was still pinned under the wheel; I hopped down and showed Mr. Hillman the angry viper. He took out his muleskinner's knife and went looking for a tree limb big enough to do battle. Finding a young persimmon sapling, he cut it down, trimmed the branches off, and killed the dangerous serpent.

Much relieved, I draped the slain reptile over the tractor hood and headed home for show and tell. Daddy proudly counted the monster's ten rattles. Momma wouldn't even come out to admire it. How's that for appreciation?

A Pig And A Rattlesnake

My brother-in-law asked me to come down to his daddy's house to help round up a pig to take to the butcher. This sounded like fun, so off we went. R.J. said he was to go down into his Dad's pasture and pick out a pig of his choice.

"You stay here while I go pick one out. I'll push him in your direction—you know what to do." R.J. handed me his little 22 rifle.

So, I'm killing time waiting for R.J. to find his pig. I decide to walk over to a tree stump and sit down. Out of the corner of my eye, I see something move.

Surely, God was watching over me. I look down just in time to avoid stepping on a Diamondback rattlesnake.

He coiled up into a ball, swinging his head from side to side. Flicking his forked tongue, he shook the tip of his tail, setting off a bone-chilling rattle, warning he was going to strike. I was in a daze, but apparently my instincts took over.

As he threw his head back to strike, his mouth flew open. I lifted the rifle and drilled him in the mouth. He went berserk, twisting and tumbling about. Then, it was all over. He turned belly up. It happened so fast I had no time to panic, but afterward, my heart was pounding and my knees trembling. I felt a clammy cold sweat, oozing out of my pores.

I crept over to a stump and sat down to collect myself. A sickening-sweet smell filled the air, that musky scent a serpent emits when threatened. While I was trying to calm down and collect my wits, R.J. ran up. He'd heard the rifle shot.

"Did you shoot the pig?" he shouts. Then, he saw the dead rattlesnake lying belly-up at my feet. Now it was his turn to get the heebie-jeebies.

"Don't move," he barks. "Where you find one rattlesnake, you'll find Poppa and Momma. Watch your step!"

Tiptoeing carefully, we eased ourselves out of that snake-infested pasture. I honestly don't know what became of R.J.'s pig that day. Maybe God was watching over it, too.

A Bicycle Lost

One Christmas, older brothers and sisters pooled their money to buy me a bicycle. To a penniless kid, it was a miracle from heaven. A fire-engine red B.F. Goodrich bike with 24-inch wheels, it was. I can still see it leaning against our Christmas tree that morning.

Learning to ride it proved painful. By the end of day one, my straddle was bruised purple. No matter, this was a mission worth suffering for.

I could hardly wait to show it off to Cousin Clem, who'd lorded over me with his Western Flyer. Soon, we were tearing up and down country roads. Clem lived across Bear Branch from us. Spring rains caused the stream to swell so wide we couldn't ride our bikes across. We decided to build a bridge.

Borrowing axes, saws, hammers, and nails, we set out. At the edge of Daddy's pasture, we leaned our bikes against the fence. Pitching our tools across, we climbed over the barbed wire and sat down in the woods to palaver.

Our eyes strayed to a rabbit tobacco bush, a native weed used by American Indians for smoking. Stripping off dry leaves, we rolled them into crude cigarettes to smoke as we dream-planned our bridge.

Using brown paper bags to roll our homemade cancer sticks, we lit them with Momma's kitchen matches. Inhaling the first puffs, we fell into coughing fits. Snuffing out the rancid smokes, we shouldered our tools and took off down through the woods to Bear Branch. Clem took over as straw boss.

"Let's find two saplings long enough to cut and drag across the stream. We'll lay them three feet apart. Then, we'll cut smaller poles to nail across the two big ones."

We sawed down two tall young pines near the creek, dragging them beaver-style across the stream. Chopping down smaller trees and nailing them across our two main support logs, we worked at fever pitch. Soon we'd be pushing our bikes back and forth across the new bridge. The swollen waters of Bear Branch would never again keep us apart.

Suddenly, we heard a loud pop like a gunshot, followed quickly by a second one. We looked up the hill through the woods and saw billowing smoke.

"We've set the woods on fire!" Clem yelled.

Dropping our axes, we raced uphill to find the underbrush blazing. Stomping and beating out the burning brush and grass, we swallowed so much smoke we were nauseated. Not until the fires were killed did we notice our bicycles. Clem's old Western Flyer, leaning against Daddy's pasture fence, was barely scorched. My shinning new B.F. Goodrich, leaning against a combustible heart pine fence post, was burned to a crisp.

Dumbstruck, we stood staring at the charred remains of my miracle bike: tires and tubes melted, leather seat consumed, wire spokes burned out. When it cooled off, Clem kindly offered to go home with me to face Armageddon. We rolled it home on metal rims.

"What will we tell Momma?" I worried as we neared home. We quickly made up a fib. We'd been playing with firecrackers; they sparked in the dry grass. Momma wasn't born yesterday. She could smell a kid's whopper a mile away, but, seeing my prized bike destroyed melted her heart. Instead of punishing me, she used it to teach us a valuable lesson.

"We can't afford to buy you another one, but we'll help you earn money to restore it," she promised. Looking at that burned out junk heap; Momma's offer seemed like an impossible dream.

"Do you have a better idea?" she asked. We didn't.

She handed us a Sears's catalog, "Go figure the parts you'll need and how much they cost."

Warming up to the task, we searched her catalog for tires, tubes, leather seat, rubber handlebars, burned out spokes, chain, tail light, and basket. Oh, yes, and a can of fire-engine red paint. Just finding the replacement parts and pricing them eased our pain. Life would go on; maybe this was doable. Momma handed us a list of chores.

"When you've earned enough money for the parts, we'll mail your order in." We planted Momma's garden, pruned her shrubs, transplanted flowers, and ran errands. Momma was showing us how to help ourselves.

Spring came and went, then summer and fall. By early winter, after much sweat and toil, we'd earned enough money to mail in our order. Then, we waited, day after day hustling down the road to meet the postman only to return empty-handed. Momma used the waiting time to teach me about responsibility, that our actions have consequences— that we must learn from our mistakes.

After an eternity, the parts arrived. We set to work scraping, sanding, and replacing the burned-out parts. Once reconstructed, we repainted the salvaged bike fire-engine red. Finally, we had new wheels on the ground and a new bridge to cross.

Grand Ole Opry or Hit Parade

Who would have dibs on our battery radio? This turned into a running battle with my sister. She was into the Hit Parade, a fluffy program featuring popular music of the day. For me, it was the country classic: Grand Ole Opry.

The problem was both broadcast only once a week, at the same time on Saturday nights. Being a romantic teenage girl, Gerry was naturally attracted to those silly Broadway show tunes from New York.

Such fluffy fare, of course, held zero interest to a red-blooded boy. No, sir, give me Nashville's Little Jimmy Dickens' "Sleeping at the Foot of the Bed" or "Taters Never Did Taste Good with Chicken on the Plate (But I Had to Eat 'um Just The Same)." And who could forget this one, "I Always Get the South End of a Chicken Flying North." Need I mention country-western idols Hank Williams and Minnie Pearl?

Surely you get the point. Who in their right mind would switch the dial from such golden hillbilly hits to listen to swirly-girly stuff like "It Had to Be You," "Sentimental Journey," or "Peg of My Heart"? I'll tell you who: my sister.

Momma settled it with Solomon-like wisdom: "You get half-an-hour of the Grand Ole Opry; she gets the same for the Hit Parade." You can bet we were both watching Big Ben on the wall, making sure nobody cheated.

A Cup of Cold Water

Daddy hired farm workers to help us in the fields. Working in the hot sun, we often needed a shady place to cool off. God must've been looking out for us: Down a hill from our fields, a spring of ice-cold water flowed out of the ground.

Field work in summer heat can be deceptively dangerous. Daddy tried to protect us from heat stroke. So, we wore wide-brim, straw hats and took breaks to cool off. Every couple of hours, he called for a water break, leading us down a wooded hillside to the spring. A tin dipper with a long handle hung on a tree limb over the spring.

What a relief to escape the sun for a few minutes, relaxing in a cool woody shade! Who would be first in line? Where the spring flowed out of the hillside, Daddy had shoveled out sand and dirt, creating a pool of water to quench the thirst of our work crew.

Dipping carefully, so as not to stir up sediment, he passed the dipper to the kids first. As each cup of water was guzzled down, Daddy rinsed off the dipper with fresh water, refilling it, passing it on. What a special treat that icy water was on a sweltering day in the fields. For a few blissful moments afterwards, we plopped down in the shade and rested. Soon, too soon, the preacher's chain gang would be marching back uphill to face an open furnace.

The preacher never knew what happened to our drinking water one day after he led his pickers back up the hill. To cope with the blazing heat of those cotton fields, Lee Roy waited until everyone was out of sight, pulled off his tee shirt, threw it in the icy cold spring, let it soak a few seconds, dragged it out, and put it back on, wringing wet. I didn't dare try it for fear Daddy would become suspicious, but it surely looked tempting.

Years earlier, Daddy and my older brothers had carved this farm out of wilderness. Once the land was cleared and ploughed for planting, we began finding American Indian arrowheads and artifacts. Near this refreshing water source, we found a pile of rock shavings where Choctaw hunters chiseled out their weapons, knives, and bowls. We kids roamed the woods, pretending to be savage Indians on the warpath. No whiteface settlement was safe from our marauding attacks.

Cousin Clem caught a Goggle-eyed perch, and we begged Daddy to let us drop it in the spring. Surprising both of us, the preacher agreed. We named him Flip Flop. Once he settled into his new home, we began "training" him by placing our hands into the water under his belly, gently lifting him out of the water.

He seemed to enjoy our game, lying quietly in the palm of a hand while being lifted out of the water. After a few seconds, Flip Flop would suddenly flounce into the air, landing with a splash back into our drinking water.

We were eager to show him off to our field hands. After Daddy had dipped everyone's water, they gathered around for the show. Flip Flop didn't disappoint, bringing squeals and applause every time with his dead fish imitation followed by his unexpected flounce and disappearing act.

Flip Flop entertained us for only one summer. Then he vanished, possibly a Happy Meal for a hungry varmint.

First Shotgun

My brother, Ray, knew I was old enough to go hunting, but Daddy's shotgun was off-limits. When the first hammerless shotguns were made, Daddy had tried to buy a 12-gauge L.C. Smith. The mail order house was out of their famous Smith shotguns so sent him a double-barreled Ithaca. Daddy used it for 50 years. He was not about to turn it over to a kid.

By then, Ray had left home and gotten his first public job. One day, our rural postman delivered a mysterious package with my name printed on the label. With the postman watching, I tore into it. Inside was a brand new 410-gauge shotgun with a box of shells. No letter. No instructions. No return address. The moment I opened it, I knew it was from Ray.

"Do you know how to shoot a shotgun?" the postman asked.

"No, but I'm about to learn." I bragged.

That very day, Daddy taught me how to load, unload, aim, and fire it. "Now, go see what you can do," he challenged. That afternoon I proudly returned home with my first squirrel to contribute to Momma's menu.

That night, I slept with one hand resting on my new shotgun. Later, Momma let me drive two nails in a bedroom wall to hang it on. That's where Daddy kept his, loaded and ready to protect us. Plus, we "men" like to admire our weapons 24/7.

Momma floured and fried that first squirrel in her iron skillet, serving it with hot buttermilk biscuits and gravy. Wonder if it would taste as good today?

Wild rabbits in Southern swamps grow into heavyweight jumbos known as Cane Cutters. When frightened by a hunter, they leap into the air, pop their hind feet together, squealing loudly. This sudden pandemonium shocks one's heartbeat. Feeding on sugar cane shoots and tender grasses, Cane Cutters grow fast, sweet, and tender. Floured and fried southern style, this delicacy is redneck manna from heaven.

My brother-in-law taught me the delight of hunting them by fastening a carbide headlight on one's cap, shining it into pastures where they came out to feed at night. We called it headlighting for Cane Cutters.

A rabbit's eye is unique when reflected by a light. For some reason, a rabbit sits sideways to an approaching hunter so only one eye is seen. Also, a rabbit's eye is unique, reflecting as a large red orb. On a dark, moonless night, brother-in-law R.J. would wear the headlight to spot a glowing red eye and then drop to his knees so I could aim and fire with my little 410 gauge shotgun. R.J. carried a burlap sack into which we dropped the rabbits. When the hunting bag grew heavy with Cane Cutters, he'd suggest, "John, it's time to knock off and go clean rabbits."

This was our cue to call off the hunt and return to skin and dress our game. Next morning, Momma would fry them for breakfast to serve with her buttermilk biscuits and fig preserves. Umm!

Ole Pete, Daddy's demon mule, lived in one of the pastures where we hunted. One night, the old boy spotted our headlight. Braying like a foghorn, he came thundering down upon us. In the black of night, we could not see the crazy beast, but his pounding hooves told us he was charging. We ducked behind a large tree as he roared past and circled to come back. To avoid being run over, we dashed to the pasture fence, jumping over it just as the deranged beast came roaring by. After this adrenalin-pumping escape, we hunted for Cane Cutters in greener pastures.

Shooting Irving's Sow

When it came time to go away to college, I dearly missed this whacky sport. So, on weekends back home I reverted to my roots. Firing up a carbide headlamp, I'd grab my shotgun and take off searching for Cane Cutters.

The farm next to us was planted in winter wheat, gourmet food for rabbits. Mr. Irving Shows, whose farm bordered ours, allowed me to headlight in his pasture.

A strong wind was blowing one Saturday night as I climbed his fence searching for the distinctive red glow of a single reflected eye. When the wind is blowing, wild animals are jittery. Every time I caught a rabbit's eye reflecting in my headlight, he dashed away.

Trying to get closer, I threw the light beam up in the air and dashed toward him, but before I could raise my gun and fire, off he dashed. This guy was playing hard to get. I gritted my teeth and cocked the shotgun. Holding the headlight skyward, I took off running toward the elusive Cane Cutter. When I guessed he was in range, I stopped abruptly, threw the headlight beam ahead of me, found a reflected red eye, and pulled the trigger.

The shotgun blast was followed by high-pitched squeals and what sounded like a stampede. Too late, I realized my mistake. I'd chased the rabbit all the way to Mr. Irving's barnyard and shot one of his hogs.

Lights began coming on inside his house. How was I going to explain this? Was Mr. Irving going to be in any mood to listen? Chickening out, I turned my light off and ran for home.

Daddy had already gone to bed. Having no choice, I woke him up and told him the whole sad story, expecting him to jump in the car and drive over to tell Mr. Irving what happened.

"Go to bed and get some sleep," he said. "We'll take care of it in the morning."

At sun-up the next day, we took off to see Mr. Irving.

"Let me do the talking," Daddy commanded. He need not have worried. I was petrified and speechless. When Daddy honked the horn, Mr. Irving came out to greet us.

"Good morning, Irving. Bennett says he shot one of your hogs last night by mistake."

Mr. Irving was noncommittal: "Is that right, Bennett?

"Yes, Sir," was all I could offer.

Daddy jumped back in: "We want to make it right with you. Whatever you think it was worth, we'll pay you for it or give you one to replace it."

Mr. Irving mulled this over. Then, after what seemed like forever he smiled.

"Well, let's call 'em in and take a look," he suggested.

He walked over to his barnyard fence and bellowed out his hog call. Thinking it was breakfast time, hogs of all colors and sizes raced up to the fence.

Bringing up the rear was a big Poland China sow. As she came closer, one could see small bloody freckles on her snout. But, she had not been blinded or seriously hurt.

"Well, folks, it doesn't look like we have a problem, but I do appreciate you coming over to check it out."

The sweetest words ever spoken! Daddy assured Mr. Irving I would not be hunting any more in his pasture. We parted as good neighbors.

Daddy could've told me a hundred times how much he loved me. Instead, by coming to my defense after a foolish mistake, he showed me what touch-it-and-feel-it-love looks like.

Swamp Tales

Buck Junior lived on a swampy backwoods farm, bordering Bogue Homa River. We spent summers skinny-dipping in the Bogue Homa. Swinging Tarzan-style from ropes tied high in riverside trees, we plunged into the dark waters, swimming underwater until our lungs screamed for oxygen.

We lived in fear of God's other creatures calling the river home. These included alligators (more on them later), mean-spirited snapping turtles, and two kinds of poisonous snakes, Cottonmouth Moccasins and Copperheads. Otter, mink, beaver, weasel, eels, and catfish also shared our swimming holes. Despite dire warnings, we survived. We meant the swamp dwellers no harm; they tolerated us.

Buck Junior fancied himself a squirrel hunter extraordinaire. Living at the edge of the swamp, his was a hunter's paradise. He liked to invite buddies over and take us out into the swamp on hunting parties. He often came back with his hunting pockets stuffed full of game.

His guests seldom fared as well. Having no compass, we tiptoed gingerly through dense underbrush, trying not to get lost.

In eons past Bogue Homa River changed courses, creating a natural lake on his daddy's land. They called it Clear Lake; you could see all the way to the bottom.

Buck Junior's family kept a flat-bottom boat on the lake to gig fish at night. One person quietly rowed while a partner used a sealed beam light to spot fish swimming below. When the spotter whispered, "Fish!"

his buddy stopped rowing, the spear fisherman took aim, thrusting his gig deep to impale the fish.

Buck Junior tried to teach me the art of spearing fish. I kept overshooting and missing. It soon became clear we'd be going home empty-handed unless we switched places. Buck Junior and his brother seldom missed. So, they speared while I paddled. Soon, the boat was jumping with flapping bass; time to go home for a fish fry. The results were fresh bass for dinner.

A few miles east of our homestead, South Mississippi's soft rolling hills flatten into environmentally important swamp land where our food chain begins. Buck Creek Flats was a place of whispers and intrigue.

Through these swamps meanders Buck Creek. A ribbon of white sand borders the little brook. Locals call it the Flats, and it's still there, a world unto itself.

Before going to sleep, Buck Creek creeps into Bogue Homa River, which flows into Leaf River, marrying up with the Chickasawhay to birth the Pascagoula River, finally seeping and oozing into salt marshes feeding the Gulf of Mexico.

Trophy buck deer roam these swamps, fattening themselves on plentiful hickory nuts and acorns—hence Buck Creek. Wild turkeys find their own heaven, hiding deep in the thickets.

It's not just flora or fauna that make Buck Creek special. It is the captivating folks who live far back in that dense underbrush. Some people in the Flats intermarried long before segregation was outlawed. Theirs was a rainbow culture of American Indians, Afro-Americans, and whites.

Deeply religious, they filled the pews of Holiness and Pentecostal churches in the area, often disdaining makeup and jewelry, forbidding tobacco, and refusing to bend to popular customs.

Flats men were outstanding athletes: big, fast, and strong before football and basketball became sports for the super-sized only. One celebrated basketball star traveled with the House of David professional show team. Women of the Flats were often beauties, tall with gorgeous dark skin and dazzling hazel eyes.

Fiercely independent, they squeezed out a living from inferior boggy soil. Some took "public jobs" lumbering, working on county road crews, driving school buses—anything to sustain their unique way of life.

It's a tribute to their character that they found a way to co-exist decades before the Supreme Court struck down Jim Crow laws in America. They did it without church bombings, governors calling out the National Guard, bullwhips, Ku Klux Klan cross burnings, murders, or bloody beatings.

Making Molasses

Making molasses was a highlight of our Halloween season. We grew sugar cane for homemade molasses, a favorite breakfast food in Dixie because it thrives in the wet bottom lands. After cutting and stripping cane stalks in late fall, we piled them high on a wagon pulled by Ole Pete, Daddy's ornery mule. The preacher let me ride atop the load as he plop-plopped through the country, heading for the Flats.

Mr. Andrews owned a sugar cane mill, powered by one horse rigged to a wheel-shaped contraption. His horse circled this wheel while we fed cane stalks into a grinder, crushing them into raw juice. A long tray caught the juice, conveying it to a metal bin over open flames. Here it simmered and boiled, thickening into molasses.

Mr. Anders dipped the hot sugary lava into gallon syrup buckets, setting them aside to cool. At day's end Daddy and Mr. Andrews divided up the gallon cans equally.

Going to the cane mill with Daddy also meant playing with other kids whose parents were waiting in line for their cane stalks to be crushed and the juices cooked into heavy syrup. Mr. Andrews allowed kids to drink as much of the juice as we wanted. Fresh crushed cane juice has a uniquely delightful taste. We didn't know when to stop until we'd drunk too much. It worked wonderfully as a laxative. A bloated stomach and frequent trips to the outhouse followed, but by molasses-making time next year, few of us remembered the pain. Even if we remembered, the smell and taste of that delectable raw cane juice was so enticing we couldn't resist repeating our folly.

Fighter Planes

One day in the cotton field, we heard fighter planes overhead. A couple of WWII pilots-in-training were practicing a warplane maneuver called dog-fighting.

As they circled and made strafing runs at each other, one clipped a wing off the other plane, and it spiraled out of control, crash landing over in Bear Branch swamp behind our house. It was an unspeakable loss.

Daddy rushed into the swamp to the crash site. Momma forbade me to go. A pilot and his co-pilot had gone down when their plane exploded and burned on impact.

The military set up a concrete marker bearing the names of those who perished. Years later, their parents visited the site and spoke with locals who witnessed the tragedy. They needed to see the place, touch the tombstones, see where their beloved sons had fallen, and talk to eyewitnesses—anything to help them come to terms with their loss.

Someday, I'd like to hack a trail through that deep underbrush and go back to those lonely markers, stand by their graves for a few quiet moments, head bowed, remembering their goodness and faded glory, saluting their sacrifice. It would be heartwarming to go back, clear away the vines and underbrush hiding their graves, dust off the military markers revealing the names of those fallen heroes carved in cold granite, and write them down so they're not forgotten.

They paid the ultimate price, standing against evil, fighting to preserve our freedom. An unspeakable loss was suffered by parents, brothers and sisters, grandparents, and lifelong friends. We inherited liberties they died defending. Thank God for their honor, bravery, and sense of duty. Young men with dreams of their own sacrificed their dreams for us.

On a white marker in the National Cemetery of the Pacific are carved these words: *WHAT A SACRED SACRIFICE HAS BEEN HERE LAID ON THE ALTAR OF FREEDOM.* Those who paid the ultimate price to keep us free deserve our undying praise.

A Boy's Mortal Enemies

When God cast Lucifer out of heaven, we kids suspected He threw him into Mississippi's summer inferno. At the very least, we knew the Enemy set up a beachhead there. In this sizzling corner of the American South, the age-old battle of good vs. evil still rages. The same black alluvial soil so agreeable to the preacher's peaches also extends open arms to hoards of creepy crawlers, pesky grasses, weeds, briars, and bushes.

Far removed from Eden, the preacher owned a field of dreams alright—nightmares. The good Lord was making good on His verdict to fallen man—you will earn your bread by the sweat of your brow. Wendy, our Taiwanese friend, says we would've never faced a sin problem if Adam and Eve had been Chinese. Why not?

"They would've eaten the snake, not the apple," she explains. But alas, Adam nibbled on the forbidden fruit.

Here's how it played out for us: Tormentors invaded our farm, marching in lock step—Sassafras bushes, Iron Weeds, Bermuda and Johnson grass, Bitter weeds, Morning Glory vines, Saw briers, thorn vines, and blood-sucking insects.

The preacher assembled his soldiers and weapons and then launched a counterattack. The enemy came against us with cockleburs, thistles, nettles, bugs, and snakes. We came against them with axes, grubbing hoes, goosenecks, ploughs, rakes, and pitchforks.

Surely these devils were sent to tempt a boy to forget his Sunday school lessons. Sadly, calling them bad names didn't make them go away.

The *Old Testament* tells of a lawless time in Israel when every man did what seemed right in his own mind. So, while the preacher hummed and whistled his beloved songs of Zion, we kids with hardened hearts railed against our oppressors.

PART VI

SCHOOL DAYS

Why do we tell our parents we hate those dreadful school days—then spend the rest of our lives treasuring, relishing, and remembering them?

J. Bennett Easterling

Childhood Bullying

On my first school day, Mrs. Daugherty, a stern-faced disciplinarian, bared her fangs and threw the fear of God in us. After lunch she made us put our heads down on our desktops, close our eyes, and play "the quiet game." For a boy on his first day of school, pumped up on adrenalin, this was torture, pure and simple.

She followed us out to the playground at recess, eyeing us like a hawk stalking chickens. Her weapon of choice was a thick hickory paddle.

I thought she was an ogre until one day she caught two older boys bullying me. She flew into them with that hickory stick whirling like a windmill.

Oh, what a wondrous sight! She had them hopping around, yelping like they'd been sprayed with High-Life. That day, Mrs. Daugherty rose from infamy to realms of glory.

Riding a school bus is bound to involve fist fights and hair pulling. Our driver, Mr. Quinn Ready, ignored juvenile scuffles unless he saw blood.

Sister Geraldine, seven years older, became my bodyguard. One day, two tormentors in the seat behind us began flipping my hair, thumping my ears, taunting, and harassing me.

"If you touch him one more time, I'm coming back there and beat the stuffing out of you," she warned. His buddy dared him to do it, calling him a chicken-hearted slug. When that didn't work, he offered him a dime, knowing a dog-and-cat fight would be worth his money. He wasn't disappointed.

The moment he touched me, Geraldine climbed over her seat and pounced on him, pounding and flailing. The panic-stricken bully seized her beautiful long locks, holding on like a bulldog. Cheering and egging them on, the other kids had the old bus rocking.

Mr. Quinn pulled the bus over, stopping to enjoy the show. Reluctantly, he finally came back to pull Geraldine off.

"You know I have to take you both to the principal's office." So he did, but we all knew his heart wasn't in it.

One day when Geraldine was not on guard duty, I took up for a runt being picked on by an older kid. When Mr. Quinn finally stopped the bus and came back to separate us, the ruffian's nose was bloodied. In school yards, facing bullies every day, Jesus' sermon on turning the other cheek sometimes seems too hard to follow. Yes, I paid dearly, but justice had fallen on the bad guy. After paddling my backside, the principal nicknamed me "Boxer."

Puppy Love

In first grade, a black-haired little pixie named Frankie cornered me.

"Will you be my boyfriend?" Before I could decline, she sweetened the pot.

"My uncle owns a grocery store across the street. He gives me free sandwiches and cinnamon buns. If you'll be my fellow, I'll share my lunch with you." Well, she was cute, and the cinnamon buns sealed the deal.

It was puppy love for almost a year. One day, a teacher pulled me aside and confided a dreadful secret: Frankie's "uncle" was not really her uncle. Frankie was lying to me and stealing goodies from the store. Unlucky in love at such a tender age! That little ill-fated romance reminded me of a blues song eons ago in the Mississippi Valley:

> *Love, o love, o careless love*
> *Love, o love, o careless love*
> *Love, o love, o careless love*

You see what careless love has done.
It's gone and broke this heart of mine
It's gone and broke this heart of mine
It's gone and broke this heart of mine
It'll break that heart of yours sometime.*

    (*Possibly the first blues song in America; sung by his mother to famed song writer Alan Lomax in the 1940s.)

After we finished picking cotton every fall, after-school chores kept us busy. We filled kerosene lamps, trimmed the wicks, and chopped kindling wood for stove and fireplace. We hauled buckets of water up-hill from a hand pump and helped Daddy feed and look after livestock. The girls helped Momma cook supper, wash, and dry the dishes. By the time supper was finished, it was time for homework. When bed-time came, no one had to coax us to go sleep.

Some lucky days when we got home from school, Momma had a surprise waiting. We smelled hot ginger bread when we opened the door; other days, there were warm cookies made with black-strap mo-lasses.

A Lovesick Bus Driver

Geraldine's boyfriend began driving our school bus on his 17th birthday, adding danger and excitement to our daily trips. He drove like a stock car racer, leaving clouds of dust over dry gravel roads. Chickens crossing the road were lucky to make it. A cloud of flying feathers once told us someone's rooster lost his race.

The lovesick bus driver adjusted his rear view mirror to wherever Gerry was sitting, watching her more than the road ahead. Yet, we survived.

We lived seven miles out in the sticks. Momma and Daddy didn't come to PTA meetings where teachers named names and complained to parents of their kids' misbehavior. It dawned on me: what a stroke of dumb luck it was that my parents were isolated.

After Gerry graduated I had no one to spy on me—or so I thought. That proved to be a false sense of security because our next door neighbor's daughter took up the job of keeping me in line. When I fell into temptation, she reported my misbehavior to her mother who told her daddy who told the preacher. A trip to the woodshed followed, helping a wayward boy understand *your sins will find you out.*

Recess was always too short. One day Charles Courtney decided to ignore the school bell calling us back to class. This seemed a fine idea, so we ventured into nearby woods to swing on grapevines.

As the day wore on, it dawned on us that this ill-conceived little episode was not likely to end well, but we put on a brave face. To make sure neither of us chickened out, we pricked our fingers, rubbed them together to become blood brothers, and vowed never to set foot in another schoolhouse.

The powers that be were not enthralled by our alternate curriculum. They hardened their hearts, narrowed their eyes, and set out to get us. By this time, we knew we were in big trouble. However, as often happens when a law is broken, it's hard to un-break. We must face consequences. Would Principal Garrett whip us with his leather belt or his hickory board?

"We're toast, and it's your fault," said I to the instigator.

Says he: "I didn't see anyone twisting your arm."

A search party of angry teachers searched the woods. Commandeered and sent out to capture us, they quickly closed in, making the arrests. Our escapade came to a sorry end when Mr. Garrett did what big burly principals do to keep unruly boys in line.

New Sheriff in Town

His Daddy dubbed him Bozo after a cartoon Billy goat. Phil Junior's photographic mind soaked up facts like a pig swilling slop. Teachers put him on a fast track, letting him skip a grade and moving him up into my class. One day, he just showed up unannounced.

To say he was warmly embraced would injure the truth. We were uneasy with this new kid on our block. I especially had cause to worry. Before Bozo came along, I was entrenched as chief mischief-maker,

Kind of like a Chicago ward-heeler. Did this Bozo-Come-Lately intend to challenge our pecking order? This had to be settled quickly. Never one to sit and hope for the best, I challenged him to a fistfight. He agreed it was the only way.

To keep out of trouble with the head spear-chunkers, we agreed to use boxing gloves and do our fighting in the gym. So, next day in PE class, we squared off, every kid looking for an excuse to get out of running laps or doing push-ups gathered round.

Like two bantam roosters, we lowered our heads and began circling. Neither of us wanted to throw the first punch. Bozo kept circling me and smiling.

At ringside, fans were getting restless. "Come on, you chicken-livers, what is this—a love-in?" We kept circling, looking for an opening, dreading the moment of truth.

"One of 'ems scared and th'othern's glad of it!"

This was not helping my reputation. Things were sliding downhill. Finally, I saw an opening and struck the first blow. When it landed solidly, Bozo looked like he was quitting, but he shrugged it off and resumed circling. Soon, he was smiling again.

I noticed that his stomach was not as mushy as it looked. In fact, my fist bounced off like I'd punched an armadillo's shell. This was not a good sign. I closed in for another shot, but he kept just out of reach. This was like chasing a merry-go-round. Plunging in, I hit him with my best uppercut.

"Like taking candy from a baby," I recall thinking.

Bozo still hadn't thrown a punch. Round and round he circled, still backing away, still smiling.

"This'll be over before he can say calf-rope," I'm telling myself. Bozo just kept up his frazzling circling.

"What's he up to?" I wondered. "Does he think he can circle me to death?"

Just as I was beginning to feel sorry for him, he unloaded. Just one punch. I never saw it coming. Someone told me later it was a haymaker to the gut. Whatever it was, it doubled me over, taking my breath away.

Where had that come from? Bozo resumed his smiley-circling. I'm still gasping for breath, my knees doing an involuntary rope-dance. Some kind soul jumps between us yelling, "Fight's over!"

Kinder words were never spoken. I'd lost all will to go on. With one killer punch, this new kid settled the question: Who's going to be Cock of the Walk?

Had a boxing match ever before been decided by just one punch? I honestly don't know. Until someone proves otherwise, though, I'm claiming the honor for Bozo.

To his eternal credit Bozo never held a grudge. He was willing to let bygones be bygones. When it became obvious that Bozo's brain was brainier and his fist harder, negotiations began. He needed a buddy, and I was ready to team up. We became best friends—to this day. (After living a thousand miles apart for six decades, when we do manage to see each other, we couldn't be happier.)

Since Bozo lived near our high school and we were both on the basketball team, he often invited me to stay overnight on game nights.

His Daddy hunted with coon hounds. A big boar coon is more than a match for most dogs, but Mr. Phil's dogs had no quit in them. They fought until dog or coon died—usually the coon, but often not until he had bitten off a dog's leg or gauged out an eye. Seeing a three-legged dog hopping about or a one-eyed lame dog trying to walk straight, one knew they'd fought their battles at close quarters.

Yes, it was a savage blood sport, one that would hardly be tolerated today—maybe even illegal—but in the Post-Depression South, surviving and raising a family on a one-mule farm was dicey. Coon skins were worth ten dollars. Two hides paid for a week's groceries. Before judging these pioneers too harshly, we might try walking in their shoes.

Coon hunting was not the only creative way Mr. Phil found to earn a living. He ran a garbage pick-up business. Servicing restaurants, sandwich shops, and grocery stores, he agreed to pick up their garbage cans twice a week, leaving empty cans for them to refill.

What to do with all that garbage? He built a long vat and installed gas burners under it, cooking the garbage until it was germ-free. The sanitized slop was fed to pigs he was raising for market.

Bozo would take his Dad's International Harvester truck over to Hattiesburg, pick up the liquid gold, and bring it home to cook. As soon as their piglets were weaned, they fed them this gourmet food.

When we were not hauling garbage, Bozo and I sometimes used his Dad's slop truck on double dates with country girls. Romance never smelled better.

I discovered too late that lifting all those heavy garbage cans had hardened his muscles, giving Bozo an unfair advantage. Bozo just kept on smiling.

Shaking With Mrs. Frazzle

What happened to Mrs. Frazzle was shameful. (Name changed to protect her memory.) She was a substitute teacher, handed the task of drilling real English into plow boys and knuckleheads.

By the time she arrived, we'd been shifted from one teacher to another. Discipline hadn't been enforced, so the class was out of control. Things went downhill from there.

Mrs. Frazzle came to us with a mop of frizzy hair, looking like Kramer in the Seinfeld TV series. Her high-pitched voice traveled up the octave scale, growing shriller as her anger rose. Shameless agitators mocked her, answering her every reprimand with pipsqueak squeals and snorts.

The cowlicked kids in overalls were not ready for English—or their wild-looking new teacher. Word got around she'd once suffered a mental breakdown. A gentle soul by nature, she quickly lost control. The situation spiraled into chaos. We should have seen disaster coming but didn't. It was like *Lord of the Flies*, but in this case the victim was our teacher.

One day, a big corn-fed farm boy defied her face to face; she flew into a nervous rage and grabbed him by the shoulders, shaking him. He managed to stand up, grab her shoulders, and begin shaking back. They danced around like two circus bears wrestling. Breaking loose, she stormed out of our room to the principal's office.

An uneasy calm settled over us as we awaited our fate. Not a culprit was stirring when the red-faced principal charged in to rescue her.

"Who's giving you trouble?" he growled.

To which Mrs. Frazzle answered honestly, "All of them."

"Okay, you're all on detention for a week. I'll expel the whole bunch of you if I have to!" With that, the bear ambled back to his den. Mrs. Frazzle was left to cope.

The next day she didn't show up—and that was the last we heard from her. Rumors flew that she'd suffered another mental breakdown and had to be committed to an insane asylum. If that's true, it should've been us.

She could've sued the school for allowing uncircumcised heathen to bully and intimidate her. Instead, she simply faded away. She was a gentle soul who deserved better. Not everyone tormented her, yet we all failed to speak out or come to her rescue.

It's a tragic memory to carry, one we regret to this day. Thankfully, the sad episode convicted our juvenile consciences and taught us a life-lesson: never take advantage of one in trouble and don't stand by and let it happen.

Faded Dreams

What do quarterbacks Bret Favre and Archie Manning, superstar running backs Deuce McAllister and Walter Payton, and the greatest wide receiver in football history, Jerry Rice, have in common? All are legendary sons of Mississippi.

With stars dancing in my eyes, I, too, dreamed of gridiron glory, but my early school days did not portend well for a budding National Football League career. I was younger than most of my classmates, skinny, clumsy, slow, and unfocused, but, whoever said a glory-ladder was paved with pillows? Determination, hard work, and perseverance will overcome, right?

So, I lifted a few weights and ate like a bear getting ready to hibernate. By freshman year, my chances didn't look much better. I'd beefed up to 130 pounds in winter clothes after Thanksgiving dinner. Unfazed, I signed up for football, basketball, baseball, and tennis. If underwater basket-weaving had been offered, I'd have tried that, too.

I became the water boy's best friend. A few other wannabees were also dreaming impossible dreams. We sat on cold benches, waiting for coach to call our names.

Finally it was the last football game of senior year. Deep into the fourth quarter, my big moment came. We were playing Petal: a big school against hayseed grasshoppers. Our team, as always, was losing, but this day we were losing hopelessly. Coach was pacing up and down the field. Hundreds of times he'd paced by me by without a glance, but today, he stopped. It took me a moment to notice him looking my way.

When you've never played in a game, you don't expect lightning to strike. My eyes had glazed over. Someone punched me in the ribs. Coach was looking at me and wagging his finger. I jumped up, trembling with anticipation. He was sending me in at left tackle.

I grabbed my helmet, rushed out onto the field, ready to get this job done, slay the dragon, win this game, and prove Coach had finally made the right choice.

Our opponent hiked the ball to a bruising fullback. It was a cold winter night, and fog was shooting from his nostrils. He charged out of his backfield like a rodeo bull poked with an electric cattle prod.

Good Lord, he was rumbling my way. Did someone tell him about me? I didn't even get a chance to tackle him. He hit me like two Mack trucks colliding head-on, flattening me like a nail-punctured tire. As I got up, shaking hummingbirds out of my ears, our opponents were on their feet cheering, another touchdown.

That's nothing, though, compared to what happened next. When I got back to our bench, Coach and all my teammates were holding their sides laughing.

God works in all things for the good of those who love him, right? Maybe, just maybe, He had other glories in mind for me.

Still not in touch with reality, I joined the basketball team. Being short, clumsy, and thin as a stick should've given me a clue this was destined to become just another dream for the Biggest Loser., but coach, out of the goodness of his soul, gave everyone, including the water boy, a black and gold jersey with a big R pasted on our chest. So, I was "on the team," so to speak. At the time, being one of the guys seemed terribly important.

"Big Ben" dreaming of gridiron glory

Chicken Train to Glory

I'll never forget the day we boarded that chicken train to glory. Technically, it wasn't a chicken train but a coal-burning freight train, and Chicago, not glory, was stamped on our tickets. Nonetheless, it was like being airlifted to heaven. Four tow-headed farm kids, Bozo of pugilistic fame, a distant cousin Lizzy Sue, Sassafras Sandford, and yours truly were venturing into unknown worlds.

Okay, it was merely a trip to the Windy City, but to us it was the Milky Way. We were flying the coop, conquering Mt. Everest, blasting off in a rocket ship from Cape Canaveral to Mars. But I'm getting ahead of the story.

Our 4-H Club sponsor hatched up an idea to form a poultry judging team, and fingered us. We had no idea what a poultry judging team did. All we knew about chickens we'd learned from Colonel Sanders. With visions of Kentucky Fried Chicken piled high for us to sample, we said "Why not?"

Sadly, neither Popeye nor the Colonel showed up. Too late, we discovered that judging poultry meant probing around in places embarrassing to us and the chickens.

Here's how it works: You take a gentle hen, tuck her under your arm while examining her anatomy. Pressing your three middle fingers between her pelvic bones, you measure the space between her private parts. This tells you how well she's equipped to lay eggs.

Of course, there's more to judging chickens. A laying hen must be clear-eyed, sport a rosy comb, and have bleached white legs and feet. Her coat must be clean and glossy. Her disposition must be sunny and serene—that's asking a lot when a stranger is ruffling your feathers.

So, we became chicken-judgers by learning to burrow, wheedle, and cajole innocent hens into giving up their bodily secrets. We must've become good at it because we won every contest we entered, plus the State championship; earning the right to represent Mississippi in the national wingding.

The good news was not every teenager is interested in probing around a hen's hiney. So, our competition was weak. The bad news was that our sponsor morphed into a slave driver. He jerked us up at daybreak to eye, probe, and measure the ladies. With classmates sleeping or scoffing down eggs and bacon, we were busy in the henhouse, getting dirty and smelly.

Imagine the ribbing we took from classmates: "Here comes Chicken Man. Ask him to crow!" Or, "Go look in a mirror; you have egg on your face!"

Well, we had the last laugh! While those hayseeds were out feeding their pigs, we were inside a warm Pullman, seeing the world.

Momma sold eggs to buy me a felt hat. Red, my six foot tall brother-in-law who managed a clothing factory in Hattiesburg, took his own wool coat, cut off the sleeves, and trimmed six-inches off the hem to keep me from freezing.

"It's not called the Windy City for nothing, John," his pet name for me. "When a nor'easter blows in off Lake Erie and howls down the streets between those skyscrapers, you better grab a lamp post and hold on!"

Red was right. Gale force winds ripped through his retreaded old overcoat, chilling my blood, gnawing at vitals, freezing body, heart, mind and soul. Oh, how we cowered as it shrieked and moaned, slamming us up against concrete walls and buildings! Taking on the dark personality of an ice-breathing dragon, its evil breath clobbered us in the face, or when it hit us only a glancing blow, it pivoted and came roaring back looking for us, slamming us again and again. Bozo allowed as how drinking all that sweet milk, buttermilk, clabber, and whey may have thinned our blood.

Southerners, like Labrador Retriever pups, are friendly and outgoing. So, when no one spoke to us, smiled at us, or even acknowledged us, we felt like foreigners in a hostile land. Were they still holding a Civil War grudge? Finally, it dawned on us we were judging them unfairly. They were not cold-hearted. They were frozen stiff. If they opened their mouths to speak to us, their tongues would turn to icicles. Like us, they had only one goal in mind: surviving.

We didn't exactly win glory for the Magnolia State in Chicago that day. The chicken-judging authorities gave us gold-plated pens just for showing up. The pens failed to write, but, hey!, for a day we were Cocks of the Walk. We had loads of fun, and when it was all over our feathered friends were relieved.

First Wheels

Was it to get away from the preacher's strict rules or because we lived so far back in swamps and hollers only the hoot-owls knew my name? Or maybe it was merely a boy needing to cut Momma's apron strings. Who knows? What I know is, at 17, getting wheels of my own became an obsession.

A brother-in-law, seeing a lonely country boy struggling to get to high school ballgames, helped me buy a 1947 Ford Club Coupe, making me the envy of classmates.

That $275 hot-rod was a ticket to freedom. It was also a clear and present danger. Some shade-tree mechanic had shaved the carburetor points, tinkered with the engine, and tuned it for racing. A NASCAR threat it was not, but it had way too many horses for a kid who'd never driven anything faster than a John Deere tractor.

Don't ask me why, but the previous owner had ripped off all the door handles, pouring melted lead into the holes, sanding and painting over them. The only way to get into the crazy thing was on the driver's side by pushing in the vent pane, reaching inside, and lifting up the door handle. I will say this, it was fun to offer friends a ride and then watch their faces when they came up to the passenger's side and reached for the missing door handle.

Daddy knew that car spelled trouble but he swallowed hard and let me buy it. Young and foolish, enthralled by a souped-up Ford but with zero sense of responsibility, I was not ready for wheels. Driving too fast is never a good idea; over loose-gravel roads, it can be deadly.

The big thrill was in seeing how fast we could take a curve without losing control. The secret was learning to keep it steady going into the curve and then slam the pedal to the floor. Wheels screaming, engine growling, and gravel flying, it would spin around and finally straighten out. In my misguided dreams, I was practicing for the Daytona 500.

Coming home late at night, I would begin slowing down a couple miles from home, thinking I was fooling the preacher. Daddy was not oblivious to my schemes.

"I was not born yesterday," he reminded me. "I was once a boy. I heard you slowing down last night when you got to Mr. Clarence's place."

So, he began taking me aside before I could escape from the house. To my discomfort, he would sit me down to pray, asking God to protect his foolish son from harm, danger, and evil and give him the good sense to be careful.

"Just remember I'm praying for you," he'd conclude, giving me a hug. I recall thinking, "Why do I have to endure this? How can I have any fun when Daddy's on his knees praying?" Too late to thank him, I now realize those woodshed prayers likely kept me alive.

A Cultural Epiphany

Finally, we were seniors—something our beleaguered teachers had been dreaming of for years. Where should we go for our senior trip? Nashville beckoned—that glittering jewel of country music and home of the Grand Ole Opry.

To earn money for this mountaintop cultural experience, we skipped school and chopped firewood. We tripped over the rules, though, by riding a school bus to class, then playing hooky. Instead of going to class we piled into someone's pickup truck with saws and axes. Some spoilsport reported us.

This did not go down well with higher-ups. We were forced to stay after school for a week to make up lost lessons. What happened to the pioneering spirit that made this country great? Obviously, it had not penetrated into the hinder reaches of Runnelstown High School.

The day finally arrived for our dream trip. For us, it was that once-in-a-lifetime journey to Mecca, the Louvre, the Taj Mahal.

Sure enough, our heroes were there: Hank Williams, Little Jimmy Dickens, Roy Acuff, and Minnie Pearl. What a dream come true—worth every block of chopped wood, bake sale, pigs slopped, and cows fed to finance this epic trip! We'd reached for the stars and conquered the moon!

Sister Edith was our long-suffering class sponsor. She coaxed her husband, Marcus, into tagging along to keep us in line. I don't recall any hanky-panky so it must have worked. Edith and Marcus managed to conceive a lovely daughter, Lou Ann, while the rest of us were celebrating. So, it seems, a good time was had by all.

Too soon our dream trip was over, time to go home. Even this proved adventurous when our bus driver ran over a deer on the highway. We talked him into letting us stuff it into the bus baggage compartment to bring home.

We took the still warm deer to Daddy who butchered it. The next week, Mamma cooked the venison in a huge barbeque pan, inviting our senior class over for a farewell picnic. A glorious ending it was—except for the deer.

A Pumpkin-Head in College

After Mrs. Daugherty waylaid the bullies with her come-to-Jesus hickory stick, I decided school was okay. At least, it beat cutting okra or picking cotton.

"One day you're going to college!" Momma kept drilling it into my head. She proved to be a prophet or a drill-sergeant—maybe both. As far-fetched as it sounded at the time, I didn't want to disappoint her.

When decision-day came, I shut my eyes and fell into Jones County Junior College. Arriving on a wing and a prayer, I'd saved just enough cash to pay first quarter tuition.

Someone pointed me to Dean Ogletree's office. He knew desperation when he saw it. Upon hearing my story, he leaned back in his swivel chair and closed his eyes.

"He's thinking of some way to let me down easy," I guessed. When he opened his eyes, I felt myself flinch.

"I don't see why we can't work something out." He began running down a checklist.

Can you raise the flag every morning? Yes, sir! Can you pull the curtain at our daily chapel service? Yes, sir! I will need you to learn how to run a projector. Yes, sir!

He walked me over to the editor of the campus newspaper, *The Radioanian*. "Here's your new cub reporter and go-fer," he told him.

Dean Ogletree was not one to beat around the bush. When that editor graduated next year, Mr. Ogletree told me, "You're running for editor." Apparently, no one else wanted the job. I ran unopposed and barely won.

Mr. Ogletree changed my life. He was mentor, defender, and true friend. One day, his students showed up at a projector room and found the door locked. It turns out they were waiting for me—I'd forgotten to come show them a film. Instead of firing me, Mr. Ogletree just shook his head when I confessed.

"Bennett, you're going to be a professor—you're too absent-minded to do anything else!"

JCJC turned out to be my kind of school, full of country boys with honest dirt under their fingernails, grease on their jeans, and boots muddied with barnyard manure. A goodly number of the fair lasses milked cows or slopped pigs.

The big social event of the year was the annual Chitterling Dinner, sponsored by the Jones County Chitterling Eaters Association. The gala was held in the college cafeteria. (I'm not making this up.) If you don't know about chitterlings, let's just say you won't see them when a pig's walking or wallowing.

The chitterling-cook-off raised money to buy band uniforms and equipment for the football team. Being editor of the campus newspaper, I was given a press pass and a heaping platter of deep-fried pig intestines.

College president J.B. Young and the Board of Trustees commanded a Head Table. Parents, professors, distinguished alumni, and sponsoring angels (heavy givers) were properly toasted. The football team applauded loudly and then ate heaping plates of the boiled, baked, and fried chitterlings. The band played with their food. Some cheerleaders turned their noses up.

Fun, fellowship, and Pepto-Bismol flowed freely. Yessiree, if you're getting an education, might as well get some culture with it.

Working on the school paper convinced me to major in journalism when I moved on to the University of Southern Mississippi. Mr. Frank Buckley, chair of the journalism department, darkly hinted that I should expand my vocabulary beyond the swamps of Perry County. I must've hoodwinked him because when I graduated he offered me a scholarship to come back and teach a freshman course while going to graduate school.

One morning, Mr. Buckley came in and demanded, "What have you done now, Easterling?" When he used our last names we knew we were in trouble. I pled ignorance.

"The FBI came by asking about you. They wanted to know if you were red or even pink!"

That was the first I knew that the Atomic Energy Commission was offering me a position in Oak Ridge, Tennessee, if I passed a 30-day top secret security clearance. It was time to move on.

PART VII

YOU CAN'T MAKE THIS UP

*Of Axe murder, giant cow lice, ten cent watermelons,
boyhood heroes, and facing consequences*

J. Bennett Easterling

Edith, the Axe Killer

Daddy was away from home, preaching on the sawdust trail. Momma was left alone with a houseful of scary kids. After we'd blown out the kerosene lamp and gone to bed, we heard a loud ruckus out in the chicken house.

Edith, being the eldest, screwed up her courage, grabbed a flashlight, and went out to see what was going on. Passing Daddy's woodpile, she grabbed his double-edged axe in case she needed to defend herself.

When she opened the henhouse door, the flock seemed to have settled down. She counted the hens to make sure all of them were safe. That's when she realized, "There's an extra hen on this roost."

Slowly, she swung the flashlight back over each one. This time as the beam passed over the flock, something about one of the hens caught her eye. One of them had feathery ears and big round eyes. It dawned on Edith this fellow was a Great Horned Owl—and he wasn't there for a friendly visit. Her protective instincts taking over, she chopped the chicken-killer off the roost with Daddy's axe.

Aunt Maudie's Mistake

Daddy's old-maid sister, a sweet but simple soul whose mind stopped developing when she was about eight years old, took turns living with her siblings. We kids loved her, teasing Aunt Maudie about getting married, telling her a rich bachelor was dying to meet her. She knew we were joshing but loved it.

She was eager to help Daddy and Momma so they made up simple chores for her. Feeding farm animals was her joy. She fell in love with every pig and calf. She enjoyed gathering eggs so much the poor hens hardly found time to sit down.

Several times a day she slipped out to the hen house collecting eggs and bringing them back to Momma in her apron pockets.

Auntie adored children and was a fine babysitter. She made up fairy tales with colorful characters, enchanting us with heroes and villains, talking animals—and always a beautiful damsel and handsome prince.

One summer when Auntie came to live with us, Daddy had planted a fine patch of tomatoes in a new garden spot. Tomatoes love virgin soil. Daddy admired his "new ground tomatoes," which were dark green and growing fast, and was expecting a bumper crop.

Auntie had seen us fertilizing Momma's garden. So, she understood fertilizer makes things grow. One day, when Daddy was away, Auntie decided to surprise him.

Taking a bucket of highly enriched nitrate of ammonia, she slipped down to the tomato patch and piled handfuls of it around the roots of each tender plant. When Daddy got home, Auntie couldn't wait to show him her handiwork.

"I fertilized your tomatoes!" she proudly told him.

With sinking heart Daddy followed her out to see the results. Sure enough, every plant had wilted. The preacher's walnut-size green tomatoes had hung their heads; leaves lay limp on the vines. Shriveled blooms looked like a child's bouquet that'd seen too much sun.

Daddy frantically scraped nitrogen away from the stems, but it was too late. Furious with his dear sister, he nearly forgot his own sermon lessons.

"She'd worry the horns off a butt-headed Billy goat," he told Momma.

Momma's cool head prevailed. "Just remember, she was trying to help you."

Daddy quickly came to terms with the disaster and forgave his simple sister. He helped Auntie set out a whole new patch of tomato seedlings. Not taking any chances, he gently warned her not to fertilize them without his supervision. With Auntie's help, Daddy's second tomatoes were as good as his first. Plus, she had given us quite a story to remember.

If Aunt Maudie were living today, with all the advances in medical knowledge, her limitations would be better understood. Mentally and socially challenged, she was just different enough to remain isolated. She would've loved hanging out with girlfriends, going to public schools, getting a job, dating, marrying, and having children, but it was not to be.

Today's world is a friendlier place for those with special needs. Mentally challenged workers are finding more opportunities to contribute. Even so, Aunt Maudie found great joy in loving her family and being loved.

Ray Becomes a Man

Ray was a middle child. Momma and Daddy were busy feeding and raising three boys and three girls. Sometimes Ray felt lost in the shuffle.

When he was a teenager, Ray joined up with Baseball, a mentally-challenged friend, to run away from home. Turns out, they were simply being boys. They'd grown tired and bored. Really for no reason except to escape, they walked out of the fields one day and just kept walking. On a lark, they took off hitchhiking.

Momma nearly collapsed from worrying, sure they'd be hijacked, kidnapped, or murdered—possibly all three. She sent the preacher off in one direction and us in the opposite, asking, "Has anyone seen Ray or Baseball?"

They took no knapsack, no change of clothes, not even a toothbrush. They'd scrounged up some loose change—soon spent for pops, sardines, and a box of saltine crackers.

They hitchhiked 250 miles north to Memphis and were sleeping under highway overpasses and in highway culverts. Warm summer nights were a blessing since they had no sleeping bags.

After several days and nights hobnobbing with derelicts and ho-bos, Baseball grew homesick. Ray heard him sniffling in his sleep one night.

Next day he asked, "Ray, is we still in the United States?"

"No Baseball, we're in Kalamazoo, almost to the Arctic Circle."

That did it for Baseball. "I wanna to go home."

Ray wasn't hard to convince. He knew Momma might have crews dragging the rivers for their bodies. They turned tail and headed home.

"We ate watermelons and peaches, snitched from farms along the highway, but we needed a bath and a warm bed. Plus, we missed our family," Ray explained.

So, Ray was a loner. Something happened, however, when he was in high school—something that put him on center stage. Times were so hard that winter that Daddy abandoned the farm to go find a "public job." He landed one building warships in Mobile where he was also shepherding a church. But what would happen to his livestock? And who would raise his crop? That's when Ray's big opportunity came. Daddy knew how much Ray loved farming and taking care of our livestock.

"Do you think you could keep the farm going?" Daddy asked Ray. What he was asking was, "Can I trust you? Will you let me down? Are you old enough, man enough, strong, and responsible enough to step into your father's shoes?" What red-blooded boy wouldn't love to hear his father asking those questions?

Slipping around behind Daddy's back and making possum grape wine was about the only success Ray had enjoyed up until that day. He knew our family depended on the veggies, fruit, and meat produced on the farm. This was a "big deal."

Even more important to Ray was that Daddy was willing to take a chance on him—to put this huge responsibility in his hands. Daddy obviously believed in him and thought he could do it. Never had Ray felt so needed. Daddy told him that his brothers and sisters would help—that everyone would work—but he would be in charge.

Ray jumped at the opportunity. Rising at daylight, he threw him-self into this dream job of saving our farm. Daddy, of course, coached him from long distance, but, Ray hardly needed his advice. He was determined not to blow this once-in-a-lifetime opportunity. He would show Daddy his confidence was not misplaced.

When the time came for spring planting, Ray was ready. Hitching up Ole Pete, Daddy's heathen mule, he worked sunup to sundown. When Pete was too tuckered to buck him off, Ray unhitched him from the plow, crawled onto his back, and rode him home at night.

Have you ever kissed a mule? No one is saying Ray did, but Pete helped him save Daddy's crop. Ole Pete didn't have many friends, but he helped Ray pull off a miracle—and Ray never forgot it. It was the year God answered prayers for Ray that he didn't even know to pray. That was the year Ray became a man.

Cow Lice Attack

What's the "baddest" thing that can happen to a girl at that super-sensitive age when she's changing from child to woman? She's watching her body daily, sure she's going to be an ugly duckling. But we're getting ahead of the story.

Sis was her Daddy's joy, a tender young rosebud, unfolding into full flower. Her dark brown tresses were drop-dead gorgeous, the envy of her friends. Naturally curly, they hung in long ringlets down her neck and shoulders.

Farm chores were passed down from one sibling to the next. So, when she was sixteen, Sis inherited milking duty. When she stepped into Tip's stall that morning, Sis never imagined what hellish demons were lurking.

Sitting on a three legged stool, she milked with both hands; the top of her head pressed into Tip's side to keep her balance. Holding her milk pail firmly between her legs, she grabbed a teat in each hand, pulling back and forth on them in sing-song rhythm.

Mamma Cat sat in a corner, watching, and waiting for her treat. Sis squirted a stream of warm milk her way. She opened her mouth like a newborn bird, inhaling the sweet nectar, licking her whiskers, smiling.

Tip contently munched on grain in her trough while Sis drained her dry. Soon her udders would refill to feed her calf and be ready for tomorrow's milking.

Sis took the fresh milk to Momma who strained it through cheese-cloth, putting it aside to cool. As it cooled, cream rose to the top. Momma skimmed off the cream, pouring it into her hand-cranked churn to make butter.

After milking, Sis felt something crawling in her hair. Running to a mirror, she found her head covered with lice. Not human lice—these critters were enormous cow lice.

She went ballistic. For a young girl in those sensitive years of adolescence, this was an unspeakable horror. She rushed to Momma who swung into action. Momma doused her head with vinegar and then poured her hair full of powdered sulfur, mixing it up into a slimy bubbling froth.

This was too much for the monsters. Discouraged by this sizzling bath, they began abandoning ship, but hold off celebrating. The eggs were still incubating. Every few days a new batch hatched out, sending Sis into new frenzies.

The creepy crawlers infested her dreams and kept her in a perpetual state of terror. Sis would never again breathe the sweet air of freedom—not until the last cow louse was cold-dead, and she had seen its corpse.

She and Momma were at wit's end. Finally, they did the unthinkable: They cut off Sis's beautiful long tresses so they ccould inspect her scalp after every vinegar-sulfur shampoo. Daddy was heart-broken when he saw Sis's beautiful locks scattered on the kitchen floor.

Nearly dying of shame, Sis suffered nightmares: What would happen next? Would Momma be forced to shave her head? Would friends find out her dreadful secret? Finally, the invaders were defeated. Sis's silken locks would return. Seeing how tortuous this had been to his precious girl, Daddy took over milking duties until those dreadful memories faded.

"Don't even think of kidding her or telling anyone," Momma warned all of us, but her flashing dagger eyes were locked on me.

The Preacher's Watermelons

The preacher hired a man with a bulldozer to push down five acres of hardwoods, clearing a new field for planting. Across Bear Branch from our house, Daddy's new field was blessed with rich top soil. He decided it was a great spot to grow watermelons.

So, we broke up the new ground, planted Congo watermelons, and waited for them to grow. Sure enough, the seed germinated, and the young plants took off fast. To give them a boost, we poured on extra fertilizer.

The Congo is a long, green melon with darker green stripes running end to end. Daddy was right: the rich new soil produced a bumper crop. The giants were so heavy, they were hard to lift.

There was just one problem: by the time they ripened in mid-July, the market was glutted. It seemed every farmer was growing watermelons, and theirs were ripening at the same time as ours.

It was a farmer's worst case scenario: a bountiful crop of high quality produce that nobody wants. Even peddling them door to door in nearby towns, we could hardly give them away.

In desperation, Daddy teamed up with a neighbor. We loaded a truck, and then he and Daddy traveled all the way into Arkansas and Tennessee, trying to sell them. They finally got rid of them but at such low prices it hardly paid for their gas.

Still, our field was overflowing with gorgeous, ripe melons. Daddy appealed to our County Agent for help. After much searching, he came back with this proposition:

"I found only one buyer. Here's his deal. He's willing to drive his Mack truck and trailer into your field, unhitch the trailer, and leave it. If your family will harvest the melons and load them in the trailer, he'll give you a dime apiece."

Momma said his offer was an insult. Siblings had grown up and left the farm. I looked at that sea of humongous melons with sinking heart—and quickly agreed with Momma.

However, Daddy explained, "We have no choice. It's the only way we can recover the costs of our seed and fertilizer." We piped down, knowing he was right.

Daddy went to see his go-to friend Bones Courtney, who responded as he always did when the preacher was in trouble, bringing his strong clan to help us load those giant Congo melons on the buyer's truck.

So, we recovered our seed and fertilizer costs. We also learned to plant watermelons earlier so they'd ripen before markets flooded. Our bodies cried out in protest, but we did what had to be done. Guess what? It didn't kill us.

Lord, Send the Rain!

Before automatic irrigation became common, people planted their crops and waited for rain. Rain, to a farmer, is the one absolute. It makes his year or breaks his back. Without it, crops wither in the fields, dry up, and die.

Lacking moisture, cotton plants full of blossoms begin casting off their tender blooms, squares, and bolls. Corn is most sensitive to drought when it begins to tassel and put on tender ears.

As spring turns into summer, rain often becomes less frequent. Baking in the hot sun without rain can destroy one's entire crop. How did farmers cope? For one thing, attendance at midweek prayer meetings showed remarkable growth.

Normally, women did most of the praying. In dry season, men were not ashamed to cry out to heaven, "Lord, send us rain!"

One year Daddy's corn was suffering from drought. His dark green corn stalks were shriveling up and turning brown. Each day without rain was critical. Unless rain came soon, his crop would be lost.

Less than two miles from us lived a wicked man. His reputation was well known: he was cruel to his animals, abusive to his family, and mean to his neighbors. People tried to avoid him.

For some reason, he took a liking to the preacher. When they saw each other, both would comment on the weather and the fate of their crops.

One afternoon, a heavy rain cloud arose, promising salvation to those faithful prayer warriors. Daddy watched the dark clouds gathering, praying more fervently with every gust of wind. Then, he watched helplessly as it blew over our farm, throwing off fearsome lightning bolts and ground-shaking thunder but no rain.

Daddy was reminded of the proverb, "One who makes a promise but refuses to keep it is like a cloud blowing over a dry desert without dropping any rain."

"Well," said the preacher, "The good Lord didn't actually promise us rain, but He sure got my hopes up!" An hour or so later, this wicked neighbor drove down our country lane. Daddy went out to greet him.

"Well, Brother Ira, I see you didn't get any rain" he gloats.

"Nary a drop" Daddy agreed. "How about you?"

"Oh, come see for yourself. It rained so much my fields couldn't hold it. Water's still standing in the middles." Then he winked at Daddy and said, "Well, preacher, I guess you're going to have to pray harder!"

Daddy laughed with him, knowing what a scoundrel he was. Later, Daddy reminded us that God sends rain on both the just and unjust. "But," the preacher mused, "it does make one wonder if He got our addresses mixed up."

Who Needs a Hero?

Every boy needs a big brother he can look up to—his very own hero. Bruce was anointed. Tall, dark, and handsome, instead of short, skinny, and pimply like his kid brother, Bruce had it all.

He played basketball at tiny rural Runnelstown High School the year they beat all the big city teams to win a state championship. A decorated veteran of WWII, Bruce returned home as a war hero. After the war, he fell in love and married his soul mate, a high-scoring beauty from the school his team made famous. Their gorgeous daughter grew up and became an athletic sensation, the highest scoring player on her basketball team.

In two years of varsity basketball and football, yours truly dejectedly warmed a bench. We shared the same parents, genes, and dreams. What's wrong with this picture?

If bullies threw sand in my face, I could run to Bruce. He was Charles Atlas! No, sir, while I was huffing and puffing uphill—I think

I can, I think I can—and petering out, Bruce was The Big Engine That Could.

"Do you ever feel like the world's a black tuxedo—and you're a pair of brown shoes?" comedian George Gobel once asked Johnny Carson. He could've been pointing at me.

So, big brother Bruce became my Superman, Batman, Roy Rogers, and John Wayne all rolled into one. It's a good thing Bruce never knew how he was idolized. He may have ruptured a gut, trying to live up to his image.

When Daddy began preaching, Bruce wanted to do everything he saw his father doing. He decided to become a preacher. So, he rounded up his brothers, sisters, and cousins and then borrowed a *Bible* from Daddy's shelf. Of course, he couldn't read, but that didn't slow him down.

Taking his congregation out in the back yard, he climbed up on a stump, waved the Good Book at them and thundered: "Brothers and Sisters, this is the *Bible*! Now, I don't know much about the *Bible*, but I do know there *is* a *Bible*!"

Daddy suggested some preachers might find Bruce's honesty refreshing and try it themselves. Bruce proceeded to preach a creative sermon about things he imagined were in the *Bible*.

Our nickname for him was Boby. Drafted into the Army for WWII, he was a mere boy when he left us. He came back from the war with a black moustache. As a four-year-old, the only way I remembered him was by an old photo on a bedroom shelf.

The day he returned was both wonderful and traumatic. At first, I was confused and frightened by this stranger. Everyone ran to hug and kiss him. Not me. I took a good look at him and ran into Momma's bedroom to check his photo. Then, I burst out crying, sure the Army had gotten mixed up and sent us the wrong soldier.

It didn't take Boby long to win me back with his fun-loving capers, like chasing me down to get "Gaw Gaw bites" or goosing me in the ribs until I wet my pants. Bruce's homecoming lives on in our hearts. He'd survived the War and came back to us. We couldn't wait to tell the world.

Daddy never force-fed the *Bible* to us, but when Bruce and our American military were in mortal combat half a world away, Daddy gathered us in a circle every night after supper to read the *Bible* and "pray for our boys."

The preacher turned often to the Psalms, appealing to God as our Refuge and Protector. Bruce was convinced God answered Daddy's prayers by saving his life and bringing him back home. The preacher no doubt hoped those gatherings around the fireplace would teach us the value of family devotions.

When Allied Forces were recapturing France from Nazi occupiers, fighting was heavy, often hand-to-hand. One day, Bruce was standing sentry on the perimeter in front of his army regiment when a Nazi recognizance team slipped up and surprised them. Years later, when he'd healed enough from the wounds of war, he told us about it:

"I was reading my GI-issue *Bible* when I looked up and saw them. At the same time, they spotted me and started throwing hand grenades. I threw that Bible in the air, grabbed my rifle, and jumped into a foxhole.

I was trying to return their fire, but every time I stuck my head out of the foxhole to shoot back, here comes another grenade. Their lobs were coming closer and closer.

By this time, my army unit had been alerted by all the exploding grenades and rifle fire. They came to our rescue, and the firefight ended. Later that day, I went back out to that foxhole looking for my *Bible*. I never found it."

In another pitched battle, a shell exploded near Bruce's head. This time, he was hit by shrapnel and severely shell-shocked by the explosion. He spent the rest of the war plus many years afterward recovering from his wounds. He never complained. Like countless others, he simply answered when his country called.

Brother Bruce came back from
WWII twice wounded, to a hero's
welcome. L to R: Iris, Bruce,
author, Geraldine

Learning to Face Consequences

Honestly, we didn't intend to set the woods on fire, but we soon
learned that even boys with good intentions can still get in a mess of
trouble.

Cousin Clem and I were playing in a pile of pine needles. A winter
chill had driven thermometers into the teens. We didn't want to stop
long enough to go inside and warm up. So, we struck a match and lit
the pine straw.

Full of resin, the tinder-dry combustible straw exploded; shooting up flames like a roman candle. What a great idea for instant heat!
Stretching cold hands to the flames, we enjoyed the spectacle but a
moment. Then, fireballs leaped from our pile of straw into the woods.

Flames gobbled up the dead pine needles, spreading rapidly. Scurrying around for something to fight the flames, we broke off green branches and tried to beat out the brushfire. Adrenalin pumping, we fought the flames and seemed to be winning. Then, the wind kicked up, fanning the fire out of control.

Daddy was away from home on a preaching trip but what to tell Momma? We needed to think up a whopper—and quickly. Every excuse we made up sounded pathetic: lightning struck, other kids did it. With no believable tale coming to mind, we pleaded ignorance.

"We don't know how it started." Momma wasn't thinking about fibs; she was watching the wind whipping the fire toward us.

"Go ask the neighbors to come help us," she ordered, "before we lose our house!"

We jumped on our bikes, racing for help.

Neighbors rushed to our aid. With their heroics, we finally brought the fires under control; averting tragedy. Momma thanked them, apologizing for the trouble "my son" caused. Clem suddenly remembered he was needed at home.

When Daddy came home, he smelled the still smoldering flames and saw the blackened woods. Momma told him what happened—and of our lame excuse.

"Son, I think we'd better have a little talk." This was code language for using his leather razor strap.

"Let's get it over with," whispered the guilty.

Daddy, however, had a surprise: "I'm not going to punish you for setting the woods on fire." I breathed again—too soon, it turned out.

"But for lying about it." Daddy went on sadly, "I'm not going to whip you tonight. I want you to think about it and come see me first thing in the morning."

So, began a miserable night for the condemned culprit. As soon as I heard Daddy roll out of bed at daylight, heading for the barn, I dragged myself out and went to meet my fate.

When I approached, Daddy was milking a cow. "Well, Son, have you been thinking about this—how wrong it is to lie to your parents?"

I was ready: "Daddy, I've been thinking about it all night." I truthfully told him.

"Well, I've been thinking too. I've decided not to whip you because you've been punished enough. You've had all night to think about it and learn from your mistake." With that, he set his milk pail down and gave me a Daddy Bear hug.

Sweet Love and Dobbers

Our Grannies knew a thing or two about raising kids, right? They would be mighty tickled if we adopted their secrets.

Before Gerber spewed out strained peas and prunes, weaned babies needed solid foods, but, the little dears had no teeth. What was a mother to do? Before moms could breeze into Giant or Safeway to grab baby food off the shelf, their babies had to be fed, but where did their pureed liver and veggies come from? Can you deal with the unvarnished truth? Granny said it's just the way things were: moms prechewed their babies' food into little cuds, calling them "dobbers." Yes, Virginia, there were "dobbers."

Any mom worth her salt knew how to do it because her mom had also chewed dobbers. Foods too hard for her toothless little tykes to swallow, she chewed into soft balls, feeding them to her small fry.

Your great-grandmother knew all about dobbers. She could tell you whippersnappers a thing or two—they were tastier than anything Heinz ever whomped up!

Yessiree, healthier, too. Why? Because there's no way she could chew up those dainty little delicacies without some of her own sweet saliva juices mixing with them.

Dear Granny's saliva was a far sight healthier than anything coming out of Heinz or Gerber's sanitized stainless steel kitchens. She did it out of pure love. It would sadden her to see you screwing up your noses and looking disgusted.

In fact, you might as well know it—your grandmother probably did it for you. Oh, she'll never tell you her precious little secret. She knows you couldn't handle it.

Can you argue, though, with her logic? What was good enough for her Granny and Pappy was good enough for you. So, don't go round putting on airs and trying to pretend it didn't happen.

Young ladies, if you really love your babies, you'll do the right thing by them. You'll breeze past those stewed prunes on the grocery shelf. Your precious ones are too good for that mass-produced pabulum gunk. Yep, if you love them, you'll do right by the little darlings. It's a heritage your family can be proud of.

Just look at you now. You've come a long way, honey child, and it all began in Granny's mouth. Write it down, sweetheart: Before Gerbers, there were Dobbers!

A Twister From Hell

"We first noticed a fresh breeze kicking up, like a summer wind blowing in from the ocean. We thought it was merely a rain cloud passing by." (Daddy was reminiscing.)

Poppa (the preacher's pet name for his father), my brothers, and I were working in our cotton field in Perry County, some 50 miles east of Purvis, Mississippi. Leaves and twigs began falling from the sky. Then bits of newspaper, ticking from mattresses, and clothing came floating down. By then, the sky was turning black; lightning was flashing and distant thunder growing louder. The year was 1908 when the infamous "Purvis Storm" nearly destroyed the whole town.

A bank of tornadoes spawned out of a huge hurricane came boiling out of the Gulf of Mexico. Those terrible twisters traveled across several states, killing people, and leaving monumental devastation in their path. (The preacher's voice cracked with emotion as he retold the story 75 years later.)

Poppa had every reason to fear the weather. He knew a twister can wipe out a crop, kill one's livestock, and destroy a house in minutes. If one escapes with his life, it's by God's mercy.

Poppa feared droughts that threatened to burn up his crops. He feared boll weevils and corn weevils, but mostly he feared those tremendous winds howling in from the Gulf of Mexico, breeding destruction.

Kids don't have enough sense to worry about storms. Not so the adults—most of them had survived one of these monsters. They had seen up close the tragedy left in their wake.

Shell-shocked survivors who have seen a twister up close are never the same. They nervously pace their floors all night, praying and watching out their windows as lightning flashes and thunderstorms roll by.

A widow lady was working in her field next to us the day of the Purvis Storm. She was a cyclone survivor. As winds picked up, with lightning and thunder approaching, she flew into a tizzy. Every time a crash of lightning shook the ground, she spun around in a half-circle to face the direction she knew the deafening thunderclap would be coming from. She grabbed the bonnet off her head, burying her face in it, whimpering pitifully. As an 8-year-old, I remember hoping the lightning would strike closer so the dear lady would jump higher, picking up the tempo of her little jig.

'Let's get out of here!' Poppa yelled. He'd seen enough.

The widow was glad to follow us home, knowing Poppa had dug a storm cellar in the side of a clay hill. The wind grew still. In the blackness, everything became eerily quiet. We raced to the cellar where my mom met us with a kerosene lamp.

We'd barely closed the door when we heard that train roaring. It was a noise I will carry with me to the grave. Within a few minutes, the killer whirlwind passed over us, and the hot sun returned with a fury.

We climbed out and found our house still standing. God had spared us to live another day. Soon, we learned of the terrible blow suffered by the people of Purvis. Survivors were pleading for beds, baby food, and children's clothes

Poppa joined volunteers filling a train with emergency supplies and then rode the train to Purvis to aid the destitute. Poppa helped them bury their dead and rebuild their homes. Neighbors opened their hearts to shocked survivors.

Church groups came to comfort those who lost loved ones, to extend God's love as they fought to reclaim their lives. It was heartbreaking but also heartwarming, something I'll never forget."

Sister's Red Dress

Sister reached those teen years when a girl's body begins to change. Dreaming of being swept off her feet by a charming prince, she began primping and preening like Cinderella.

Pouring over mail order catalogs from Sears & Roebuck, Penney's, and National Bellas Hess, Sis found a gorgeous red dress. She showed it to Momma, pleading "all my friends have pretty store-bought clothes."

Momma, always sensitive to our needs, was a push-over. Sure enough, Sis won her heart. Soon, egg money was being squirreled away for that do-or-die-must-have-dress. When Momma sold enough eggs, Sis mailed off her order and waited. When it arrived, Sis couldn't wait to try it on.

"It looks like it was made just for you," Momma told her.

When Sis showed it off to Daddy, though, asking him, "What do you think?" she was shocked.

"Yes, honey, it's nice, but it shows your shape a little too much." Of course, Daddy's opinion was super-important to her. The idea that someone would be looking at the shape of her body instead of her dress was terrifying.

Frightened by the miracle of puberty, Sis was super-sensitive to the way her teenage body was changing. Her worm was becoming a butterfly, but the last thing she wanted was to bring attention to it. She stuffed her dream-dress in the closet and refused to wear it.

Big sister Iris couldn't resist kidding her:

> *Sister has a fancy dress.*
> *See Sister's little red dress*
> *from National Bellas Hess!*

Thank God for Mothers

In late August, Mississippi's cotton bolls begin bursting open, signaling they're ready to pick. Nobody was spared this chore except Momma, who was cooking our meals.

She sewed together a little cotton picking sack and sent me out to join Daddy's crew. Only four-years-old, I cried pitifully, pretending to be sick to get off the hook. Momma had seen it all before and was wise to my tricks.

"And even, I can't find my sack!" I wailed. The sack was soon discovered where someone had hidden it. Off to the hot fields I was sent, singing a hopeful little ditty:

> *"Look at the clouds*
> *I think its gunny rain!"*

Meanwhile, Daddy was praying for fair weather so his crop could be gathered. Every sibling was also praying for rain, but, he was a preacher so our prayers didn't stand a chance.

Japanese POWs in WWII, forced into work gangs, cut timber near our farm. The young men sweated in the hot sun, naked from the waist up, their golden skin glistening. Their close shaven heads shined like bowling balls.

Our womenfolk, especially the girls, were ill at ease with the POWs working nearby. We kids were also afraid of them but so curious we couldn't resist following them around, watching as they worked.

They spoke no English and were forbidden to talk to civilians, but, they didn't seem to mind us hanging around. Some even smiled at us when the guards were not watching. Maybe we reminded them of their siblings and families across the ocean.

When I was a toddler, Momma discovered pinworms on my bed sheets. A closer inspection showed them in my pajamas and underwear. Also called seat worms, these unwelcome guests often attack poor people, but, if it makes you feel better, a medical guide says they're found even "in the seats of the mighty."

Momma went on the attack, dousing me with home remedies. When nothing worked, she appealed for Daddy's help. The preacher took his flashlight and a pair of tweezers and bent me over his knees for a visual exam. Daddy's flashlight and tweezers worked like a charm.

A Woman's Work

Try to imagine a world without electricity, gas, or indoor plumbing, no air conditioning or central heat, no washing machines or dryers, no refrigerators, TV's, telephones or vacuum cleaners. This was Momma's world.

She often lamented, "A woman's work is never done." Looking back at how many duties landed in her lap, one might wonder if everyone else was loafing. Truth is, the preacher commandeered the rest of us as field-hands.

Monday was wash day, ruling Momma's life from morning 'til night. Momma's wash pots were moved downhill near her hand pump to avoid lugging those heavy pails of water uphill.

She filled two big cast iron pots with water, stacked kindling wood under one, adding Octagon Soap and a sprinkle of Red Devil Lye to soften dirt and grime from our field clothes. When the water was smoking hot, she dumped our clothes in. With a wooden pole, she poked and stirred them to loosen dirt. Next, she lifted them out, scrubbed them across a galvanized tin scrub board with ridges, rinsed them in cold water, wrung them out by hand, and threw them across a rope clothesline to dry in the sun. Dirt didn't stand a dog's chance against Momma.

Next, she attacked her whites and the preacher's church clothes—soaping, agitating, scrubbing, rinsing, wringing them out, and hanging them to dry.

Tuesdays found her starching, ironing, sorting, stacking, folding, and putting away clean clothes. Wednesday was her main housecleaning day, but since field dirt doesn't respect a calendar, she faced housekeeping chores every day.

Cooking three hardy meals a day six days a week for her field workers, she was running from one job to the next. Summers found her canning hundreds of jars of vegetables and fruits and picking potato bugs off her Irish potato plants and cutworms off her tomatoes.

Wooden floors she scrubbed with a mop Daddy made by boiling corn shucks, then twisting them into holes in a flat board and fashioning a handle. Somehow, she found time to gather eggs, feed and medicate turkeys and chickens, yet tend a lovely flower garden. She even swept the yard with a brush broom. She drew the line at emptying chamber pots, delegating that smelly job to her boys.

Sundays was a rest day for us but not for Momma. This was her day to cook a groaning-board style meal for the extended family. If this wasn't back-breaking enough, she patched our clothes with a foot-pumped Singer sewing machine.

To catch her breath, Momma liked to slip out to our front porch with a cup of coffee, sit in her hand-made wooden swing, sipping her java and stirring the suffocating hot air with a funeral parlor fan.

"Show me a mother, and I'll show you one tired soul," Momma said. Remarkably, it was all done willingly, cradled in love.

Proverbs says it best, "May her good works follow her. May all her children rise up and call her blessed." Yes, indeed, God bless our moms!

Big-Hearted People

Every child needs to be surrounded by big-hearted people like these:

Mrs. Boutwell ran our country grocery. She found a silver cap pistol that shot real caps and sent it home by the preacher. Momma outlawed it inside the house, but hordes of attacking savages were shot dead in nearby woods.

Curry and Pearlie Grantham, a childless couple heard Ringling Brothers Circus was coming to town. They asked Momma if they could take me. Who knows if they liked the circus, but they did it for a kid whose wide eyes took in the wonders.

Brother Bruce and his wife Hazel drove out to the country on Sunday afternoons to take us swimming in Leaf River.

Neighbor Alton Dixon gave us free haircuts. He kept a barber's chair in his home, hand-cranking it up and down. He used a board for little ones to sit on. Mr. Dixon's clippers, scissors, and straight razor kept needy kids from looking so shaggy as to need dog tags.

Sister Edith became a surrogate mom, gave me money for school lunches, tried to iron the country hick out, and taught me the King's English. Her husband, Marcus, invented chores to help me earn money. Edith also dreamed up projects to keep me afloat, for example, hiring me to move the same rose bush so many times Marcus joked that we were wearing it out.

Sister-in-law Hazel pulled strings to get me a job as night watchman in a pecan plant to help pay for college and introduced me to the love of my life. Dot and I tell people we met in a nut house. They nod and smile knowingly.

Momma sold eggs to buy me a gold class ring when I graduated from college. The ring cost $90, and only the Lord knows how many of her good laying hens were worn out by the effort.

Geraldine and Red took me to Florida's snow white beaches and to The Back Porch in Destin for the world's best grilled amberjack sandwiches. When I grew up and found a wife, they took us to Panama City for deep sea fishing where Dot caught a magnificent 26-pound red grouper and had to call for the first mate's help to land it. For the next 40 years, the four of us made our pilgrimage to Destin.

R.J. drove a bread delivery truck. He took me on his route one day. His first stop was a doughnut factory. Hot doughnuts were on cooling racks, with grease and sugar still dripping off. R.J. gathered up several dozen to drop off along his bread route. Freshly baked cream turnovers were also on those cooling racks. Seeing my mouth watering, R.J. left a dozen doughnuts and a dozen turnovers in the front seat between us. Before the day was over we'd polished off both boxes. I was in hog heaven until stomach cramps set in.

Miss Nelly and Mr. Buford let us buy groceries on credit. When we needed supplies, Momma sent us across the field to their tiny store. Miss Nelly filled the order, bagged up our groceries, wrote it all down, and sent the groceries to Momma. When Daddy scrounged up the money, he'd stop by and pay off our bill. No interest, no pressure.

"How do you know who you can trust?" I asked Miss Nelly. "Oh, we learn quickly who pays their bills. We only get burned once or twice." Miss Nelly often slipped candy into my bag to enjoy on the way home.

Neighbors bought my Blair Products. Momma and I ordered supplies from a catalog, using the U.S. mail. When they came, Mom and I unpacked and priced them. Then, I loaded them into my bicycle basket, rode through the countryside, stopping at each farmhouse to show the products and give my sales pitch. Did they need my products? More likely, they were reaching out to help a kid.

Ray invited me to live with him in Houston one summer so I could find a job and save money for college. National Lead put me to work outfitting what they called doghouses, small two-man trailers for oil well crews to live in. Ray's wife, Opal, cooked my meals, washed and ironed my clothes, and sent me off to work with a full lunch pail every day.

Sister Iris loved me so much she saved my baby shoes, a pair of scuffed brogans. Iris washed off the dried barnyard manure, glazed the little shoes in bronze, and kept them with her valuables until the day she died.

PART VIII

ALL GOD'S CHILDREN

Of guinea fowl and bulldogs, donkeys playing basketball, wandering cows and a lost goose, of alligators, stripped kittens and pet roosters, of feisty dogs and chick-eating foxes, of buzzards, owls, and a pig that burst open, of turtles, terrapins and tumblebugs.

J. Bennett Easterling

Guinea Fowl and Bulldogs

Uncle Grit, a 300 pound woodsman, looked like Sampson's picture in Daddy's King James *Bible*. A quarter Choctaw Indian, he never shaved and seldom bathed. Kids were deathly afraid of him.

Everything about Uncle Grit paralyzed us. He talked loud, swearing to beat the brains out of anyone crossing his path. We believed every threat he uttered. His torso rippled with muscles. He once lifted the rear end of a car off a bulldog someone ran over.

We'd heard Native Americans can't handle the white man's firewater, that they have a missing gene, rendering their body helpless to process alcohol. Uncle Grit could've been their poster child.

Momma said he had way too much Choctaw blood in his veins to handle liquor. The demons hid deep in his DNA, just waiting for his lips to touch booze. They jumped out howling and brawling until he wrecked a honky-tonk, scared off the women, and mauled the patrons. This would go on until the law came to get him or he passed out.

When Jesus came tip-toeing into Uncle Grit's life, all this changed, and we breathed a sigh of relief. But I'm getting ahead of the story.

We can only guess at the demons he was battling. We could see red flags rising when he started drinking—a dreaded sign, a warning to stand back until the storm passed.

Before he married Aunt Bertha and got saved, Uncle Grit was a hell-raiser. Boozing every Saturday night, he picked fights with practically everyone except the cocktail waitress. The sheriff would lock him up for the night, let him spend Sunday sobering out, then send him back home Monday morning to his wife.

Uncle Grit got thrown in the jug so often the cops loved him. He was on first-name terms with the sheriff and justice of the peace. He was their kind of man's man—ruggedly handsome with a heavy black beard, big and fearless, a dangerous character with a loud raucous voice that startled strangers and left bar-hops weak-kneed, breathless, and eager to please.

Because of a volcanic temper, wiser people steered out of his way. During one carousing bar fight, he picked on the wrong man. The victim's family let it be known they were laying for him. Sure enough they waylaid him a few weeks later at the same saloon, surrounded him, and almost killed him. Two brothers pinned his arms behind his back while two more pummeled him. Monday morning he hobbled through the woods to tell Mom all about it, boasting it took four men to overpower him.

Aunt Bertha followed him to the cotton gin every fall when he sold his bales of cotton, demanding the money to buy school clothes for their kids. If she failed to intercept him before he hit the bars, he would drink and fight until all his money was gone. When he wasn't drinking, Uncle Grit was good to his kids.

He owned a pack of bulldogs, trained to fight other dogs. They were vicious, ready to maul or kill anything he set them on. All Uncle Grit had to do was yell "Siccem!" and those dogs smelled blood!

Sadly, Uncle Grit was also a racist. After drinking all night, he'd come home in the wee hours, call his bulldogs out from under the house, and yell, "I smell a nigger!" His raucous bellowing carried throughout the woods. This set his bulldogs to howling. Our neighbors deserved better. For the most part, they were good, hardworking people, minding their own business, trying to live and let live. Surely, they must have loathed his reckless bloodcurdling yells. Mom tried to shame him, but what do sisters know?

All of this changed when he and Aunt Bertha joined the Holiness Church. They preached "living above sin" so she set out to reform Uncle Grit. He never quite lived up to her lofty goals, but God sandblasted off some of his hard edges.

Uncle Grit lived across Bear Branch and through the woods from our house. His corn crib was home to a passel of half-wild cats, surviving on rats and mice.

Uncle Grit was good to me. I never believed for a minute he was a no-good bum even though he created more than enough evidence to convict him. Deep inside this terrifying giant thumped a good heart. He loved his family, his dogs, and his country. He would give you the shirt off his back.

He let his son, Clem, and me ride his frisky plow horse to our swimming hole. When I was old enough to plow, he paid me to help plant his crops and gather his turnips, mustard greens, and collards. I'd come home tired and dirty but with two greenbacks stuffed in my pockets.

A row of plum trees bordered his fields. When they were ripe folks came from miles around, picking them to eat fresh or to make jelly. We picked them off the trees and ate the sweet tree-ripened fruit until our tummies ached.

Behind Uncle Grit's corncrib grew a patch of poke weed, a leafy plant that grows wild in the south. The poorest of the poor ate it. Aunt Bertha stripped leaves off the stalks to boil with pork fatback. She once talked me into trying it. I ate the fatback but couldn't swallow the slimy green leaves. Aunt Bertha believed in miracle cures. "Ain't nothing like a good bait of Poke Salad to clean out yore pipes and cure what ails you."

Uncle Grit also raised guinea fowl, a chicken-sized bird from Africa. Quarrelsome and mean, they matched his persona. They roosted in a Chinaberry tree next to his log house. Plump and compact, they looked like polka-dot bowling balls rolling along. Grazing in flocks, they scoot across a yard pecking at stinkbugs, ticks, beetles, and flies. Organic gardeners swear the funny-looking little guys are super for controlling garden pests. (Got bugs? Get guineas!)

Those bug-eaters make noisy neighbors. The ladies are loud talkers and singers. When distressed, they throw all-night panic-parties, cackling, and squawking by the light of the moon. Up at the break of dawn, they begin quarreling or gossiping—who knows which—robbing their owners of peace and quiet.

Guineas catch their prey by swooping down on them, legs churning like windmills. Baldheaded, their ash grey feathers are speckled with white spots. Red waddles on their cheeks and long eyelashes make them look like circus clowns.

Guineas run like a blue streak. Maybe they're God's attempt to improve on road-runners or the good Lord, saying, "Let's see just how ugly I can make a chicken."

Uncle Pete swore his guineas could smell an intruder a mile away. It seemed to be true. Roosting behind Uncle Grit's house, they pitched a fit when a stranger approached, a high- pitched screeching alarm. As soon as the guineas erupted, his bulldogs viciously charged the intruder. If Uncle Grit didn't call them off, woe to the visitor. Unwelcome guests got the message.

"Tastes just like chicken, only sweeter," Uncle Grit bragged about eating them and nobody was going to argue. He also ate their walnut-sized, bluish, speckled eggs.

Since Clem was my constant playmate, the guineas and bulldogs decided I was no threat, but things were about to change. As I described earlier, my siblings gave me a fire-engine red bicycle for Christmas. When I proudly rode it across Bear Branch and through the woods to show it to Clem, I was stunned when the guineas pitched a fit instead of giving me their usual welcome. From up in their treetop roosts they spotted the red demon I was riding. They went off like a fire alarm, screaming and squawking. The bulldogs came charging from under the house toward me. I thought they would see it was me, but they circled the bicycle with fangs flared and murder in their hearts.

Just in the nick of time, Uncle Grit opened his back door and screamed at them. They slinked off but watched me with murderous growls until I dismounted from the bike. Guineas flew down from their roosts, clucking and suspiciously inspecting the bicycle.

Neither the guineas nor bulldogs ever got used to that blood-red bicycle. To keep from being mauled, I learned to dismount and approach the house on foot until Clem came out to play. They were telling me, "Come over for a visit, but leave that Red Devil friend of yours in the woods." It became an uneasy truce.

Donkey Basketball

If bulldogs and guinea fowl aren't your cup of tea, how about bouncing up and down basketball courts on a donkey?

What do the names Doomsday, Thunderclap, Lightning, Disaster, and Balaam have in common? They're all hee-haws trained to thrill would-be riders and spectators and make money for their owners. Would you believe some smart guy discovered donkeys can be trained to play basketball? Well, sort of.

Donkey basketball games were a highlight of the social season in small towns and rural communities. These dopey-looking creatures are u-hauled to schools where foolhardy folks ride them up and down hardwood courts while playing basketball.

Teams often pit students against their teachers, girls against boys, and parents against kids. The rules are simple; the riding is not. Players must shoot while sitting on the beast.

No one even tries to dribble—except the donkeys when they get excited. Referees are definitely in the donkey's corner, rewarding the mischief-makers with treats when they buck like a wild stallion or duck their heads, sending a terrified rider sliding off. No doubt adding to the sport's popularity is the chance to see principals, mayors, coaches, and preachers tossed in midair and dumped on the floor. Basketball rules are followed halfheartedly except for jump balls which the donkeys never mastered.

The funny looking critters can be cuddly and docile or rambunctious, mean, and contrary. Some kick, snort, and bite if they're having a bad day, not unlike some folks you may know. The dumb brutes came with a variety of attitudes. Most sported sunny dispositions with a few Jezebels. Some were godly, others heathen. Some were docile; others seethed with revenge. You could see it stamped on their faces. You can also see why people identify with them.

Because of the donkeys' stubborn unpredictability, the games were not-to-miss entertaining. One was trained to sit on the basketball, refusing to get up or allow a referee to touch it. This froze the game but delighted fans as both teams took turns pulling and shoving him to free the ball.

Riders never knew what to expect of their steeds. You might be ahead of the pack, streaking toward the goal when your donkey balked. Since they wore rubber horseshoes, this violent change in momentum was like hitting a brick wall. Usually, the rider flew spread-eagled over the donkey's head, losing the ball and landing in a wondrously undignified heap. Because of their temperament, picking the right floppy-eared steed to ride was a big deal. If your mount didn't cooperate, you would spend more time picking yourself up off the floor than riding.

Spectators screamed out useless advice as their team whizzed up and down the court. Game scores were low, free throws next to impossible. (Brother Bruce's all-time best was three baskets in one game.)

Fans often scooped up the tickets as soon as they went on sale. Something about seeing bosses humiliated and friends embarrassed appeals to the average Joe and Jane.

Trainers had taught one hairy performer to bray when his rider scored, delighting the crowds. The braying ass was named "Balaam" after the biblical character whose donkey spoke to him.

The smelly brigades traveled in circuits, appearing yearly to perform their magic. Spectators hissed and booed the riders—or applauded when one of their own scores.

The donkeys were well-fed and groomed; not at all reluctant to play their role as crowd-pleasers. Sponsoring schools or charities split their proceeds with the donkeys' owners. The jackass entrepreneurs traveled in caravans, feeding and grooming their four-legged stars to keep the good times rolling.

Were they potty trained? Not really. But when accidents happened, a "biscuit brigade" swooped in, clearing the courts of donkey droppings. Such accidents added a festive air of drama and were loudly applauded.

Today, this unique entertainment is still alive but on life support. Lawsuits are threatening to bankrupt this mostly family-owned sport. Helmets and pads are now standard. A few people have been injured, and some have hired shrewd, fancy-Dan lawyers to sue. Since the adorable entertainers aren't talking, lawyers are rushing to represent them. PETA (People for Ethical Treatment of Animals) claims the donkeys are confused and being mistreated. So, if you haven't yet ridden to glory on one these lovable performers, you'd better move fast. Another slice of the American pie may be vanishing.

A Lost Goose

For less adventurous souls disinclined to riding mules, how about capturing a wild goose, and turning him into a chicken?

"As the weather cooled off one autumn, a flock of wild geese were migrating south when one fell out of the sky. (The preacher was entertaining us with one of his childhood stories.)

I was maybe ten years old and had never seen one of those great birds up close. Now, there was one hopping around in our corn field. Approaching it, I saw the honker dragging a broken wing. Poppa let me take the big guy home. We made a splint, tying his damaged wing firmly against his body to heal.

We named him Gander. Poppa put him in a pen with our chickens. Gander adjusted quickly, happy to discover new friends. The chickens, taken aback by this mysterious stranger, gave him a wide berth, but when he peacefully ate with them, roosting quietly with them at night, they gradually accepted him.

Gander seemed to enjoy hanging out with chickens, but as his broken wing healed, he often turned a watchful eye to the sky. When flocks of wild geese flew over, he craned his neck, listening and watching them until they were out of sight. Then, he'd waddle back to his chicken trough for more corn.

I was hoping to keep him for a pet. So, when his broken wing healed, I clipped his feathers so he couldn't fly. Gander settled in for the winter.

By early spring, he'd grown new wing feathers. One day, a flock of Canadian geese, migrating back to their northern nesting grounds, flew over Poppa's farm. Gander spotted them before we could even see them. As his family and friends cruised over, the homesick old goose let out a forlorn, ear-splitting call.

From high in the clouds, they answered him. That was all the encouragement Gander needed. As we watched, my lonesome goose took off running, lifted himself out of the chicken yard and soared into the sky. He was likely singing, 'Ain't no chicken fence gonna hold me in.'

Poppa allowed as how it was best he rejoined his kin, and I sadly agreed. We hated to lose him, but it was thrilling to see Gander rising higher and higher, calling with every breath to his long-lost family."

The preacher said Gander taught him a bit of philosophy: "When God makes a goose; it's no use trying to turn him into a chicken."

Until the Cows Come Home

Daddy, like most nickel-and-dime farmers, didn't own enough grazing land to feed his herd of cows. Mississippi, being a farm-friendly state, allowed smalltime ranchers to turn their cows out on public lands to graze. Such free-range laws were a gift to Daddy, but not everyone welcomed them. Why not?

When they've eaten their fill, cows enjoy ganging up on gravel or blacktop roads, lying down, and chewing their cuds—a cow's noisy habit of spitting up (regurgitating) fresh grass they've swallowed, then chewing it again. This made for some exciting dates for young lover boys out for a moonlight drive—paying more attention to the pretty thing cuddling beside him—than to the road ahead. Running into a herd of cud-chewing cows could be messy, sometimes bloody, a most disheartening way to end a lovely evening.

Free-range grazing laws allowed farmers to milk their cows in the morning and then open the barnyard gates and shoo them out into the woods to feed on tender grass all day. Keeping their young calves penned up at home was sure to bring Mommas back to feed their babies at night and be available for milking next morning.

When it was time to wean their calves, the cows just forgot to return at night. Instead of coming home, they simply lay down and went to sleep in the woods. Time had come for their yearlings to grow up and fend for themselves.

Daddy watched my sisters closely when they began dating to make sure they came home at a respectable hour. If they stayed out too late, he rebuked them for "Lying out with the dry cows."

We pause now to remember two wonderful pigs:

Bruce's Guinea Pig

Daddy gave Bruce a pig of his very own. Bruce was to feed and fatten him and then sell him at the stock yards as a reward for taking care of our livestock. In a stroke of genius, Bruce named his new charge "Guinea Pig" because it never stopped eating.

Guinea Pig was a pitiful piglet, half the size of his siblings. Pushed aside by suckling kin, he squealed and waited his turn. By the time they had filled their tummies, mamma's teats were dry.

You might've been ashamed to claim this skinny runt, but Bruce was tickled pink. He could almost hear money jingling in his pockets.

Bruce concocted a plan. Instead of feeding him with the rest of the litter, he put Guinea Pig in a separate pen and brought him a bucket of wheat shorts—gourmet food to a pig.

As he watched Guinea Pig inhaling slop, Bruce noticed his stomach was growing. Clearly, this was working. Bruce mixed more swill, poured it into the pig's trough. Guinea Pig was on a roll. He sucked it up and grew some more. Bruce was beside himself.

"Soon he'll outgrow all the others," Bruce was thinking. Back at the feed bin, he mixed still another pail of wheat shorts. Not knowing when to stop, Guinea Pig kept drinking until his stomach burst open. (My sisters will tell you I'm not making this up.)

Bruce's Miracle Grow plan had backfired. Adding to his loss, Bruce had to endure juvenile poetry and kidding, "Boby had a Guinea, Boby had a Guinea Pig, Poor little Guinea Pig, He up and died!"

No one remembers what happened next. With Momma and Daddy's unconditional love, Bruce no doubt learned his lesson and was given a second chance. My luck with pigs proved to be even worse than Bruce's.

Scaring a Pig to Death

Our pigs aggravated the preacher by following us while we were hunting. This was annoying when one is tiptoeing quietly through the woods, trying to slip up on a squirrel.

Daddy got a kick out of hiding behind a tree and watching as pigs picked up our scent, coming right up to us. Suddenly, Daddy would jump out, shouting and charging toward them.

Squealing in panic, the herd scattered in all directions. For the next few minutes, they would leave us alone, but they were so dumb they soon forgot being frightened—and we'd have to repeat the lesson.

One day, I decided to go hunting while Daddy was running his trap lines. As soon as I spotted a squirrel and was trying to slip up on him, here came the blasted pigs, rooting and grunting, causing a commotion.

Why not try Daddy's trick, I was thinking. So, I hid behind a big oak tree and waited. When the pigs finally tracked me down, I jumped out like a mad dog, wolfing and howling. Panic-stricken, they wheeled around, stampeding off.

Unfortunately, the pasture fence was only a few feet away. One of the big porkers charged headlong into the heavy wire fence. Bouncing back like a rubber ball, he fell over on his side, shaking and kicking violently. I ran over to him, expecting him to jump up and run away.

His kicking grew weaker and then stopped. He grew still, deathly still. "Hello, Houston, we have a problem!"

Hitting the fence at full speed, he broke his neck. What to do? What will I tell Daddy? Knowing time was important, I ran home, abandoned my gun, and hurried off to find Daddy. By this time, he'd finished running his trap lines and was nearly home when I intercepted him.

"I think I just killed one of our pigs," I blurted.

"What happened?" he wanted to know. "I jumped out and scared him; he ran into the fence and maybe broke his neck."

"Well, let's go see about it," allowed the preacher. Taking one look, he confirmed my fears.

"Okay, let's butcher him to save the meat," decided the preacher. So, that's what we did. We dragged him back home, fired up an iron cauldron of water, scalded and dressed him out, and hung him in the smokehouse to cure. When Daddy didn't scold me, I wondered why.

"How could I blame you when I'm the one who taught you to do it?" Neither of us repeated our folly. Tell me, what are the chances of scaring a pig to death?

Alligator Alley

What most frightened you as a kid? In sluggish rivers and swampy marshes of the American South, that dubious honor belongs to alligators.

Crocodile Dundee would've felt very much at home in the dark waters of Mississippi's rivers. For kids afraid of their shadows, however, these genetic throwbacks to dinosaurs earned a nasty reputation. Male alligators grow up to 12 feet long, weighing about 500 pounds. They tear animals apart and crush their bones. Only two things could entice us to invade their territory—swimming and fishing.

We'd heard stories of bull alligators attacking dogs, pigs, and even cattle and of how they seize their prey, drag it underwater, twisting and turning it over and over until it runs out of oxygen and drowns. This is known as the "Death Roll." We'd also heard their powerful jaws can crush cattle bones, but if those jaws are shut, a man can hold them closed with his hands. Well, we were neither men nor eager to test that theory.

Yet, even these horror stories could not keep us from our beloved lakes and rivers. A popular way to fish for catfish is to string trotlines across a river with baited hooks six or eight feet apart. Camping out on riverbanks, we paddled across the rivers several times during the night in a small flat-bottom boat, checking our fishing lines.

Bull alligators, bellowing in the dead of night, sent shivers up our spines. Because of the shape of their skull, alligators can keep their bodies submerged, with only their eyes above the surface watching for prey.

On moonless nights, those evil red eyes reflecting in our headlights told us we were in dangerous waters. We were not alone. We were being watched, under surveillance by aliens.

On a family trip to Daytona Beach, Florida, last summer we were reminded of the terror alligators create. A rogue alligator attacked a local 17-year-old boy, biting off his arm. The gator was captured, cut open, and the severed arm rushed to a hospital where the boy was recovering. It was too late to reattach the partly digested arm.

So, we knew we were swimming in alligator-infested waters at our own risk. Thankfully, we never experienced those Death Rolls up close and personal.

Hunted down by men who eat their flesh or sell their hide for purses and shoes, gators almost became an endangered species. Fortunately, they're now protected by laws. The big crawlers are magnificent creatures, deserving a chance to survive. Surely, they're entitled to their tiny corner of the earth. If our reptilian brothers could speak, they might remind us they are not as deadly as many other hazards we face every day:

- More people are killed by texting while driving,
- More are killed by lightning.
- More are killed or maimed by sharks.
- More drown in floods.
- More are buried by earthquakes.
- More die in fires.
- More are killed by guns.

Compared to crocodiles, the American Alligator is a pussy cat. Some say Mississippi's alligators pose little danger. It's true. Adults are seldom attacked. Pets and children are more vulnerable, but come on down, friends! We'll leave the porch light burning.

Calling Owls and All Things Wild

Some woodsmen imitate wild animal calls so perfectly creatures are fooled into thinking their mate is calling—and can be enticed into close range. Would alligators respond to our bellowing? We chose not to find out.

Daddy mimicked wild animal and bird sounds so expertly they responded to his calls. Wild turkey, quail, and foxes were fooled by his uncanny impersonations. One day, he and I were slipping through the woods hunting when a Great Horned Owl began hooting. Daddy cupped his hands and answered his call.

"Now, be still and watch," he whispered. Presently, we heard the beat of wings as a huge owl plopped into a beech tree beside us. No sooner had he landed than another one swooped in, landing on the opposite side of us. From deep in the swamp, they'd heard the preacher's call and came to check it out.

Because owls were a threat to Momma's young turkeys and chicks, I expected Daddy to shoot them. Instead, he motioned for me to keep perfectly still. Cupping his hands over his mouth, he called to them again. We watched as they turned their heads 90 degrees both ways to follow the sound of his calling. Seeing something they couldn't believe, they seemed to be asking each other, "Have you ever seen such a poor excuse for an owl?"

A Goat That Came to Stay

One day a creature showed up on the preacher's doorstep that he had not called—and did not want. When we went out to milk the cows, a kid goat was making himself at home in our barnyard, hobbling from a birth deformity or accident.

"Or foundered," was the preacher's guess, referring to an animal that has gorged itself to the point of becoming disabled. The poor thing was hurting, walking stiff legged like an 80-year-old man with arthritis, but helping himself to the cows' and pigs' feed, he rallied. Soon, he was ripping and tearing, running around kicking and acting like, well, a rambunctious kid.

Daddy never raised goats; he never wanted one. This little guy, though, was lovable and lost so the preacher fed him, hoping to find his owner. We spread the word that someone's goat had taken up with us, and we'd be happy to return him. No luck.

"Never name an animal you plan to eat," Daddy always said. Yet, we named him Gruff, and you can guess the rest of the story. We had crossed a bridge. Momma wouldn't allow us to barbeque Gruff.

So, what was to become of our little visitor? What else but a family pet? Cousin Clem and I made a harness for him. Gruff enjoyed our games but balked when we first hitched him to a toy wagon. We refused to give up on him. Soon, Gruff was big enough to pull the little wagon. Clem and I took turns—one leading, the other riding.

Gruff enjoyed all the attention. When we didn't come out to play, he clambered over the barnyard fence and came looking for us. He became a good pet—until he reached puberty. Pining for female companionship must've driven him loony. His horns had grown dangerously sharp.

One day as Momma was hanging her washing out to dry, Gruff was waiting. With no warning the Billy goat snorted and charged. She sidestepped just in time as he ripped by and turned to come after her. She barely beat him to the back door.

She didn't tell Daddy what happened until one day Gruff slipped up from behind, butted her in the rear, almost knocking her down. That was too much—even for Momma. When Daddy found out, he was ready to kill him, but Momma was one step ahead. She offered Gruff to Clem, who was thrilled to take him home. We were afraid to ask what they did with Gruff—if they had him *to* dinner or *for* dinner.

For Love of Kittens

Momma sent Iris and Geraldine across Daddy's cotton fields to the country store to buy groceries. As they climbed over a fence, a litter of kittens appeared out of nowhere. Beautiful black and white newborns they were.

"Where's their mom?" Gerry asked Iris. They looked all around but didn't find her.

"We can't leave them out here alone," Iris said. "Let's take them home."

It seemed the humane thing to do. We sometimes used a medicine bottle with a stopper to squeeze out milk for motherless farm animals.

So, they started chasing the gorgeous jet black kittens dressed in their white tuxedos. Iris closed in on them from one side, Gerry from the other. Just as they reached out to grab the first one, he hiked his tail and sprayed a stream of hot liquid all over them. Too late, they realized

234

their lovely kittens were baby skunks. With eyes burning and holding their noses, the girls high-tailed it home to tell Momma.

"Take off your fumigated clothes, carry them out in the backyard, and burn them." Those were Momma's orders. After tubs of soap and water, Geraldine and Iris still smelled to high heaven.

A wealthy aunt and uncle were coming for dinner that evening. Momma made the girls eat in the kitchen, but she warned us not to gloat or kid them. "They were trying to do a good thing."

A Missing Rooster

Sometimes, Daddy let us claim a farm animal for a pet, name it, and take care of it. A red New Hampshire rooster became my god-child. His happy chortling earned him the moniker, Chuckles.

Chuckles seemed to know he belonged to me, following us out in the field where we were chopping cotton or thinning corn. Chuckles shadowed me, watching for grasshoppers, crickets, and grub worms unearthed by my hoe. When I tossed him a bug, he did a little victory dance, hopping around with glee.

Daddy adopted Chuckles' brother so we competed in finding and tossing goodies to our pets.

The problem with Chuckles, one that proved fatal, was his unbridled enthusiasm. He never stopped crowing. That was fine with me. That's what roosters do.

Turns out Chuckles took his duty too seriously. He crowed 24/7. No doubt, he meant well. Chuckles understood his job description: to help make more chickens and serve as our alarm clock. Simple enough, right?

Here we come to an important life lesson. Chuckles failed to distinguish between being diligent and overly zealous. He knew a farmer depends on his cocks crowing at dawn to herald a new day, to rouse him from his dreams, to call him to another hard day of coaxing a living from his soil.

Chuckles was a good rooster, a faithful loving pet, a devoted friend, who never gossiped and always expected the best. He spoke in unknown tongues on topics I knew naught of. We chatted, played, and laughed together. We bonded.

Yet, Chuckles, failing to grasp that more is not always better, grew indiscreet. What a tired farmer needs after working sunup to sundown is sleep—needs it more than love or riches or roosters.

To rouse a weary man from his feather bed before dawn is not appreciated. When a farmer lays his head on a soft pillow, he's desperate for sleep. He does not need a midnight fire alarm—or a feathered alarm clock with no cut-off switch. Chuckles crowed like a pneumatic drill.

Even the power of positive thinking has limits. Sometimes it's a crevice too wide to leap over. Chuckles' leap fell short.

One day, Chuckles came up missing. This was unusual since he seldom failed to follow us into the field for bug-hunting. Daddy didn't seem to share my concern.

A few days later, I found a pile of red feathers out behind our smokehouse. This was where Daddy took our fryers to wring their necks and pluck their feathers.

When I confronted Momma with the evidence, she explained Chuckles had grown up and started fighting with our other roosters. To keep peace in the flock, he had to go. She told me to pick out any other chicken to replace Chuckles.

On the farm, everything has its time and place. Momma knew I was old enough to face the hard knocks that life dishes out and begin coping with them. I knew she was right, but I also suspected she was not telling me the whole story.

I remember thinking, "If only I could've warned him in time, maybe he would've flown the coop."

Aunt Girt's Feist Dogs

Like all Americans, Southerners adore their pets and animals. All of them cannot be honored here because editors insist a story cannot go on forever. With apologies to those left out, these lovable and not so lovely ones earn honorable mention:

The Feist is a small mongrel dog highly favored in Dixie for no good reason. Aunt Girt kept a tick-infested bunch of them underfoot. Of unknown and unknowable parentage, full of themselves, Feists are delightfully contrary little creatures.

Thick as the fleas in some back-country regions, the little beasts are full of nervous energy. They breed like rabbits. Every time we visited Aunt Girt, a new litter greeted us. Irritable and upset by life in general, they think they're masters of the universe, touchy and quarrelsome; hence, the term, *feisty.*

Often neglected by their poverty-stricken owners, the woeful little guys become vagrants, surviving whatever fate throws at them. Could we do that?

Mangy and flea-ridden, they expect the worst but keep on hoping for the best. Any self-respecting tom cat can swat them over, sending them tumbling with one good whack. Yet, they think they're invincible. Who could fail to find humor in a puny creature with such an inflated sense of their own importance? Thank you, Aunt Girt.

Fox Attack

Momma bought 50 Indian Runner baby chicks for me as a 4-H Club project. The idea was to teach kids how to care for their animals. Club rules required me to build a shed for the hatchlings, feed, water, medicate, and watch after them.

They were off to a good start by Easter. When they were partridge-size, we noticed one or two missing. None had appeared sick, and we didn't find any dead ones in the pen. Daddy suspected foul play.

Momma helped me count and recount them. Sure enough, nearly each day we counted, another chick had vanished. Upon investigating, we discovered a pile of feathers. Next, we found a slick trail under the chicken wire fence where a thief had crawled into their pen. Next day, we found several more biddies mutilated and half-eaten. The preacher declared war.

That night Daddy placed one of the slain chicks just inside the chicken pen where the killer had entered. He set a varmint trap in the slick opening. Early next morning when Daddy checked his trap, a red fox was caught in her thievery. Daddy knew what must be done, but he wanted me to understand why.

"We can turn her loose to kill more chicks or put her down." It was a hard fact of life to confront at such a tender age. I wanted to negotiate.

"Why not put her in the back of Mr. Russell's pickup truck, drive miles away, and turn her loose?" I suggested. To answer that question, Daddy pointed to her belly. "What do you see?" he asked. Her teats were swollen, full of milk. I was still clueless.

"She has a den nearby and is suckling her pack of little foxes. If we let her go, she'll keep coming back until your last chick is gone."

Daddy couldn't let the opportunity pass without finding a spiritual lesson in it. "Remember, the thief comes to steal, kill, and destroy."

Daddy explained that the young fox kits may be old enough to come out and learn to hunt for their own food. This often happens when young animals lose their mother. Also, the male species often teach their young to hunt.

"If they survive, maybe they'll find some tasty mice and frogs to eat instead of your baby chicks," concluded the preacher;

Forgive us PETA, but we did what ranchers and farmers have been doing for centuries to protect their livestock. Still, it was heartbreaking to think of those little foxes waiting for Mom to come home, wondering, "Who's coming to feed us?"

How long did they wait? Did the father come to save them? Did they scramble out of the den and go looking for food? Why must life be so cruel?

Counting Crows

Bones said one of the strangest jobs he ever had was counting crows for a rich planter in Georgia. "De Depression done killed mos' jobs. Family was hurtin."

"But why would anybody pay you to count crows?" I asked.

"'Cause when he plants his peanuts, de frazzlin' crows swoop in and digs'em outta de groun'. Dis farmer hear de giverment is payin' farmers to trap or poisen crows if you prove to'em you hav' a big problem. Dat's when I tells de man, why don't we count'em? Nex ting ya know, I'm sittin' out in dis field ona stool, wif a water pail and a lunchbox full of peanut butter sandwiches, countin' crows. He paying me a buck a day.

All time I countin' crows, dis ole black bird sittin' up in a sweetgum tree, countin' me. I spose he countin'. He caw-caw-cawin' all day long, fussin' at me or countin' me or laffin' at me for being dum enuff to sit on dat stool countin' crows. He watchin' me, like he want to say, 'You a grown man an' all you doing is countin' crows?'

But honest-to-God, I felt no shame. Margie and me had a passel of young'uns at home. I would've counted cockleburs or cockroaches ifin he say so. Buck a day look mighty good when yo kids hungry. De Good Book say de Lord hear de young ravens when dey calls. Hit also say ravens fed de prophet Elijah when he was hongry.

All dis time dat old bird squawkin' at Bones. I gets to thinkin', is he hongry? You know what Big Ben? I wus thinkin' dis crow keepin' bread on my table but ain't no bread on his table. Nex thang ya know, I'se breakin' off crusts fum my peanut butter sandwich; thro'em over in de bushes. Maybe I was jus lonely, but I had the strangest feeling 'bout that crow. I know hit sounds weird, but it wus like God's tellin' me, 'Feed my crow!'"

Defending Buzzards

Why the preacher loved buzzards is no mystery. A man of God, he felt obligated to love all creation. They will never be as popular as tickets to a Miley Cyrus concert, but Daddy eventually convinced us that even buzzards are our friends.

I once happened upon a flock of buzzards partying over a newly-found cow's carcass: hip-hopping around a prone body, lifting their wings, dancing with delight. I froze in my tracks and watched as they paraded around their banquet table, reminding me of a folksong my Grandfather used to sing:

> *Way down yonder in the forks of the branch,*
> *the jaybirds whistled and the buzzards danced.*[1]

One of their leaders hopped atop the stiff cadaver, plucked out a beak full and began feasting. Elders tore meat off in hunks, passing it to their young. The babies promptly lay down and began wallowing in their food. Disgusted, yet thrilled and fascinated to have a ringside seat, I decided it was all in all a good day.

If you've ever been a victim of shunning, you can empathize with a buzzard. Gross is not adequate to describe him. If you've been "dissed" by friends, put down by girls, looked down on by taller people, or intimidated by bullies, join the buzzard brigade. This is a fellow you must get to know.

Begin with their habit of eating dead animals—rats, skunks, possums, snakes and road kill. Heroes of the killing fields, buzzards are a corpse's best friend. Their cup of tea is not found on a king's table or served in rose gardens. No, what really turns them on is pecking hunks of meat off decaying bodies. They stand on their food, talons gripping sun-ripened skin, drooling and dancing as they nibble and dribble. Shocking Emily Post and guardians of proper etiquette, they burp up hairballs, then wolf them back down. Sometimes their food won't stay down so there's a bit of involuntary retching, barfing, and spewing.

We call them turkey buzzards though turkeys may take offense at the comparison. Californians call their big scavengers condors—maybe this makes them less disgusting to Hollywood. The California carrion-eaters stand 50 inches tall, sporting eight-to-ten foot wing spans. Our buzzards were pygmies compared to their overgrown brothers. Buzzards, to their credit, don't really care what we call them.

"Just leave us alone to dispose of your garbage." It's true, they devour tons of disease-carrying corpses. They are not attractive neighbors unless you fancy bald-headed characters with hooked beaks and blunt claws. Ugly creatures? You be the judge. The preacher brought us up better than to make fun of others. Why not extend a bit of charity to our feathered friends' table manners? It seems a small thing to ask after all they do for us.

Soaring high in the sky on a windless day, vultures defy gravity. Gracefully riding unseen air currents, their eagle eyes spot a feast miles away—or if their eyes fail, their remarkable noses, like built-in radar devices, zero in on their next banquet.

Daddy told us this story:

"When I was a young boy I began wondering how a buzzard knows if an animal is dead—or just sleeping. I have no idea why I needed to know this. It wasn't like I wanted to be the world's leading authority on buzzards. It was just a boyish whim, and my curiosity cost dearly.

I talked a buddy into helping me trick buzzards into thinking we were dead. We went out in a field where they were circling, took off our clothes, and lay face down on the ground, watching and listening. Sure enough, they spotted us and began circling lower and lower. We could hear their wings flapping. Two landed on the ground beside us. We closed our eyes. They hip-hopped around us. One jumped on my back, took a few steps, and tried to peck off a piece of flesh. I screamed bloody murder, and they flew off in panic. My friend laughed all the way home."

The preacher liked to point out that buzzards travel in groups, sharing their food in common like the early Christians. In mating season, they insist on privacy, pairing off and nesting in caves, hollow logs, or on cliffs. Mom-to-be lays one to three eggs on bare ground. When their babies hatch, both parents bring tender hunks of delectable food in their throats, emptying it directly in little darling's mouth. What's not to admire about that?

The Lowly Armadillo

It's difficult to fall in love with armadillos. Yet, they deserve a modicum of respect. After all, they've outlasted the saber-toothed tigers.

Looking like a cross between a baby dinosaur and a Sherman tank, the low-slung armored beasts roam swamps and hills of the South, creating ill-will.

"A giant nothing-burger," someone dubbed them. Actually that's unfair—even the *World Book Encyclopedia* acknowledges they're good to eat.

Natives of Argentina, they migrated to Texas, finding their *Gone with the Wind* Tara. A popular hunch says they caught free rides in steel culverts and oil well equipment into Mississippi and neighboring states.

Not combative, armadillos try to live by the golden rule, but it keeps backfiring. Has that ever happened to you?

With long claws, they dig elaborate tunnels to escape enemies and to raise their young. This also raises something else: the ire of ranchers and farmers whose mowers, plows, and farm equipment are broken or damaged by hitting their holes.

With long, narrow tongues, they suck up ants, yellow jackets, earthworms, spiders, and snails, a habit most farmers appreciate. Surely, this repays unhappy ranchers for a few blown tires and shattered disk blades, but that's just my opinion.

At the first sign of trouble, the little guys high-tail it to their dens. Not being very swift, this sometimes fails. If overtaken by a predator, Plan B is to curl up in a tight ball. By tucking their head and feet up underneath their shell, they make it next to impossible for foxes, coyotes, wildcats, and hungry carnivores to find a place to sink their teeth.

A final word in their defense: During the Great Depression, armadillo steaks helped countless peasants, peons, and poor folks avoid starvation. Shouldn't that count for something?

Loggerhead Turtles

These big boys can grow into 500 pound monsters. One captured off Florida's gulf coast was more than six feet long and weighed half a ton. Some live more than 100 years. Also called alligator snapping turtles, they're ferocious when threatened.

The ones we encountered roaming the swamps were often recently hatched babies, but, they grow up fast. This predator can thrust out its head, striking with the quickness of a snake. The old folks told us, "If a snapping turtle clamps down on your finger, he holds on 'til it thunders."

Still, we loved to find them and live dangerously by playing with them—at a distance. We'd tickle his nose with a cattail brush, pretending to brush his teeth as he viciously attacked the brush. We swapped dares to see who would venture closest to those steel-sharp teeth.

We took no offense at them for defending themselves. Even shy Easter bunnies will punch-kick an attacker, right? We had just enough sense to keep our fingers out of reach.

Gopher Tortoises

These tortoises are upland cousins of loggerhead turtles, thriving in red clay hills of the Deep South. We searched the woods for their dens, teasing them by crawling on their backs and pretending to ride them.

Gentle and harmless, they've survived for eons, eating plants and making their homes deep underground. They dig their holes deep into the sunbaked clay; some tunnels run 50 feet long, protecting them from forest fires and predators. Gopher tortoises' powerful forefeet claws help them dig deep into hard-packed hills.

Dubbed "Hoover Chickens" after Herbert Hoover who had the rotten luck of being President during the Great Depression, desperate people found their meat, if not tasty, better than starving. Thus, man was added to a long list of predators including armadillos, coons, foxes, skunks, dogs, snakes, raptors, and fire ants.

Thankfully, in 1987, the Fish and Wildlife Commission listed them as endangered; convincing most people they're too valuable to eat into extinction. However, if the economy tanks again, watch out, gophers!

Lee Roy's Tumblebugs

Lee Roy's tumblebugs were admired by every neighborhood boy. He kept them in shoe boxes, ventilated by nail holes punched in the tops and sides.

We got caught up in Lee Roy's passion for the little creatures, helping him collect new specimens, begging old shoe boxes from our parents. Black bugs, green and blue ones, brownish golds—Lee Roy's hobby became a fun project to see how many types of tumblebugs we could find.

"Dey eats you-know-what," Lee Roy explained. "Dey rolls up de dung by tumblin' it into itsy-bitsy balls." This was fascinating science.

"Dey lays dere eggs in de balls an buries em in de groun. De babies hatch out and eat de balls and are de happiest bugs you ever saw." Lee Roy had obviously done his homework.

"Some folks calls 'em June Bugs," he explained, "dey is de farmer's friend." By this, Lee Roy meant tumblebugs see to it that animal dung on a farm is rolled into small balls and buried. You might call them the original environmentalists. Seeing our jaws drop in amazement, he was inspired to go on.

"De fee'males watch as de young bucks roll dere balls. When a sassy girl sees a ball she thinks purty nice, she waltzes over and claims it to lay her eggs in. Dey marry den and dare, rite on de spot."

We were blown away that a boy our own age had pulled himself up by his bootstraps to become an authority. Lee Roy left us no doubts. He knew everything there is to know about tumblebugs.

"Did you know dey talks to de stars? De Milky Way tell'em where to hide der balls so a thief don't come sneaking along and steal der eggs."

Lee Roy went to great pains to create a homey room for his guests, lining their shoeboxes with old newspapers, keeping fresh water in a jar lid. He supplied them daily with what he called "tumblebug manna from heaven," a concoction of dirt, mixed with fresh cow dung.

"Dey gentle creatures, don't scratch or claw or bite. Dey not fraid of peoples. Sometimes, when de moon be full, I lets 'em out and dance wiffem. Dey likes to dance for folks."

To prove his point, Lee Roy lifts a pair of mates out of their shoebox onto an outdoor picnic table. They make no attempt to fly away but seem to be waiting for Lee Roy.

Pulling a juice harp from the bib of his overalls, he begins softly enchanting them with a favorite hymn of the Bible Belt:

> *And He walks with me,*
> *and He talks with me,*
> *And He tells me I am His own,*
> *And the joy we share as we tarry there,*
> *None other has ever known.*[2]

To our astonishment, the little bugs would begin swaying from one side to the other in time with the music—or so it seemed to us.

"Watch 'em now," Lee Roy giggled. He switched to a catchy Cajun classic: "Jambalaya and a crawfish pie and file gumbo."[3] The bugs stopped, seemingly confused. A moment later, they were sashaying to the new beat, lifting first a back leg, then a front one, rocking from side to side.

We were beside ourselves. I couldn't wait to tell Momma. I rushed into the kitchen where she was cooking supper.

"Would you believe Lee Roy's tumblebugs are dancing?" I told her in a high-pitched voice, chosen to announce an earth-shaking event. Momma didn't even stop stirring her peas.

"You don't say," she replied matter-of-factly.

"Well, don't you want to come out and see for yourself?"

"Not really, I'll take your word for it."

Momma just didn't get it. Sometimes, the highest scientific achievements passed her by. She wasn't even impressed by Edward Wilson, an Alabama boy who grew up to become the world's leading authority on ants, won two Pulitzer prizes by studying his ants, and taught research scientists about ants at Harvard.

It makes one wonder, if Lee Roy had enjoyed similar opportunities, what could he and his tumblebugs have accomplished?

Sad to say, he never won a Pulitzer nor taught at Harvard. Drilling me day and night to " make something of yourself," Momma still refused to give Lee Roy's scientific research the time of day. Who will ever understand mothers?

PART IX

THE REST OF THE STORY

Like swallows returning to their nesting grounds and salmon to their spawning waters, the author revisits the old farm he left so many years ago, trying to recapture days of yesteryear. In faded memories, he hears the preacher singing, cow bells ringing, dogs barking, the WWII guns of Camp Shelby rattling his bedroom windows, and love-starved cats, begging for attention.

J. Bennett Easterling

Strangers at the Door

As the Great Depression flickered and died in America, the Industrial Revolution came knocking at our door. One day, we were chopping wood for Momma's cast iron stove. Next day, she was cooking with butane gas. One day, we were gathering pine knots for our fireplace, sawing down oak trees and stacking firewood. Next day, the fireplaces were boarded up and gas heaters installed. They burned red-hot and smutted up the grills but we woodchoppers weren't complaining.

A new day was dawning. The coming of electricity changed our lives. Farms will always demand hard work—but a different kind. No more back-wrenching trips back uphill from a hand pump, lugging buckets of water. Smelly kerosene lamps are only a memory—never again must we constantly refill them, trim the wicks, and carry them from room to room.

Sadly, some country folk refused to dance with the stranger, this new phenomenon of "lectristy". In their minds, it was a first cousin to lightning. They'd seen lightning bolts split open towering pines and reduce ancient oaks to splinters.

"I can't see it, taste it, or smell it. All I know is, it can kill you." So, they dared not touch a light switch.

"No, thank you! What was good enough for Granny's good enough for me." You were wasting your breath trying to convince them

So, not everyone embraced Reddy Kilowatt, the catchy little character PR men invented to sell electricity. Simple country folks are not always adaptable to change. Some just said "no" to the big power lines marching across Dixie. They kept lugging their water pails and sawing and chopping down trees to cook their meals and heat their homes. The poor dears kept sitting on their milk stools, pulling at cows' teats, while technology rolled over them like a tsunami. They arose from feather beds on cold nights, trudging through rain, wind or snow, making their way down dark paths to trusty outhouses—you could feel their pain.

Fear of the new strangers locked them inside prisons of their own imagination. Was this industrial genie an angel of mercy or a messenger from hell? Each family decided for itself.

Thankfully, the preacher embraced the strangers at our door. We said goodbye to our two-hole privy, infested with Black Widow spiders. The preacher's theology was as earthy as mud: If God sends you a gift, don't wait for Him to gift-wrap it. Just reach out and grab it.

Coming Home

In the preacher's house, nobody got away from God. Under Daddy's roof, we absorbed the great miracle stories of the *Bible*. However, while God was always with us, we were not always with Him. Can you relate to that?

Desperate to be accepted, some preachers' kids resort to outlandish antics. Friends are sizing them up, suspecting them of being goody two-shoes. Foolish behavior too often became my ticket to peer approval.

Over-the-top zeal convinced my pals but kept Momma up nights wondering if Daddy's reputation as a man of God would be trashed. Behavior unbecoming a preacher's kid would be putting it kindly—because peer acceptance was so huge a deal.

If you've ridden a cable car in San Francisco, you may appreciate how hard it was for me to hold on to God. You jump on a rolling streetcar as it climbs up a steep hill or plunges to the bottom. If you're fast enough to land inside the open car, you grab a sway bar and hold on for dear life. Thank you, Lord, for holding on to me when I lost my grip on you!

Somehow, I survived childhood dreaming of two miracles that never came: God's plague on rattlesnakes and okra. Diamondbacks and okra still thrive in the South. Folks seem to tolerate them better than I.

In fact, hunting rattlesnakes for sport is now a big deal. Here's how it works: In winter, when snakes are hibernating, hunters go out looking for holes in the ground where they're hiding. They pour gasoline down into their bedrooms to saturate their dens. When fumes become unbearable, the rattlers abandon their lair and hightail it out. The hunters are waiting with nets. The idea is to capture them for show and tell. If anyone's interested, you're welcome to my ticket.

Incredibly, okra has become my favorite vegetable. As for rattlesnakes, we battled to a Mexican standoff. They leave me alone; I return the favor. Please, no rattlesnake steak with my fried okra.

Years later, while working for Congressman Trent Lott in the United States Capitol, he gave me a lovely poster hanging on his office wall. He saw me admiring it and insisted I bring it home to Dot, warning me, "It's going to make her homesick!"

It shows a ship sailing back into Gulfport at sunset after a day of shrimping. The caption:

Mississippi
It's Like Coming Home

That's the way it's always been for us. After fifty years of living "up North," we still go back to Mississippi every year. Visiting family and friends, returning to our origins—it just seems right. Riding out into the country, standing over ancient graves where parents, grandparents, cousins, and kin are buried, we're like wild geese migrating back to their nesting grounds.

A nephew and I recently drove out to the farm I left in 1957. We rode down the old country lane where our mail box once stood and the rattlesnake crossed the road. We marveled at the vast cotton fields, now farmed with huge combines. Driving up to our old home site, we parked in the driveway, remembering the soft sound of rain dancing on a tin roof and hailstones pounding it, winds howling, and lightning flashing in a black night. I could still hear those WW II guns of

Camp Shelby rattling our bedroom windows. We struggled to recall how the old scrap-board house looked before Daddy added sheet-rock siding. A modern brick rambler now stands where a barnyard once overflowed with earthy sights, sounds, and smells.

Respecting the new owner's privacy, we sat outside in the car reflecting. Time has silenced the old familiar voices. Yet, we keep coming back, trying to dredge up those long-lost days. It's how we remember who we are. It's like coming home.

THE END

CHAPTER NOTES

PART I

1. John A. Lomax and Alan Lomax. 1947. *Best Loved American Folk Songs.* New York: Grosset & Dunlap.

2. *Ibid.*

3. Southern slang for "boogeyman."

4. George Gordon, Lord Byron. 1816. *The Prisoner of Chillon.* London, UK: John Murray Publishing

PART II

1. William Gaither. 1963. "He Touched Me" in Word/Integrity, ed. *The Celebration Hymnal.* Brentwood, TN: The Gaither Music Co.

2. William Pitts. 1863. "The Little Brown Church in the-Vale." Unpublished song, currently in public domain.

3. John A. & Alan Lomax. 1947. *The Boll Weevil.* New York: Grosset & Dunlap.

PART III

1. J.B.F. Wright. 1975. *Songbook of Faith and Joy.* Pleasantville, NY: Readers' Digest. Early 1900s American spiritual, popularized by Tennessee Ernie Williams.

PART IV

1. John A. and Alex Lomax. 1947. *Whoa, Buck.* New York: Grosset & Dunlap.

2. Mark Twain, quoted in various publications, among them: Budd, Louis J., ed. 1992. *Mark Twain: Collected Tales, Sketches, Speeches and Essays*, vol.2. New York, NY: Library of America.

3. Charles and Ruth Seeger with John A. & Alan Lomax. 1947. *Old Joe Clark.* New York: Grosset & Dunlap.

4. *The Holy Bible* (King James Version): Matthew 16:26.

5. Jack Nelson. 1993. "Terror in the Night" in *The Klan's Campaign against the Jews*. New York: Simon & Schuster.

6. Stuart Hamblen. 1950. "It Is No Secret [What God Can Do]" in *Family Songbook of Faith and Joy*. New York: Duchess Music Corp.

7. *The Holy Bible* (New International Version): Revelation 5:9-10.

8. *The Holy Bible* (King James Version): Matthew 23:15.

9. Woody Guthrie. "Red River Valley." ASCH Recordings, original origin unknown

PART V

1. Rudyard Kipling. 1909. "An Old Song" in book title. New York: Triangle Books.

PART VI

1. Norwood, Hermond. 1998. *Remembering Slavery: African-Americans Talk about Their Personal Experiences of Slavery and Emancipation* (book & audio set). Washington, DC: New Press, the Library of Congress, and Smithsonian Productions of the Smithsonian Institution.

PART VIII

1. Charles and Ruth Seeger. 1947. "Buckeye Jim" in book title [adapted]. New York: Grosset & Dunlap.

2. C. Austin Miles. 1912. "In the Garden" in anon., *Voice of Praise Hymnal*. Chicago: The Rodeheaver Co.

3. Hank Williams. 1952. "Jambalaya (On The Bayou)." MGM.

Selected Books from MSI Press

365 Teacher Secrets for Student Success in Elementary School: A Guide to Ideas and Activities for Parents

A Believer-in-Waiting's First Encounters with God

Blest Atheist

El Poder de lo Transpersonal

Forget the Goal, the Journey Counts...71 Jobs Later

Healing from Incest: Frank Conversations of a Victim with Her Therapist

Joshuanism: A Path Beyond Christianity

Las Historias de Mi Vida

Losing My Voice and Finding Another

Mommy Posioned Our House Guest

Publishing for Smarties: How to Find a Publisher

Puertas a la Eternidad

Road to Damascus

The Gospel of Damascus

The Marriage Whisperer

The Rise & Fall of Muslim Civil Society

The Rose & the Sword: How to Balance Your Feminine and Masculine Energies

The Seven Wisdoms of Life

Syrian Folktales

Understanding the People Around You: An Introduction to Socionics

When You're Shoved from the Right, Look to the Left: Metaphors of Islamic Humanism

Widow A Survival Guide for the First Year

J. Bennett Easterling

CPSIA information can be obtained at www.ICGtesting.com
Printed in the USA
BVOW05s0750230514

354014BV00002B/5/P